SALVATION

To Bonnie,
a fellow/sister
sufferer.
stay strong!

Katharine English

ISBN: 0692617833
ISBN 13: 9780692617830

SALVATION

A JUDGE'S MEMOIR OF A
MORMON CHILDHOOD

——

Katharine English

Praise for *SALVATION: A Judge's Memoir of a Mormon Childhood*

Salvation is a brave and compelling life story that is memorable, insightful, and a pleasure to read. Katharine English spans her years from childhood to her adult career as a juvenile judge, and moves effortlessly between the challenges of abuse-filled early years and the opportunities she finds later to make a difference in the lives of other children. The humor that erupts from time to time bears witness to the remarkable human capacity for recovery and to the hope that courage and a willingness to live an examined life can lead to healing.

—Judith Barrington, author of *Writing the Memoir*
and *Lifesaving: A Memoir*

In Katharine English's memoir, *Salvation,* set in the Salt Lake Mormon community, we learn about the evolution of bravery, the costs of survival, and the loyal ties that confirm her loving commitment to a complex constellation of characters who see her through.

English establishes the role of the Mormon Church in her upbringing—both the scarring judgment and the closeness with an ardently believing grandmother who helps carry her past the tumult of home. In reflecting back on the searing family dramas of alcoholism and neglect, English is able to enter the young girl's mind with keenly observed details of a child's wonder, sharp dialogue and her own canny adult's sense of irony. Some scenes are funny, even as they rip away all sense of stability. The slow reveal of her evolving insights and the shock of recollections of her own child abuse are hard-earned and honest.

She gives us many sides of betrayal, loyalty and love, while taking on the disappointment, rigidity and comfort of the Mormon religion she grew up with, and the necessary search for acceptance and recognition as her own person. She places the wounding events of the past into a bold telling and subtle acceptance providing the necessary vision and heart, as an adult, to understand growing up in a divided house, a divided land and somehow, coming through whole.

—Beatrix Gates, author of *Dos* and *In the Open*

Judge English willingly allows us to explore and co-experience the dark secrets of her life—a dysfunctional family, sexual drives and motivations, and the underbelly of the Mormon Church—with a raw understanding of what creates a compassionate courtroom judge. It's not for the faint of heart. No holds barred, welcome to the life of a wonderful writer who is willing to share the most sacred of life's teachings.

—Norman Zurn, author of *Self-Realization: A Journey* and *620 Ways to Wake Up Your Bucket List*

For my sons,

Greg and Nathan

The Hebrew word for *salvation* means literally 'to make wide' or 'to make sufficient.' The Oxford Companion to the Bible [says that] 'The primary meaning of the Hebrew and Greek word...salvation is non-religious... and refer[s] to victory over evil or rescue from danger in this life...When [Jesus] says to [people] that their faith has saved them, it is the Greek word for 'make you well'... that is employed.

—Kathleen Norris, *Amazing Grace*
© Penguin/Random House, April 1999

Your childhood is a village.
You will never cross its boundaries
No matter how far you go...

You who are descending
from mountains of the past,
how can you climb them again,
and why?

—Adonis, "Celebrating Childhood,"
Selected Poems, translated from Arabic by
Khaled Mattawa
© Yale University Press, 2010

AUTHOR'S NOTE

———◆———

THE NAMES OF MY ANCESTORS, grandparents, and mother are accurate. I have changed the names of my father's family, stepfather, Sunday-school teacher, and siblings to protect their privacy as much as possible. The narrative is based on my own memories, to which I have been as true as possible. But as my mother once said, "The truth moves around," so others may remember these events differently.

ACKNOWLEDGMENTS

HOORAY FOR SIBLINGS! WHAT AN indomitable tribe we are. Thanks particularly to my youngest brother, with whom I shared my journey home. An especially deep thanks to my older sister, who supported me daily, and who edited my story with an eye toward encouraging my veracity in Mormon facts. I am also grateful to my younger sister, who gave me a bump up in the beginning and to my other brother for running the marathon-long final edit with me.

Hooray for teachers! My heartfelt appreciation to the poet and teacher Beatrix Gates, for invaluable insight during the writing of this manuscript and to my advisors at Goddard College, where this book began: Michael Klein, Victoria Nelson, and Elena Georgiou.

Hooray for writing groups! Thanks to my writer colleagues: Linda Adams, Mary Lou Bean, Hydee Clayton, Terrell Dougan, Kathleen Farley, Karen Hayes, Grace Johnson, Sandy Montanino, Dave Tibbetts, Paige Upstill, and Norman Zurn.

To my colleagues, Bret Jackson and Kody Partridge, and my dear friends, George and Norma Garwood, my thanks for reading the entire manuscript and offering suggestions and encouragement.

And finally, many thanks to my long-suffering companion, Cary Griffiths, who listened, advised, and supported my writing through years of endless discussions and rewrites.

CONTENTS

CHAPTER 1

STIRRINGS

———◆———

MY COURTROOM WAS HUMID WITH the smell of coming rain. A window was halfway open. The leaves of the giant horse-chestnut tree sighed. A warning wind stirred, and I felt the dampness of Oregon on my skin.

Sitting for my tenth year as a referee and pro tem judge in the Multnomah County Circuit Court in Portland, Oregon, I presided over juvenile delinquency and child-abuse cases. I felt overwhelmed by the squalor and detritus of the troubled families who appeared before me, and I yearned to quit, to throw off the terrible burden of responsibility. But I couldn't seem to leave and felt locked in place.

At noon I planned to recess court, step into my chambers, take off my robe, don my running clothes, and spend an hour running on the streets surrounding the juvenile-court complex: through the tidy Vietnamese neighborhood, past women raking up the latest pile of leaves and young men tinkering on their cars, down Sandy Boulevard, waving at the merchants pulling in their bookracks and sale tables to avoid the rain. I would jog in place at the red light, waiting for it to change.

A lunch-hour storm might overtake me, might begin as I hit the final hill back to court, might wash me clean. Looking forward to the noon respite, I was able to bear the brutality unfolding before me now.

Today's case concerned a mother's abuse of her constantly wailing infant daughter by yelling and cursing, hitting, and finally, in desperation, beating her baby into silence.

I remembered myself, twenty years earlier, standing over my nine-month-old son, who was crying from a bleeding diaper rash no doctor could diagnose. "Shut up! Shut up!" I screamed. Over and over. I nearly hit him once, frantic to end the noise, but instead threw a lamp across the room. One cold winter night, I escaped from the house for an hour, oblivious to the sleet that slapped me in the face, leaving my crying child alone on the floor.

I finally turned to a naturopath, who kindly assured me, "It's his diet, dear, I'm sure. Let me help you." She did, radically changing his menu. His rash was gone in days. I remember the spectacular relief I felt.

My son believes he remembers my screaming.

I remember my own mother's screaming.

I recessed court at noon. To move among beauty and normalcy, I jogged under the darkening sky. I breathed in the fresh, damp air and felt the mist on my face. I saw a woman deadheading roses, another taking clothes off the line, and a man hauling groceries from his car—the ordinary tasks of ordinary lives. I would shower after my run and return to the courtroom, to a father making excuses for missing his alcohol treatment, to bickering spouses locked in a fight over the placement of their abused children, to a sixteen-year-old begging for emancipation from her neglectful parents.

The storm broke. The rain soaked me, and I returned to court refreshed. But not washed clean.

CHAPTER 2

ERIC

———◆———

MY BROTHER ERIC, TEN YEARS younger than I, came up with the plan that would change everything.

In 1994, he came to visit my courtroom, eager to see me at work on my juvenile-court cases, which, in Oregon, are open to the public.

Eric is an Adonis. Because he had a different father than I did, he looks nothing like me. Whereas my father gifted me my height (four feet, eleven and a half inches) and width (stocky and square), Eric's father gifted him with the towering good looks of a Greek god—a sculpted face, high cheekbones, deep-set blue eyes, and thick golden hair. Tall and ruggedly handsome, he is also slim and muscular. He earns it: workouts at the gym every day; superb hygiene; careful coiffing through brushing, fluffing, and coloring his hair; and good nutrition.

"I use my looks and charm," he jests in half truth, "to cover up my fear of failure. If I look good, I'm in control."

We both understand the irony—our need for control spins us frantically. We can both be bossy, easy to irritate, and judgmental.

But Eric usually has an ever-cheerful, optimistic personality and a dazzling smile. He has never been married, or generally monogamous, but he lived for many years in San Francisco and Los Angeles with his lover, a man we both adored, who tragically died of AIDS.

"Oh my god, he's gorgeous!" My court staff swooned.

"Of course," I said, laughing, resigned by now to such exclamations. "He's my brother."

Only one clerk missed the irony and insisted. "But you're so short and...and..."

"Plump?" I laughed.

"And the most gorgeous woman on earth." Eric put his arms around me and hugged me, lifting me up off my feet. He flashed his smile at the clerk. "Don't you agree?"

"Stop that!" I said as I reddened, delighted. "So unjudicial!"

"Speaking of which"—he set me down—"let's go see you judge, Kittens!"

Eric is the youngest of my mother's five children. We have always been good friends. He was my confidant through my failed marriage, custody quarrels, single parenting, difficult relationships, law school, litigation practice, and now, my judicial career. I was his confidante as well, through his placement in foster care at fifteen, through his senior year in high school when he lived with me (during my early marriage), through his coming out, through the death of his lover, through his discovery of his own HIV-positive status, and through his difficulty in interpersonal and professional relationships. We shared our adult struggles. We listened. We advised.

I built my career as a teacher, trial lawyer, and judge as I proudly watched him build his own. He was editor of the University of Utah paper, and then he was a journalist and television reporter during the rise and assassination of San Francisco's Harvey Milk. He began his own company in Los Angeles, where he created innovations for sports and weather television. He invented the Weather Wand (the small remote controller weather reporters hold and press to move clouds and wind around on the map) and contributed to the development of the first "virtual" sets (the blank screens behind television reporters and talk-show hosts that show imaginary settings). He currently develops devices that will radicalize advertising on network TV. He is brilliant, a workaholic, and exceptionally eager for success.

Both of us buried our Utah childhoods, or so we thought. We left behind our mother's alcoholic rages and physical abuse. I retreated from my father's abuse and his subsequent cool indifference, while Eric recovered from his father's abandonment. Eric fled to his prominence in television technology in Hollywood; I fled to my courtroom. Each of us needed desperately to land on both feet, but we often stumbled. When we fell flat, we helped each other up.

I was depressed and in need of help when he came to watch me in court. "Let's see what's getting you down," he said. We hugged.

He entered and sat in the courtroom. I went through another door and entered my chambers to change into my robe—a thin, worn cotton drape I was loath to exchange for the heavy brocaded gowns other judges wore. I was afraid to discard old friends; even ex-lovers remained in my life.

I delayed. I watered my years-old climbing philodendron, buried my nose in the pungent Double Delight roses cut from my garden, and gazed at the reddening leaves outside my window, briefly gathering fortitude to face the sorrow that confronted me in the courtroom.

If the Oregon Children's Services Division received a report of child abuse or neglect and, after investigating, believed there was a serious safety concern for the children, a petition was filed in juvenile court, charging the parents with abuse or neglect and asking for state intervention. It was the judge's duty to determine whether the charges were true. If they were not proved, the children returned home. If proved, however, the state took custody until the parents successfully completed services required by the state. At review hearings, the judge ruled on whether the parents had succeeded at rehabilitation. Sometimes the family was reunited. Sometimes, never.

Many of the cases seemed routine and were quickly resolved—dirty houses, children left unsupervised, excessive discipline. But many cases were difficult and profoundly sad—grave injury, sexual abuse, appalling neglect, abandonment.

On the afternoon when Eric visited, my docket included several initial hearings and a panoply of review hearings. Eric seemed to be in a cheerful mood, proud to watch his sister at work, anxious to be of help in lifting my faltering mood. He sat in the front row and gave me a smile and a thumbs-up, which I appreciated but was professionally obliged to ignore. I appointed lawyers for the parents and children, and the hearings began.

As the hearings continued, Eric began to slump. He looked shell shocked, his mouth partially open, his eyes wide. Before the afternoon was over, he rose slowly, as if in a daze, and left the courtroom. He told me later that he'd left the courthouse, dispirited and raw, walked around in a drizzle of rain, found a private place to sit, and wept. He had seen our own parents, our siblings, and our childhood passing before him.

I dismissed court for the day and hung up my robe. Eric and I went out to dinner, but he ate little. His agitation erupted in questions about the cases he had observed.

"Why did you leave that poor baby in that filthy home?" and "What will happen to that twelve-year-old when he runs away again?" and "Can't you sterilize a woman after she's had seven kids taken away?" He exhaled, turned away.

One case in particular troubled him: "Why did you take that girl away from her mother?" After a pause, he came to the point. "She looked like Mom, didn't she? The mother?" His voice caught. "You could tell they loved and depended on each other. They just needed help." He pursed his lips. "Why did you seem so...unmoved?"

I wanted to tell him that it was more complicated than that. I was required to "exercise judicial restraint" and remain calm and neutral. My personal feelings could not enter into my weighing of the evidence— that wouldn't be fair or just. But those answers felt too cold, and they weren't the entire truth. In reality, my heart broke every day.

I couldn't speak. The waiter filled our water glasses. His apron was soiled. Tomato sauce? I began to think of recipes I wanted to try. How at one time I'd wanted to be a waitress. Anything. Anything.

"Well..." Eric pulled himself up straight and sighed. "I see why you're blue, Sis. It's so grim." He was not going to let this go, my baby brother; he was determined to save me.

We were silent for a few minutes. He pushed the spinach salad around on his plate. "I couldn't do it." He shook his head. "Lord, it's just not for me." He looked at me and I held his look. In that moment, our eyes read each other's histories. I didn't flinch, though I knew what he was about to say.

"And how can it be right for *you*?" He reached for my hand, and I gave it. Outside, the drizzle turned into a steady rain. His large tanned hand covered mine. "Why don't you quit?"

Eric's gentleness undid me. He, like no other person, understood that in my public and professional life I was cheerful, optimistic, and competent, as was he. Both of us seemed successful, respected, and well liked, even happy. But we carried a deep sadness. With each other, we could let loose the grief.

"I'm immersed in this tawdriness, and I can't seem to get out," I admitted. "It's good pay and great status. I like my staff and coworkers. I'm good at the job." I looked down and noticed my untouched food; I hadn't eaten either. "But I feel like this is my punishment for some terrible childhood transgression and that I have to endure it, like a whipping."

"Hey, Kittens," he said soothingly. "You aren't alone. As my therapists say, we carry the child forward." He paused. "Did you do something that deserves this punishment?"

"Not that I've ever talked about," I said.

Eric was about to speak, but the waiter appeared. He had on a fresh apron.

"Is the food not to your liking, miss?" he asked.

———————

Over the years, Eric and I had counseled with several therapists, read books, and analyzed ourselves. To little avail, it seemed.

As my years on the juvenile-court bench passed, I often attempted to put my friends and family at ease by recounting humorous moments in the courtroom.

"You'll like this." I chuckled, recounting a hearing in which I had to decide whether to commit an allegedly mentally ill man to confinement at the state hospital. He had stabbed his mailman, claiming him to be Captain Hook. "I had to assure this severely disturbed man that I was Peter Pan and that I didn't like Captain Hook either. Only then did he feel safe enough to confess the attack."

My friends laughed and began to slide into the comfort zone. "So what did you do?" one asked as they leaned forward, all ears.

"I forgave him." I poured more beer from the pitcher into our glasses. "And committed him to the state hospital." I paused. "His daughter was actually named Wendy."

"No!"

"Yes!" Now they were engaged, softened into pleasure. They relaxed into the evening's gaieties.

The conversation with my friends moved on, but I kept thinking about Wendy's father, the furrowed confusion on his face as he was gently led out, and the clerk's forlorn gaze as she and I looked into the future. We knew what awaited Hook's killer—Neverland. He would never live with his daughter again, never be free of Thorazine, and never be released from his illness.

Court was rarely the forum where parents and children, the mentally ill, or divorcing spouses found their dignity or human wholeness. Yet this was where I sat, doing my life's work, wondering whether I was in the right place, the right profession.

When I first started, I looked forward to my work. I wanted to learn and understand, to craft a solution to these troublesome problems. I relished moments of humor, friendly cooperation, and success. But I was increasingly pained by the tragic circumstances of so many families. I was intensely affected by the immensity of the sorrow. Dysfunctional families appeared before me, and the facts of their lives poured out, poignant and raw: a young girl intentionally scalded in boiling water; an infant left suffocating in a hot car while his parents drank in the local bar; parents lost in a fog of methamphetamine, locked in denial and arrogance, defeated; refugee families in cultural conflict, a daughter in a miniskirt and spiked hair, a son refusing traditional worship, the Vietnamese parents awash in the shame of being summoned before a judge.

Sometimes a case ended in a welcome success: parents rehabilitated, families reunited, children adopted into caring families. Although I knew there were many players in this drama of families saved, I felt a too-keen possessive interest. I wanted it to be true that it was because of *my* competent legal analysis, judicious planning, and clever securing of resources that dangerously dirty houses were cleaned up, that addicts sobered up and regained custody of their children, and that abandoned children found new homes. I wanted it to be true that because *I* insisted on social workers, lawyers, parents, and children doing what was needed, performance was improved and success followed. *I* made it possible for traumatized children and trapped parents to be treated and trained so that the family was made whole again.

I knew I was not solely responsible for the triumphs, yet I highly valued my part. And for many years, I did the job well. Firm but kind. Compassionate but demanding. I needed the successes for survival. I collected the victories, held them close, took from them immeasurable satisfaction, and used them to heal the pain.

Sometimes, however, I could not control a growing outrage. In the last year, I had become increasingly frustrated. My irritation surfaced on the bench. I became impatient, sarcastic, blaming. Outbursts in the courtroom were happening more often. Recently, I'd lost my temper on the bench, hurling my anger out at the litigants—the lawyers, the parents, and the social workers.

In one case, two neglectful parents shouted insults back and forth as they fought over the custody of their teenage children, who were present and sitting red eyed and numb. Ordinarily I would have spoken to the parents kindly: "I know you want to be good parents. All parents want to do well by their children. Tell me what you think your children are feeling at this moment." Instead, I yelled at them. "Shame on you, in front of your kids!" I snapped. "How insensitive! What kind of parents are you?" I'd thought them disgraceful, and I'd behaved disgracefully in my turn.

I was two people: one yelling, and one watching myself and saying, *Why are you yelling? Where is that coming from?*

In another case, parents who had relapsed on cocaine defended themselves against child-abuse charges, claiming it was "no big deal." I scoffed, "You might as well take your child into the backyard and stab her through the heart. Your drug use is just as damaging."

A lawyer once came to court woefully unprepared. I had received no summation or report. But rather than set the hearing over to a later date to allow for better preparation, and take the lawyer aside during or after the hearing to suggest improvements, I lost my temper and chastised her in open court.

"We are privileged to be lawyers, privileged to have food, shelter, and opportunity. How dare we neglect our duty to perform well for our clients, especially when our clients are children or hapless parents?" The courtroom quieted, surprised at the lecture. I climbed on my high horse and continued. "Even parents at fault should be served vigorously, be-cause the reuniting of a safe and healthy family is the primary goal of the juvenile-court system," I ranted. She and the other people in the courtroom were stunned into silence. I learned later that she had in-tended to ask for a setover—her own mother was dying, and she'd had little time to prepare—but my immediate paroxysm had prevented her request.

A judge is required to maintain a "judicial demeanor" and behave as a respectful and calm decider. But that year I had gained a reputation for losing my temper. I was overcome, particularly when incompetence, irresponsibility, and ignorance seemed so obvious, so preventable. When I lashed out, I was frightening, terrifying, and intimidating to those who were so much less powerful. Even if the anger was justified, showing it was hurtful—and rarely productive. After each scene, I grieved over my own uncontrolled behavior.

I confided to a colleague. "What the hell is happening to me? I used to be so reasonable and kind."

"I don't know." He sympathized. "But you need to get control of yourself."

I was ashamed of losing the reasonable, neutral demeanor required of a judge. But what was even more puzzling to me was that I knew *while* I was doing it that I was wrong. I knew it even *before* I went off on a tirade. Still, I felt helpless to control myself.

My especial fury was reserved for the state social workers who were responsible for the care and safety of children in state custody. I was blinded by a growing, almost tyrannical need for children to be well served by the agency.

The day before Eric's visit, I'd heard a case in which a social worker had failed to monitor or visit a foster child who had subsequently been abused by the foster parent. I raged. "How dare you come into this court and tell me that the state has the power to take this boy from his family, and then can abuse that power by neglecting him in foster care? We haven't cared for him any better than the parent did!"

This was the fury I felt most justified in expressing. While many case-workers are excellent, an incompetent one can damage a child's life and destroy a family's hopes.

"You aren't a parent yourself," I said, castigating one worker, "yet you've formed a knee-jerk judgment on this parent without any empathy for her or any understanding of her challenges."

I confronted another worker who was insisting I remove a Vietnamese child with bruises on her legs. "You recommend removal of this girl, and you haven't even talked about the damage this sudden and frightening change might cause to her!" I went on and on. "Where in your report is there any mention of cultural and racial differences? Did you ask if those bruises are from coining? Do you even know what that is?"

Another worker neglected to visit children in foster care to assure their safety and determine their needs. Yet another refused to write a timely and detailed report, and forward it in advance to the parents so they could prepare. Many crafted reports in boilerplate language rather than prose specific to the family. Most infuriating to me were the workers who assumed an air of righteousness that was rigid and impenetrable. The social workers had such power over other people's lives that any failure to do their jobs reduced me to blistering in-court lectures, subsequent public criticism, and private tears of embarrassment and shame for my injudicious fits.

At these times, I knew that my anger was excessive. After all, social workers in the juvenile-court system are seriously underpaid and vastly overworked, burdened with caseloads too large to manage effectively. Where was my sense of proportion, balance, and reasonableness? Where was my compassion for the professionals? I felt dislocated and abandoned.

———◆———

During that desperate year, Eric began to talk me through the dark times. "There's no need to show your anger," he cautioned. "You're the judge. You can order whatever needs to be done." This calmed me but certainly didn't cure what was beginning to feel like an illness.

His most perceptive insights took the form of questions. "Where is that fury coming from?" I didn't know. "You do this work that makes you sad and so angry, yet you seem to thrive on it. Why?" This paradox was true.

Why had I spent my professional life drenched in the impoverishment of human life? What had pulled me into the river upon which I was floating? What was the source of the river and what moved it—that force below the surface, that undercurrent of *why?*

I could sketch the surface of my river. While every job I'd ever held was for the money, desperately needed at home, there were other more profound reasons for my choices.

When I was eight, I picked raspberries at Bear Lake, Utah—not just for money, but so I could get out of the house. I would rise before dawn to work in the sweet smell of the raspberry patches and eat the fruit until I burst.

At ten, I worked for my grandmother, the director of the University of Utah costume department, so I could find relief from my chaotic home and invent new lives in the costumes and theatre.

At fifteen, lying about my age, I became a night filing clerk in a medical clinic. I relished the walk to and from work in the comforting dark, and I dawdled, not wanting to reach home too quickly.

Then the switchboard at American Oil fell under my complete control as I juggled fifty telephone cords into holes and learned the thrill of organizing, controlling, and successfully satisfying fifty callers at once—a sense of power I didn't have in my house.

As a teenager I worked at the House of Music as a record salesgirl, so I could escape into music and to make a connection with customers who seemed normal, cheerful, and stable, compared to my unpredictable, ulcerous family.

And in college I worked midnight to eight at Western Airlines, consulting massive books of flight schedules for drunks and suicides calling to plan imaginary trips around the world. There, I imagined my own flights.

At twenty-one, I married to escape my family and Utah. I worked year after year and job after job. I put my husband through college by brokering lumber, answering phones in an accounting office, and greeting patients who came to the dentist for root canals and gold crowns.

But I was restless, dissatisfied. The women's movement inspired me to return to college. I became a middle-school teacher, and then a trial lawyer in family law, and then a state family-court referee and judge pro tem, and then a tribal-court judge. I found a focus: children and families.

That was the surface of my river. Families and children were my river. As time went on, they began to hold me like undertows, hidden logs, submerged boulders. I didn't explore the depths, where the question persisted: Why did I need to help families and kids?

I became immersed. Students slouched or studied at their desks; clients wept or celebrated in my law office; dysfunctional families came into my courtroom, imploring and trusting or angry and resistant, their stories wretched or rewarding. And symbiotically, their lives nurtured and sustained me. My life was theatre. I didn't have to be me. I had a family—two sons—yet that life was too real. I became, instead, the families and the children I served, living their lives, not mine, as though my own life depended on it.

I *thought* I was moving along in this river, but as though caught in a whirlpool, I saw only the foam. Something else was roiling.

———◆———

Eric's visit to my courtroom, and the words spoken and unspoken between us that evening, affected me profoundly. My unadmitted past had fiercely coiled its arms around me, holding me in place. I had to break free.

"Katharine, you and I have been in therapy for years. I don't know about you, but whatever is holding me back needs to be found out." He stirred his coffee, leaned across the table. "Let's take a trip to Salt Lake City and find it together, shall we?"

It was 1994. Contemporary self-help authors urged us to break free from the chains of childhood. Eric thought it was reasonable, in this discover-our-true-selves atmosphere of the nineties, to look back to our childhoods. The professionals I'd consulted had asked me, "What secrets have you been keeping?" I always said I had none, but I knew it wasn't true.

When I looked back to my childhood, it was to Utah, to Salt Lake City, a seemingly benign city in the lap of Mormonism, at the foot of the majestic Wasatch Mountains, in a desert where toiling pioneers turned the sand to soil; grew trees, corn, and industry; and flourished in their faith. In my childhood Mormon Church lessons, I learned how God had promised this gentle valley to the Mormon pioneers. The Church, in turn, promised me the family I yearned for on earth and a promised family ever after in eternal life. But "thy kingdom come" never came.

What *did* come were questions. Though I'd left the Mormon Church when I was twenty-one, how had it not left me? How could I exorcise my mother yet carry her still? How had I deeply loved a monstrous father who deserved derision and blame? And why did I seem successful as an adult and yet feel so utterly lost?

Eric and I made our plans. We would return to Salt Lake City. He would explore the root of his desperate need to be liked and in charge. He would find out what made him into a fearful adult who, in order to be loved by all, took care of everyone's needs but his own. He would face his demons, no longer emerging as the powerless, unworthy child. He would be set free.

I would go back to confront my Church and my parents. At heart, I knew they had somehow propelled me into this miasma of anguishing juvenile-court work, and their legacy now held me tight. As we planned the trip, I felt my repressed anger rising. I shouldered it like a weapon. I would return, armed with the maturity and cynicism of age, shielded by the sobering distance I had placed between my past and present, and I would find the evidence with which to blame, convict, and punish my father, my mother, and my Mormon Church. Thus, I would emerge avenged. I would be set free.

But it didn't happen that way.

CHAPTER 3

INTO THE VALLEY

—◆—

ERIC AND I DROVE SOUTH into Utah from the Idaho flatland and traveled along the skirt of the Wasatch Mountains.

I was never able to put a finger on what it was about those mountains that so held me to them. I'd loved them from the moment I was conscious of them as a small girl. After I left Salt Lake City to live in Oregon, I still longed for them, as did Eric, living in the belly of Los Angeles.

I believe I felt protected by these massive mountains, the Wasatch Range, on the rugged western edge of the Rockies, marching 160 miles south from the Idaho border through the center of Utah. For a religious child, the highest peaks rose like astonishing prayers, twelve thousand feet above sea level. They were all around me, 450 square miles of them. I felt like a miniscule supplicant at their feet. "Suffer the little children come unto me," I heard them say.

Maybe it was how violent their origins were, how old and wise they had become. As many as twenty-five million years ago, the plateau was a forest, a peaceful plain. But thousands of feet beneath the earth, the land collided and shifted, like a furious family fighting and then fragmenting, and the Wasatch Mountains pushed their way up, escaping through the plain. The mountains reached up to the sky, temples of stone. Then the land groaned in sorrow, faulted, and tore apart, finally stretching and falling into a vast and peaceful steppe. Like my family.

I knew that some part of my genetic makeup was stamped indelibly with my pioneer origins in this Great Basin valley. My ancestors had migrated here, following their faith. In 1847, the Mormons fled from persecution in Illinois to Wyoming. Then they veered south to Utah, blazing a path down Emigration Canyon. Led by God, they said, they descended into the valley, calling it Zion—a gathering place for people "pure in heart." This barren place was soon to be a lush and thriving oasis. In 1861, my Mormon great-great-grandfather settled there.

As Eric and I drove out of Snowville, on the western hem of the Rockies, the sight of the jagged peaks looming up in the distance thrilled me, even though I hadn't seen them for decades. Voluptuous, magnetic, and powerful, they seemed to eclipse all history.

As the car hummed along I-15, past the Golden Spike National Historical Site and the northern tip of the Great Salt Lake, a primal ache tightened my throat. This was home. It didn't matter how eager I had been to leave it.

———•———

Eric and I had been on the road since four that morning, eating from the cooler, stopping at rest areas. It was two in the afternoon when we reached Brigham City, an hour north of Salt Lake City.

"Let's stop," he proposed, "and go to Maddox for lunch."

I laughed. "For old times' sake."

So we did. Maddox Restaurant was on an offshoot highway that led to Bear Lake, a deep, multihued blue lake, half in northeastern Utah, half in southeastern Idaho. This "Caribbean of the United States" was where our maternal grandparents, Ninyah and Baba, owned two cabins on the lake—our childhood vacation spot, a place of joy and respite. The adults gathered on the porch of the Big House and left the children alone to inhabit the Little House. We were free of adult supervision, free to climb Gus's Hill, or swim around the lake bend, or walk to Ideal Beach down the road and listen to the jukebox.

On our way to and from Bear Lake, Ninyah and Baba often stopped at Maddox for out-of-this-world fried chicken, rolls, and chocolate shakes.

Though we were often hungry at home with our mother, at Maddox we were sated, happy, and hopeful.

Eric and I ordered the usual chicken and shakes. We sat in the familiar red faux-leather booths, surrounded by pine walls and smiling waitresses. I missed my grandparents. I'm certain Eric did, too. But we were lost in the silence that had become part of our defenses as children, keeping us safe from discovery or punishment. Even as adults, our ability to talk truthfully and intimately to each other had not fully formed.

"Soon we'll see the Great Salt Lake." Eric pointed. "So many good times. And so much sadness. Remember the time—"

I interrupted him. I wasn't ready yet to delve into the morass of memory. "Yes indeed," I said, "Saltiest inland lake in the world."

I never enjoyed the Great Salt Lake, thinking of it as cold, and rejecting. My grandfather, Baba, told me how eons ago glaciers had formed and begun to move, a tale that terrified me. As the earth warmed, icebergs broke, calving into what became the massive Lake Bonneville. As a child, I could see myself drowning. My child self was saved when the huge lake diminished into several smaller lakes, which eventually disappeared. But one lake remained—the Great Salt Lake, a breathing survivor laid in Bonneville's grave, surrounded by miles of dry salt flats. I didn't want to go near it.

"Hey," Eric persisted cheerfully, sucking the last of his shake as we had done as children, making a loud slurping noise and causing heads to turn. "Remember that monstrous castle the Mormons built on the Great Salt Lake?"

"Of course. Saltair Resort," I recalled, smiling. Taking cover.

The Mormon Church was intent on bringing culture and healthy recreation to its members: concerts, plays, and hearty social activity. To that end, the Church built a large Moorish-style pavilion, with garish domes, wraparound porches, game rooms, and a chandeliered ballroom for dances and musicals. On the fairway, barkers summoned players to toss rings and win teddy bears, and carnival rides beckoned for a nickel. We donned our swimsuits in the changing huts.

As if thinking the same thought, Eric and I shuddered—the dirty lake. "Mom wanted to lie in the sun," I grumbled, "so she made us go into the lake in spite of the brine shrimp."

Eric imitated Mom: "Leave me alone. Scram! Go swim with the brine shrimp."

I laughed. "Did you know brine shrimp eat their own?"

"Ha! How appropriate. And ugh! The fecal pellets." Eric began to laugh, too.

"Phytoplankton," I added. "And algae."

"Brine flies!" We laughed uncontrollably, though there was nothing funny about brine flies. They swarmed around us, flew in our mouths, landed on our salt-crusted skin.

"She asked, 'Having fun?' when we straggled back. We were desperate to go home."

"I remember." Eric nodded.

Other diners were looking at us, so we tried to stifle our laughter, but we were helpless, as though in church.

We weren't laughing at brine flies, of course. We were avoiding talking about the sorrow that so often underlay our laughter. Eric pulled himself under control and reached across the table to take my hand. "Well, I guess we better get going, no?"

We finished our lunch and headed south again. I was uneasy and fearful. I slowed to fifty-five miles per hour. I chewed my nails. The lake was now on our right; we passed Willard Bay, where young people watched the speedboat races. In Farmington, further south, we could see Antelope Island rising in the lake like a giant getting up from a nap, a huge brown hulk in the afternoon sun. I'd gone on a field trip to the vast acres of the island, petted the sheep on a farm there, and watched the antelope roundup.

When we ventured to and from Bear Lake as children, I-15 had not yet been built, so we drove on Highway 89, in our grandparents' old Studebaker, through small towns like Clearfield and Layton, Centerville and Kaysville, and the aptly named Bountiful. Eric and I recalled the old highway fruit stands, the roadside rodeos, the quaint gas pumps, and the sweet smell of my grandfather's pipe as we snuggled in for a nap in the backseat. Now those towns zipped by, and as we approached Salt Lake City, I felt a paradoxical mixture of fear and anticipation. Sadness enveloped me; at the same time, I felt eager and joyful. I had said nothing, and though the car had been wrapped in silence for some time, Eric suddenly said, "Yes. Me, too."

I knew that sometimes people decided to do daring and bold things. I was doing such a thing now. Promise moved me forward, but a paralyzing reluctance stalled me. As if in a daze, I acted determined and calm. Yet mountains were moving inside, and I felt like I was drowning in the geology of fear.

"It's going to be OK, Sis," Eric soothed. It wasn't, and I knew it then, but it was too late to turn back.

And then there it was: the vast Salt Lake Valley spread before us. We stopped the car and sat in silence looking at the expanse below us.

The ancient climate had warmed and dried. Conifers replaced hardwoods; bunchgrass and Gambel oak blanketed the canyons and foothills. Streams gathered water and sped, tumbling down the Wasatch Mountains between patches of bared earth, shaping the cliffs and walls. Six carved canyons cut and wound their way down through the mountains to the plain, and creeks danced over the rocks. These streams brought the Mormon pioneers their precious, lifesaving water, allowing them to transform the dry salt desert into verdant Salt Lake City, nestling in a thirty-mile-long half-halo indentation at the foot of the range, a city that now shelters the center of the Church of Jesus Christ of Latter Day Saints—the Mormon Church.

Eric and I loved those canyons: florid with greenery in the summer; thick and fragrant blazing autumn leaves covering the canyon floors in the fall; bare, jagged cliffs of granite and sandstone towering over them in winter; and the creeks rising to rivers in the spring.

"Shall we go for a hike in Millcreek Canyon one day?" I asked, breaking the silence.

"I was just thinking of that," he replied. "It's an amazing story, isn't it?" Eric mused. "How the Mormons turned this barren place into paradise."

When the original Mormon prophet Joseph Smith was murdered in Illinois, the Latter Day Saints escaped to the Salt Lake Valley, led by the Church's new prophet, Brigham Young. Trekking across the midwestern plains, down the Wasatch canyons, to the western front of these mountains, the immigrants settled where five mountain creeks emptied into the parched and dusty valley. Big and Little Cottonwood Canyons gave up their timber, granite, and essential water to the pioneers, who built houses and stores, dug canals and irrigation ditches, planted gardens and trees, and started businesses. Settlers harnessed and named the fifty-one-mile-long Jordan River, which ran through fields and low marshes. The wetlands, thick with cattails and grasses, were home to slinking foxes, burrowing groundhogs, and hundreds of birds of varying species, trilling and barking. The desert bloomed. The Mormons folded their arms around their faith and their people. They thrived, and the land became fecund with food, towns, and children. This is the land where I was raised and to which I now returned. I was unaware of the truths that were about to unfold, but I sensed them looming.

"Here's an irony," I told Eric. I explained that when the Mormons escaped to the Salt Lake Valley, it was part of Mexico, a wide stretch of arid and secluded land. They were relieved that the US government and its bigoted citizens would leave them alone to worship and live as they believed. But a year later, at the end of the Mexican-American War in 1848, the territory became part of the United States. Thereafter, the concerned territorial government kept watch over this band of religious renegades, building Fort Douglas and dispatching US soldiers to contain the Mormon fervor for independence.

Eric and I drove into the city as the sun slipped down toward the Oquirrh Mountains to the south, a range that joins the Wasatch to complete the circling arc protecting the valley. On a hill to the north stands the Utah State Capitol, a fine, sturdy building overlooking the entire city below, housing mostly Mormon and conservative legislators since statehood, gained in 1896.

Temple Square, a double-size city block in the center of the city, on which the Latter Day Saints built their temple, the number of which eventually spread to over a hundred Mormon temples throughout the world. Lush, park-like landscaping surrounds the Temple, a holy place, the House of the Lord. Only those who are especially worthy are allowed entrance.

In the Temple, sacred ordinances, such as everlasting eternal marriage, are performed, and covenants—promises between the member and the Lord—are made and bestowed. For righteous Mormons, all paths lead to the Temple.

We headed for the motel.

"We'll go to Temple Square first?" I inquired. "Walk around?"

"Why not?" Eric smiled. "First and last, no?" His irony unnerved me a little. What if the Gospel of the Church was true? What if "first and last" was right, and Mormons were, as I had been taught, the only people to go to Heaven?

"Did you ever go in the Temple, Eric?"

"No. I never believed in the Church, really. But I had to join to be a Boy Scout." He paused. "Did you?"

"Only once," I said, "to be baptized for the dead."

No Mormon may enter any Mormon temple without a temple recommend, given by the Church's high authorities, guaranteeing the member's worthiness. Any member may enter the Temple basement, however, to be baptized by proxy for deceased non-Mormons who hadn't heard about, or accepted, the Mormon Church during their lifetime: relatives, friends, strangers, and even those of other faiths such as Jews, Catholics, and Muslims.

When I was thirteen, I did this.

Although I was scared, I felt mature and was also oddly proud to be part of the vicarious baptisms. That day I was vividly aware of the cool Naugahyde seat in my mother's car. I fretted at how the back of my legs began to sweat and dampen my skirt. I worried that the breeze would muss my hair on the walk through the Temple grounds. But my greatest fear was that the lay priest, startled, would look at me and exclaim, "Not worthy!" He would lean into my face and say, "I can tell that you are a liar and a thief, and you don't pay your tithing." I would die on the spot. I knew it.

I was led to the basement of the Temple, where a large font of water was surrounded by twelve huge golden oxen symbolizing the lost tribes of Israel, of which the Mormons believed they were one. I had changed my clothes and was dressed in white. I took off my slippers and climbed down several steps into the water, where a giant of a man stood to receive me. He made no accusations, and I was filled with relief. Still, I shuddered at his hugeness. He put his great hand on my back, pinched my nose shut, and lowered me into the water. He prayed in a dark, deep, rumbly voice, like God's, mumbling the name of a dead person. Then he did it all over again for yet another dead person. And over and over. I don't remember how many times or how many souls I saved. I do know I was drenched, and cold, and very much fed up with the whole thing by the time it was done. I was very glad to be out of there, and I never went again.

"I've always thought that ritual was weird," Eric said.

"That's what Olive said, too," I said. "And because I loved her, I was torn."

My best friend at that time was Olive, a girl whose name fit her. She was dark, plump, and round breasted at age fourteen. She had a faint odor of salt about her; her parents called her "ripe." Her family was poor, Italian, Catholic, and outspoken. I met her when I was eleven and selling Girl Scout cookies; she asked me whether I would come back to visit. I went to her house, where we listened to music, drew pictures of naked women, and hung laundry on the indoor clothesline, which was strung from her kitchen to the bathroom.

After I was baptized for the dead, I believed I was superior to her and said so. But she scoffed at my pride. "That's so corny," she said.

"You are just jealous," I retorted. I wanted to change the subject. "Here, let me comb your hair." Olive's hair was long and black, and she enjoyed my "coiffing" it. She sat between my legs, and I brushed her hair a hundred strokes.

But I couldn't let the matter go. Olive needed instruction. "I am a servant of Jesus, and I am gathering souls into the everlasting Kingdoms," I explained.

"No, you aren't." She shifted in my lap. "You're just forcing people who can't fight back to be Mormons. That is so creepy."

"Not so." I was sad for Olive. "You can't get into Heaven unless you're a Mormon," I argued.

She warned, "Don't you ever get baptized for me, OK?"

"But then we won't be together in Heaven."

"Yes, we will." She turned and wrapped her legs around me. "We'll all be together: Catholics like me, Episcopalians like your uncles, Jews and Arabs and sun worshippers. God loves us all, and Jesus means for us all to be in Heaven."

That seemed reasonable. So I asked Mom whether it was true. What if some dead person hadn't wanted to be a Mormon? What if she was a Catholic or Jew? What if all those people I was baptized for had liked their own religion? Wouldn't they be mad when they woke up? I mean, why didn't we ask them when they were alive? Could we undo it?

"Stop asking so many questions," Mom grumbled. "Listen to me. There are a hundred paths to Heaven. Olive will be there, too."

"How do you know? That's not what Sister Mallow taught me at Sunday school." I paused, resentful and unsure. "She said there's only one path. You have to be Mormon."

"Well, Sister Mallow is not the most saintly of Sunday-school teachers," Mom sneered. "Where is she now, after all?"

"What do you mean?" My mom could not possibly be right. Sister Mallow had been an angel. I didn't know then where she had disappeared to, though I would find out later.

"Go read, or write your stories. You'll figure it all out someday."

My mother was a paradox, sometimes criticizing, sometimes defending the Church. She rarely clarified my doctrinal confusion. This muddle fueled my doubts. Was the Mormon Church right? Or was Mom? Was there one way to Heaven, or many? I loved my mother, and I wanted her to be right, but why had she sent me to be baptized for the dead if it wasn't necessary? And why did she send me to church every Sunday, even though she didn't go herself? But then there was Sister Mallow at Sunday school, who, as far as I knew, never told a lie. So who could I trust if not her? Myself?

I wanted Olive to go to Heaven with me. So that was that. I decided I would convert her, which would satisfy both Mom and Sister Mallow. But I never did, and when she moved away the next year, I lost her. I harbored a secret hope that there were many paths to Heaven, and I would meet her there.

As we drove closer into the heart of Salt Lake City, Eric said, "But I do remember the Tabernacle." I welcomed the shift in subjects. Yes, the Tabernacle. "You didn't have to be a good Mormon to go there," he continued, and then he fell silent in memory.

Temple Square also enfolds the LDS Tabernacle, home to the world-famous Mormon Tabernacle Choir. Unlike the Temple, the Tabernacle is open to all, Church members and visitors alike. The elongated dome, shaped like a silver bread loaf, stretches 250 feet long and 150 feet across, and is held aloft by forty-four sandstone piers. Seven thousand people could comfortably fill the pews in the audience, the gallery, and the balcony. From the pulpit, in front of one of the world's largest pipe organs, the leaders of the Church deliver speeches during conferences to a full house of Latter Day Saints, who come from all over the world to attend.

"I remember that running through the pews was like being lost in a vast maze." Eric smiled. "My friends and I put tacks on the seats."

Not me. As a child, I sat reverently in the straight-backed pine pews or played happily on the Temple grounds, racing along the paths bordered with bushes and flowers circling the buildings. Although the Church eventually purchased surrounding blocks for its multiple buildings, I recalled the genealogy building on the Square, where we traced our ancestors, and Brigham Young's old house, which housed his fifteen or more wives.

I was taught that the spirit of Jesus came only to Mormons. And on those grounds I felt Him, and I felt blessed to belong to what we fervently declared to be "the Only True Church." Even though I left that Mormon community in my early twenties, I still thought of it as a "family of origin."

Eric, however, did not have that family, and he felt the loss as he grew up. "I was surrounded by the Mormons and the Church," he said, "but I wasn't really a part of it. I just stood outside and looked in." He paused. "I longed for it, but I knew I didn't belong." Suddenly the car seemed too warm. I cracked the windows, letting in the cool autumn air. "You know. Mom and Dad, and all that." I did, but I didn't want to talk about it yet.

We intended to head directly to Temple Square, to the heart of the faith in which I was raised, from which I had departed, and in which Eric was immersed but not integrated. We determined this was the place to begin, the sacred place that had permeated my childhood and adolescence and, as I believed, had profoundly betrayed me. But I drove instead in a long detour around the city. "This is OK," Eric said, without my asking.

We were subdued as we drove to the East Bench. The afternoon sun shadowed the mouths of the many canyons. We drove into the tree-lush Federal Heights neighborhood, which rose to the foothills in the northeast. Our maternal grandparents had lived there above the old Fort Douglas site, in the city's wealthiest neighborhood, now overabundant with cottonwoods and aspen. Years-old maple and cherry trees hung over wide front porches; long lawns sloped to the street. Our grandparents' house stood austerely at the top of one hill and at the bottom of another, looking smaller than I had remembered it.

We drove past Ninyah and Baba's house. How we had loved it. Every Christmas they set up a tree so large it filled the music room. In the vast kitchen, Cook made scones and fried rice for lunch when I stayed over, and in the master-bedroom suite, Baba sat in his overstuffed chair, smoked his pungent pipe, and pulled the tasseled cord to ring for the butler to bring more coal for the fire.

When I was ten, my father (whom my grandparents disapproved of) divorced my mother. So we came to live in my grandparents' house on their displeased sufferance, relegated to the dark and damp basement. Then, during my mother's brief marriage to Eric's wealthy father (whom my grandparents did approve of), we bought our own mansion right across the street. I had my own bedroom with a balcony, where I sat reading the Mormon magazine *The Children's Friend*. Our maid and her daughter lived with us. Christmas was a spectacular affair, amid smells of cinnamon and the taste of eggnog, and Eric was born there a few months before his father left us all.

Mother was divorced again, this time with five children. We moved to the lower, less-affluent Avenues. Like many in the neighborhood, our house shared a pocked driveway. The second-story porch was converted into my chilly bedroom, and the backyard grew thick with weeds. Apartment buildings and small stores congregated and socialized with the houses. People dumped trash in the fields; adults parked their cars on the lawn. Children played kickball in the streets and chalked hopscotch squares on the sidewalks, pushing a rubber hoppy taw from square to square with their toes. We lived there until Eric was seven and I was seventeen.

Eric had taken over the wheel, and he drove us into these lower Avenues, moving ever closer to town center. We passed the now-vacant corner of T-Street Market, where Eric had once bought candy and I had stolen it. We drove by Reservoir Park, where we'd played on the swings and tricky bars, and imagined dead bodies in the reservoir. And we saw Wasatch Elementary School, where I attended one day rich from Federal Heights (driven there by our live-in maid) and the next day poor (walking to school). In the latter days, I took a sack lunch, and after school, I played at my new friend Joan's house, where she and her mother lived in a basement with no windows.

Now, thirty years later, our ragged 1st Avenue neighborhood was gentrified, with small art galleries, a spa, and an antique shop on a corner. But progress did not dull for me the memory of dry, prickly, and browning lawns, or erase the smell of cabbage cooking, or diminish the feel of the potholed streets as we bumped down them in my mother's beat-up Ford. The once-lovely heave of hills far above to the north was now obese and acne-pocked with modern megahouses, whose windowed eyes stretched floor to ceiling to lord over the suburbanized valley.

Eventually, Eric and I turned west on a street far north of the Temple, completing a wide path around the Temple block. We repeated this square, each of us on edge, each circle bringing us a bit closer in, turning down street after street until the Temple was four blocks away on every side.

Then we stopped. I was exhausted in a fearful way. Eric, too, seemed tense. Without discussing it, we went no closer to the Temple.

We had reservations at the Stansbury Suites, so we drove over, parked the car on the hot asphalt, and disgorged ourselves. Blocks away, on the top of one of the Temple's many spires, the golden statue of the Angel Moroni rose into the sky, blowing his horn high above the city streets below.

"Good old Angel Moroni," I said. "The bearer of good news."

Eric began to unpack the car.

In 1834, an angel appeared to young Joseph Smith in upstate New York (so the story goes) and revealed that the True Church of the Lord had been lost to all who had come before, and that he, the Angel Moroni, would deliver the Restored Church to Joseph. This was the only true Gospel of Christ; an old priest named Mormon had written it years earlier in foreign script on golden plates. Moroni led Joseph to the Hill Cumorah, where the plates were buried. With the help of his friend, Oliver, and two magic stones called seer stones, named Urim and Thummim, Joseph translated the plates into the Book of Mormon. Thus the true Gospel was restored to the world. The plates subsequently disappeared. Now a gold statue of Moroni adorns the highest spire of all Mormon temples. The angel is blowing his horn in celebration and welcome.

That day I felt a strong sense of power in refusing Moroni's pull. He would have to wait until I cooled off, rested, ate, bathed, laid out clean clothes, slept, gave the Toyota a good scrub, and washed the car windows so I could better see the truth.

"I hate the Church," Eric offered as we loaded up the suite's kitchen with our boxes of food.

"But you weren't really an active member," I said, curious.

"But it was all around me. Everywhere," he responded. "All my friends were Mormons. Everything happened around the Church. Everyone knew Mom was a Jack Mormon, smoking and drinking, and that our dads had dumped her. They teased me. I felt so helpless. A nobody." He stopped, looked at the loaf of bread he held in his hand, not seeing it. "I was so ashamed." I went to him, and we hugged, standing still for a long time.

"You aren't a nobody," I said. "You've always been a somebody."

We didn't go to Temple Square the next day either. It fact, we didn't go until the end of the trip, when I went not for memories but for good-byes of an unexpected kind.

Eric and I shared a bond made of thread needled so deep that we felt lockstitched together forever. When I married at age twenty-one, I left him with Mom's third of five husbands and the man's two wild sons. During the next four years, Eric fell into a deep depression, turning abusively against Mom and her new family. Mom placed him in a boarding academy and, when that failed, in a foster home, where he attempted suicide.

At age sixteen, he called me and begged me to rescue him, which I did. He lived with my husband and me in Oregon during his senior year of high school, where he finally found success: vice president of his class, an advocate for disadvantaged students, a scholar, and a popular young man. After graduation, he went back to Utah to attend the University of Utah, where he did well. After college he left Utah and did not return. Until now.

We planned obsessively for the upcoming days, as all five of my mother's children had learned to do. Planning was order, order was control, and control was power.

Eric and I made separate lists of the places we would visit. Some places we would go to together: the government buildings that housed our histories; the Salt Lake County Courthouse, where we would read transcripts of our mother's court hearings; the Utah Real Property Division, for the deeds to our houses; the Latter Day Saints Genealogical Society, for our family's genealogy charts; and the public library, to view the *Deseret News* archives during the years my great-great-grandfather was the fiery, polygamy-supporting editor. We scheduled interviews with my mother's last living sibling, Uncle Thurston, and our two widowed aunts. We would go to the canyons. We would visit the houses we'd lived in, the neighborhood churches, the schools we'd attended.

When we weren't together, we would come and go in each other's shadows, or touch briefly for stories and comfort, lingering over food, sharing laughter and information we had gleaned. We each had the memory of a different father to confront. We had unique memories of Mom and of the Mormon Church. We would roam our city and our pasts.

From each place of despair, we would take a token. Then we would travel together to Bear Lake. To throw them into the deep.

In a sense, we made this trip together. In a very deep sense, we each made it alone.

Everything went according to plan. Almost.

CHAPTER 4

PIONEERS

———◆———

OUR ANCESTRAL MORMON STORIES WERE passed down over the years. Baba told us the facts about the Church and our history, and Ninyah infused them with faith and color. My mother, when she was in a rare good mood, elaborated and dramatized them. My father just laughed and said we had all been "hoodwinked by a darn-good con man." He said the founder, Joseph Smith, was a "water finder, a woman chaser, and a charlatan."

Baba took all the children on Sunday rides, where sometimes, instead of listening to the radio, he would tell us about his grandfather's life. I thought the story rich and exotic, and I made him repeat it again and again.

"Your great-great-grandfather, Charles William Penrose, was born in England in 1830," Baba recited. "When he was eighteen years old, Mormon missionaries converted him to the fledging religion. That means 'new.'" He looked at me. I knew what it meant. After all, I was five. "Now, imagine this..." Baba continued.

As I grew older, I learned the wonder of the story. Grampa tramped through Great Britain for over ten years, preaching the Gospel and seeking converts. He met and converted the mild Lucetta in an English country house. They married, and in 1861, when Grampa was thirty-one, they crossed the ocean in a long and perilous journey, immigrating to America. They followed the trekking Mormons to Utah in answer to the worldwide call from the second Prophet, Brigham Young: "Come to Salt Lake City, all ye faithful. We Saints are building Zion!"

In a covered wagon carrying his pregnant wife, their three living children, and everything the family owned, Grampa Penrose pioneered across the continent to the hot and salty Utah desert, where he became a leader in the Mormon Church, a composer of hymns, and the editor of Salt Lake City's *Deseret News.* Mom told the story best.

When Mom and Daddy fought (over religion, money, the children, and each other's deficiencies), Daddy slept on the couch, and Mom let me sleep with her, unless I wiggled too much.

"Be still," she'd grumble, and I lay quiet as a star so I could stay there, listening to her talk in the dark, the orange glow of her cigarette piercing the shadows.

I always felt slightly guilty about Daddy on the couch, but I was too eager to be close to Mom and hear her tales to refuse her invitations. One evening, when I was six or so, Mom had one of her headaches and went to bed early.

"Tell your mother she's wrong," Daddy said as I walked by him to the bedroom.

I rubbed Mom's head while she talked to me from her pillow. "That feels good," she said. I was happy I'd pleased her. After a while, she pushed up on her elbow and took a long drink from her glass. Suddenly she turned to me. "Grampa Penrose became a Mormon in England," she began, and I waited for the good part. "He was really, really old when he got baptized, you know…about eighteen." Mom chuckled and smoked some more.

I didn't puzzle long over that. Mormon children are baptized at age eight, but I was pretty sure I knew why Grampa had waited. When you get baptized, the Holy Ghost comes into your body. That's pretty scary! I thought I would wait, too.

Mom fluffed the blanket up and threw it back. "Rub my temples again," she said.

"Great Britain must be a very big place if it's called 'great,'" I joked. "Is it as great as Great-Great-Grampa?" I liked my own jokes.

"He came from England in a boat," she continued, ignoring me. "That's clear across the ocean, thousands of miles from here."

I was impressed. The librarian showed it to me on a round globe. She said it was hundreds of times farther than Bear Lake. It took hours to get to Bear Lake, so I knew England must be forever away.

Mom waved her arms and shook the quilt up and down in waves. "Waves crashing! Thunder! Lightning from the sky! The boat nearly tipping over in the wind."

I shuddered. A gray ash fell on the sheet. She brushed it off.

The summer night was warm and dry. A hot breeze blew in from the open window. "Great Britain is three whole countries." She took another drink.

I wondered whether Grampa's shoes had holes in them.

"Then," she said. I took a deep breath. "Imagine this! They came clear across the Wild West." She murmured into her glass, "Looking for what?"

I looked at my mother that night, in the deep dusk light, her cigarette glowing. Usually her face was ragged and mean-streaked, especially during her angry tirades, when she ordered us about and when she complained about Daddy. But that night she was breathtakingly beautiful. Her face softened when she told stories or sang songs. I have a photo of her that reminds me of that night, when I sat up on my elbow and gazed at her face in the moonlight: her pink skin as smooth as a tulip petal; her eyebrows arched in perfect half moons; her hair blond and downy; her lips, slightly opened, still red with the dark lipstick she always wore. I didn't dare kiss her, though I longed to do so. "Get away," she would have said.

Suddenly Mom interrupted my gazing, putting her cigarette down in the ashtray, sitting up straight, and leaning close to me in the deepening dark. "Gramma was so scared. Wolves lurked at the edge of the

forests." She lifted her body up in a dark arch over me. "Owoooooooo!'"
she howled. I shuddered with terrified pleasure.

"Grampa had to swim rivers, go miles through deep tunnels." I'd
seen pictures of miners with lights on their heads and soot on their
cheeks. That was Grampa! "He had to climb high cliffs, finger by finger,
grabbing at the cracks." Mom lifted her arms over her head to the bed-
stead; her fingers crawled up the wood to the wall.

"Did he fall?" I was thrilled, part of me hoping he had.

Mom laughed. She was enjoying herself as much as I was. She offered me a sip of her drink. It tasted like bitter orange juice.

"No. He was well hung." She laughed, and so did I, imagining
Grampa hanging on for dear life, but safe.

"And we can thank God," Mom breathed out. "'Cause otherwise we
wouldn't be here." She tickled me. "Wouldn't that just be such a shame?"

It felt wonderful to be in her bedroom, in her lilac sheets. The smell
of her Tabu powder floated in the air and mixed with the smoke, and
willow fronds swished across the window screen. When her humor rang
out, I took it as the affection I so craved. Once I grew up, I figured that
she was probably drunk, or on her way, and sarcastic. But that didn't
change my sweet memory of her then: happy, pleased with herself.

She drained her glass and picked up her burned-down cigarette,
took a long drag on it, and stubbed it out. She lay back and blew out the
smoke in a slow exhale. "He went on, brave in his faith." She sighed.

The breeze blew gently in. I smelled her smoke rise at my side and
felt it curl warmly around me. "They fled to the West," she murmured.
"Fled. Bled. Dead." She rolled over and went to sleep.

Mom was grumpy when she woke up, her headache still pounding.
She wanted a beer and didn't feel like talking while she drank it.

I wonder now whether Grampa Penrose had been caught in the
Kansas-Missouri debacle over whether those states would be admitted
to the Union as free states or slave states. Kansas had only just been admitted to the United Sates as a free state in 1861, but violence from pro-
slavery rebels lingered. President Lincoln had signed the second part of

the Emancipation Proclamation in January 1861, although the Civil War was still in full flower. The Battle of Gettysburg occurred in July, the very month Grampa had pioneered across the country to Utah. Immigrants weren't required to fight in the Civil War, and Grampa had no desire to do so. He may have skirted Kansas altogether, setting his narrow focus on the Mormon Zion.

That trek across the plains was the good part of the story. I made Ninyah, Baba, and Mom repeat it over and over again: Grampa leaving President Lincoln and the Civil War behind, searching for a place where he was safe, walking hundreds of miles to get there!

Mom taught me how to remember all the eastern states Grampa went through. "You know how I say 'Poor me!' when I'm tired?" Yes, I knew. "Well, think it three times: 'Po' me, me, me.' Except think 'Po' I, I, I.' That's *P* for Pennsylvania, and *I* three times for Indiana, Illinois, and Iowa." I remembered "Po' I, I, I," but I couldn't remember the states. I just thought about Mom, rubbing her bunions and groaning "Po' I!"

Grampa Penrose's family walked about fifteen hundred miles. With their wagon, livestock, and draft animals, they crossed the Mississippi River from Illinois and then forded the Missouri River out of Iowa and into Nebraska. They followed the Platte River to Wyoming. Prairie flies buzzed at their heads and ate the grass out from under the cattle. Gramma's skirts and petticoats soaked up the dew and became filthy and heavy. They trudged along, day after day. Mosquitoes chased them and feathered their faces. When it rained, the wagon got stuck in the mud. Sometimes they found notes left by others who had gone before, written on white buffalo hides and tied to a rock: "Welcome, new Saints." Baba and Ninyah told me that the Indians were a source of trouble, but Mom told me they were friendly, protective, and eager to trade fishhooks and beads.

They stopped at Fort Laramie. Gramma sewed and cooked while Grampa danced, played horseshoes, and wrestled. The children played draughts, ball, and tag. On Sundays, everyone rested, prayed, and sang hymns all day long.

Even today, Mormons spend Sundays in worship and are prohibited from play or commerce—although a Mormon friend secretly gives me money to buy things for her, and with her blinds drawn, she watches movies on Netflix.

The Saints followed the Oregon Trail to Fort Bridger in the lower corner of Wyoming, near the Bear River Divide, through sagebrush and bunchgrass, which sometimes caught fire and licked at their wagon wheels. They passed herds of buffalo, and Mom said they saw antelope, hares, and wolves. "Gramma had a lovely perfume called Le Skoonk," Mom joked. I thought she was serious and marveled at Gramma's foresight to carry it across the prairie.

The Donner Party had come this way before, so my Grampa followed that trail. When I was a child, no one told me that the Donner Party was not a festive group that had ultimately met tragedy. I imagined all the Donners dancing and stomping until all the brush was knocked flat and the path was cleared. Grampa turned off the Donner trail at Weber Canyon and down East Canyon, which flamed out that autumn in a wide palette of color, spreading over the hillsides and down into the promised valley.

Recently I read Wallace Stegner's *The Gathering of Zion*. He movingly describes the "suffering, endurance, discipline, and faith" of the immigrant Mormons. Even though I no longer belong to the Church, I am deeply moved by the pioneer stories and have emerged with a fierce pride in my ancestors. I understand more fully the origins of my work ethic, my fortitude, and my strong determination.

———•———

"I'm tired," Mom protested one night when Daddy was on the couch and I was in Mom's bed. I asked for the story again. "You tell it. But first fix me a drink." I did.

I came back and snuggled in under the quilt. "Well…" I said dramatically. This theatricality, encouraged from the time I was three, would carry me onto the stage for the next decade, then into the classroom, and then into the courtroom. On that winter night, though my audience was only my mother, I gave it my all.

"Oh, the trip across the plains was hard, hard, hard!" I held my hand to my forehead, thumb pressed against my temple, and sighed a mournful moan.

"Grampa Penrose clawed his way up the steep cliffs, hacked through thorny brambles into ravines, chased after his stolen horses, and wove through meadows white with Queen Anne's lace and red with Indian fireweed." I shook my body, bumping up and down. "His wagons rattled down the rugged Pony Express trail. The pioneers camped at the foot of the looming granite peaks, surrounded by wolves. Thousands of miles they plodded, until, finally, at last, thank God, the wagon train creaked and wheeled and rolled into the sandstone basin."

Mom had fallen asleep, but I went on.

"Grampa started campfires on the trail and shot his rifle into the trees. Bang!"

Mom rolled over, mumbling slurry words.

"He sat on the buckboard and cracked his whip over the oxen. 'Hyah! Hyah!'" I sat up and cracked my imaginary whip on the quilt. "Gramma stirred a big black pot of deer and rabbit and prairie-dog soup with a wooden spoon as it hung over the campfire." I stirred with an imaginary spoon. "Mmmm!" I licked my lips. Then I scuttled under the covers and put my leg up against Mom's bum. I closed my eyes.

My breath felt warm, like handholding, as I talked into Mom's nightgown. "They roasted marshmallows on aspen twigs. Grampa cut one for each child." I could smell the sap. "Let's see…Ernest, Jessie, and Kate played with stones in the creeks. They threw sticks for the puppy. They chased grasshoppers and jackrabbits. They played hide-and-seek in the boulders and up in the trees."

I was tired of talking. Still, I couldn't leave them, so I dreamed them.

I dreamed it was bedtime in the belly of the Wasatch Mountains that stood guarding us from danger. The full moon threw itself over the wagons like gauze. Grampa's puppy settled his chin on his paws. Ten thousand stars shone overhead.

I was falling asleep, and I dreamed that Grampa became Daddy. "Come, Ernest and Jessie and Kate and Kathy," Daddy said, "and look at the stars with me." We lay on our backs in the meadows, looking up to see where Daddy was pointing—to the cup, the bear, and the man with a bow and arrow.

I told him he didn't have to sleep on the couch; he could sleep with me. We slept under the wagon wheels, where Daddy tucked us all in. "Here's your favorite song, sweet girl." He brushed his hand on my head, twined his fingers in the strands, and sang softly. *Without a song, the road will never bend.* The rhythm of his voice was like a stream.

I imagined his voice wrapped around me, warm, steady, fragrant with campfire smoke.

I dreamed I fell asleep in my father's arms.

———◆———

Years later, when I was eight, Mom was sitting at the kitchen table, doing her books. It was my turn to fix dinner, and I was opening the spaghetti cans. Suddenly she looked up from her books. "You know what?" she asked.

I knew by the challenging tone of her voice that something was coming. I waited. Mom sat forward and leaned on her hand. "What?" I said, turning, alert.

"Lucetta was just the first of three wives Grampa had in his lifetime." She paused and took a drink, and then looked slyly at me. "All at the same time."

She let this sink in. Why hadn't I heard about this before? Three mothers for three kids!

I turned back to the stove, surprised and oddly upset. I emptied the cans into a pot and turned the burner on. Something occurred to me. "Did they have more kids?"

"Yes, indeed. They certainly did."

"How many?" I assumed a casual air.

"Well, in England, Charles and Lucetta had four—one a year. But one died before they left Essex. They came across the ocean with three. Lucetta was pregnant, but the baby died in Emigration Canyon."

I felt a tug in my throat. No one had told me.

I could feel Mom smile. "Charles had more, though," she teased.

"How many?" My friend Susan had thirteen brothers and sisters. Most of the families in the Church had seven or eight. Some had a dozen or more! We had four so far. But that was enough for me.

"By the time Grampa was a little older than I am now—" Mom paused until I had to turn away from the stove and look at her. Satisfied that I was paying attention, she went on. "He had twenty-eight children!"

I was stunned, and I lost all pretense of indifference. Where did they live? Where did twenty-eight children sit? Who got the bedrooms? I tried to figure out how many children that was to each mother.

"Go on, Mom," I encouraged her.

"That's all." She looked down and picked up her pencil. "I guess they lived happily ever after." She chuckled and went back to her books. "Stir the spaghetti."

That was it. I could get no more information from my mother. I was deeply disturbed by this news, worried that the children would get underfoot, be trampled, starve, get lost. Why did my Grandfather Penrose have so many kids?

I finally asked Baba.

"Great-Great-Grandfather Penrose was a very important man," Baba responded, rocking in his chair. I played with my dolls at his feet.

"That doesn't answer my question very well," I complained.

"He wrote hymns for the Church," Baba went on, "and he talked to President Cleveland when Utah was trying to become a state."

"Why?"

"Why what?"

When I look back at this conversation, I see where my mother and then her children got their talent for denial and obfuscation.

"Baba!" I refused to let it go. "Why did Grampa have twenty-eight children?"

Baba sighed. "Well, he went to the president to argue that Mormon men should be able to practice polygamy."

He wasn't going to answer my question.

"What's polygamy?" I asked irritably.

He sighed again. "It means that men can have more than one wife."

I perked up. "Why do men want more than one wife?"

Baba smiled but was silent. Ninyah, who had been sitting in her own chair, quietly sewing, interjected.

"So the women can replenish the earth with children, dear," she said. "There are little spirit babies in Heaven waiting for bodies. They have to have a body first, before they become a Mormon and go to Heaven. So women have lots and lots of children."

I was perplexed. There were little souls cluttering up the sky? I had been one?

"Come here, Kathy," Baba said sternly. "I'll sing you one of Grampa's hymns." Baba picked me up, settled me into his lap, and then launched into "School Thy Feelings," which only the men sang, though I didn't know why. My mother and father should have both schooled their feelings every day.

I waited patiently for the singing to be over. Then I asked, "Why can't wives have more than one husband?"

Although a separate non-Mormon sect named the Fundamentalist Latter Day Saints (FLDS) preaches and practices polygamy, Mormons no longer do. Originally, however, the Mormon Prophet Joseph Smith received a revelation from God that directed members to practice multiple marriage. He himself married about thirty women, ten of whom were already married. Brigham Young had fifteen wives and was "sealed" to fifty-seven, all told. By sealing the women to him, he ensured that they would be with him in his eternal family in Heaven. This troubled me.

What if a woman he married was already sealed to her own husband? Who got her?

However, in spite of my Grampa's advocacy, and as a condition of Utah's admission into the United States, polygamy was outlawed. Yet it is still practiced in offshoot factions of the Church, the best known of which is the FLDS (of Warren Jeffs fame). Ironically, however, the revelation has not been removed from, or contradicted by, the Church's second-most-sacred text, *The Doctrine and Covenants*, one declaration of which commands multiple marriage. So it seems that, although prohibited on earth, men will have multiple wives in Heaven, if there are more women than men in the afterlife. As a child, I had a question on that point.

"What if there are more men than women?" I asked, but I received no response.

It's a tricky subject, then and now.

———◆———

Ninyah invited us to dinner whenever she was on good terms with Mom. Over roast pork, fried potatoes, and steaming vegetables, the family carried on spirited discussions about the Church. I was primarily interested in the food, which was far better than we had at home. I usually paid attention to the oft-repeated tales, though anxiety crept over me when Dad sneered and Mom yelled, their voices rising, which caused Baba to slap his palm on the table and roar, "Enough!"

One Thanksgiving, after several cocktails, our family sat at Ninyah's long mahogany dinner table, feasting on Cook's roast turkey, mashed potatoes, rich gravy, buttered asparagus, baked apples, and pumpkin pie. Baba carved; Ninyah served. Alternately, they corrected our manners and instructed us on the meaning of Thanksgiving.

"We are thankful we are Mormons," said Ninyah, "and for our plenteous bounties."

We then each listed our gratitudes. Sandy, then eleven, refused to say; Lucy, then six, was grateful for her doll; Clark was only four, but I expect he was grateful to finally be potty trained, which had taken forever. As for me, age nine, I was thankful for the food. Eric wasn't born yet—lucky Eric.

"I am *so* thankful for my screwdriver," Mom chuckled, to Baba's dismay, "that I think I'll be thankful for another."

Baba ignored Mom. "I'm thankful for my lovely wife," he said lovingly, "and dear grandchildren."

Cook answered the buzzer, which was discreetly hidden under the lip of the dining-room table. She served up the dessert and poured Grand Marnier for the adults. Before Cook returned to the kitchen, Mom tapped her glass for a second fill-up, ignoring Baba's displeasure. She turned to me. "Would you like to have three husbands when you grow up, Kathy?"

I had thought about this. "No," I said. "I want to marry Olive."

Even though Olive was Catholic, we had talked about joining religions and becoming Mormolic. I liked the idea of praying to a woman, and she liked the idea of being sealed to your family for eternity—especially to me if we married.

"You can't marry Olive," Ninyah said. "It's a sin."

Daddy agreed.

"Men can't marry men," said Baba.

"And women can't marry women, darling," sniffed Ninyah in her most aristocratic voice.

"Who gives a shit," said Mom.

I said I didn't understand why grown-ups who loved each other couldn't marry, even more than one person at a time, so long as they all agreed.

Mom turned to Baba. "So," she said slyly, "Kathy wants to know something." She smiled at me. "Will women have several husbands if there are more men than women in the afterlife?"

I held my breath.

"There won't be," Baba said, dismissing the question.

"And why is that?" Mom was loud and sarcastic. I stopped eating and feared what was to come.

Ninyah said soothingly, "Because women are more spiritual than men. More of them will go to Heaven."

Mom laughed. "Right. Well, who'd want more than one husband anyway? One is bad enough." She looked at Daddy and took a long sip of her after-dinner cordial. "Me, I wouldn't mind having a few working wives."

"It's all poppycock," my father said sullenly.

"What's 'poppycock,' Daddy?" I asked.

"Mormonism, that's what, little darlin'," he soothed, turning to me. "Golden plates, twenty-eight wives, sealings, Kingdoms, God living on the planet Kolob, sacred undergarments—"

"Henry, I won't have this," Ninyah said, trembling. "Please refrain from—"

"Here, Hank. You want poppycock?" Mom threw her drink at Daddy. "Have *this* poppycock."

I was glued to my chair, the woven bamboo of its high back pressed into me. Sandy rolled her eyes. Lucy put her hands over her ears.

"Well, now, isn't that so typical?" Daddy sneered. "You're all drunken hypocrites."

He stood abruptly, left the table, and slammed out the front door. Mom pushed back her chair and stomped off to the living room—to the liquor cabinet, I supposed.

Baba rapped on the table with his fork. "Here now, children. Let's sing 'Over the River and Through the Woods.'"

When we were done singing, Ninyah said sweetly, "Now, let's talk about something pleasant, shall we? More pie, dears?"

I was all for that.

There were many disturbing scenes of that sort when the family was together for a meal. I often joined in, teasing Lucy, who was quiet, vulnerable, and frightened by the language and the tone of the voices. Sandy yelled at Mom, and Daddy derided us all. When Clark was born, we called him a cipher. "Pass the ketchup to nobody," we taunted.

We passed the cruelty down.

———◆———

Even as I grew older, I played at pioneering. I pretended I had three wives and twenty children. I bent and cut branches for guns, ate flowers to keep from starving, and dragged my wagon over Ninyah's yard in the rain, cutting ruts in the grass and digging myself out. I was under attack from Indians. I slapped at the rain, crawled on my knees, and clawed out a valley in the middle of a big lilac bush, where I hid all my wives and children. When Ninyah called me in and sat me on the hearth, I warmed my hands over the fire and said brightly, "We've all frozen and gone to Heaven now."

I often closed my eyes and imagined the thousands of faithful pioneers who, over the years, pioneered to Zion. Ninyah talked about how some of the wagon trains had to plow through high drifts of snow. They plodded on, soaked to the skin in deluges of rain, sucking through mud so deep the wagons sank to the hubs. They crossed rivers that swept away stoves and cows—babies, too, I imagined. And wives. In all, seven thousand pioneers made the trek. Two companies were caught in early winter and ended up walking, pushing handcarts. Caught in the snow, some were rescued, but over two hundred people died —starved or frozen.

I could see Grampa and Gramma coming down the pass. In my imagination, the children skipped alongside the creek, the puppy dog wagged his tail, and they all sang hymns as they rumbled along. They came with their wagons and bedsteads, bureaus and buckets, animals and cooking pots, children, old folk, baby coffins, and Books of Mormon. They came right down those majestic mountains to this dry and treeless plain, right here to this city where I grew up. As a kid, I felt like waving: "Hello there, Grampa! It's me, Kathy!"

Ninyah tells me my great-great-grandfather looked out over the Great Basin to the small oasis the early pioneers were building, to the damming of the creeks and irrigating of the valley, to the planting of potatoes and grain, and to the silvery Great Salt Lake far off to the north and west. He turned to Lucetta and said that Brigham Young had been right when he proclaimed, "This is the place." That's what the

Prophet had said, and Grampa said it was so. It was the Lord's place, the Mormons' place, and my ancestors' place. It became my place, too.

This was my genealogy, and even as young as three and four, I luxu-riated in the stories. I began to feel that I had been born too late, that my pioneer family was my real family, and that my little soul had been dropped to earth too far in the future. I pulled my beloved ancestors around me, and they held me close to their ardent fires. More than any-thing, I wanted to be heated by the religious flames that warmed them. I wanted to believe in the faith that burned in their hearts.

But as early as I can remember, I had questions.

CHAPTER 5

THE DARK HOUSE

———◆———

IN THE MOTEL, I SLEPT poorly. I had a nightmare about the Dark House and a temple of gold with no doors. I dreamed of my grandmother cutting endless reams of cloth with children's scissors, and my grandfather's pungent pipe tobacco poured into a glass of orange juice. I dreamed of a table covered with plastic food and woke in terror when my mother's rage erupted in a dank garage. I rose before sunrise. Although I was sweating, my feet were stone cold.

I unpacked a dark-blue canvas laundry bag. In this bag I would place the tokens from each place I chose to visit. Something to throw away.

Eric still slept. The car was mine this morning, and I planned to visit the house where I was born. But after packing the cooler and filling the car with gas, I was still reluctant to throw myself into the quest, feeling surprised at the recklessness of descending into the past. Now, after all the years of forgetting, I would remember.

As a girl raised in the Mormon Church, I had rebelliously become an inquirer rather than a follower. I was still looking for answers. I wanted to find them; I didn't want to. Somehow I was finding the courage to complete this quest, but I was afraid. I didn't realize how much more afraid I should have been.

Breathless with anxiety, I thought coffee would center me. At Starbucks, I sat quite still, sipping a latte, trying to settle myself. The sun rose, ticking away the time. I waited for my panic to subside.

From the patio where I sat, a slight breeze threatened a scorcher. The mountains shimmered in waves of heat. I imagined I could see the settlers descending. Although I was no longer a Mormon, I still took heart, and my cue, from those thousands of Mormon pioneers who had come so bravely through those mountains and into this desert valley.

Salt Lake City is the heart of the Mormon Church, officially called the Church of Jesus Christ of Latter Day Saints. In Utah, it is simply called the Church. The members call themselves Latter Day Saints, or just Saints, but everyone else calls them Mormons, after the scribe who wrote the book restoring the lost true Gospel, the book translated by Joseph Smith, the founder of the Church.

My maternal ancestors were Saints. I know this because they tracked our genealogy, an important practice in the Mormon Church; knowing your genealogy means you know who you are. The family also tracked our non-Mormon ancestors so that we could be vicariously baptized for them. This "baptism for the dead" ritual is essential, because Mormons believe that only Mormons can enter one of the three Kingdoms of Heaven.

For many years I was told that being Mormon was the most important thing about me, that I was blessed. But did I know who I was?

I knew that my great-great-grandparents were Charles and Lucetta Penrose, who came from England to Utah, where Charles gained great wealth and status. Grampa and Gramma Penrose's daughter, Jessie, married my great-grandfather, William Jones, also a rich and high-placed Mormon. They bore a son and gave him what was then a man's name— Shirley. This was Shirley Penrose Jones, my beloved grandfather, Baba, a gentle, soft-cheeked, cinnamon-tobacco-smelling man, who continued the family tradition as a wealthy, high-ranking member of the Church in spite of a new doctrine prohibiting his drinking and pipe smoking, which he did in secret. He was an attorney, revered and beloved by his colleagues, his friends, and his grandchildren.

While at Georgetown Law School in Washington, DC, Baba met the elegant Sereta Taylor, who was attending a girls' finishing school there. Her father was first the Oakland city treasurer and then a wealthy California real-estate magnate. She became my adored grandmother, Ninyah, a name Sandy bestowed on her when she couldn't pronounce "grandma."

An aristocratic sense of entitlement floated about Ninyah. She walked erect, was perfectly coiffed, and dressed fashionably, even when she wore pedal pushers in the garden. The faint smell of Stargazer lilies drifted around her, and she swept through life as though she had wings, open and ready to enclose me.

Baba and Ninyah bore my mother, also a Sereta—Sereta Taylor Jones—and then three sons, who were jealous of their doted-upon sister. My mother was beautiful, smart, and musical. But she was often aloof, or simmering. When her crimson lips curved softly and enigmatically, you could decipher the meaning only by looking into her eyes, which were a sultry hazel with gold flecks twinkling when she was gay, muddy brown when she brooded, and stormy gray when she was angry. As time went on, her life disintegrated. Buried in disappointments and suffering her parents' cold rejection, she was often enraged at my father, at her parents, and at her children.

My father, on the other hand, was slow to anger, though he had a quick and stinging riposte for each of my grandparents' insults. He was a short, squarish man, dark and handsome, quiet, and affectionate to his children. His wit was sometimes caustic, often sardonic, but his delightful sense of humor often bubbled up and cheered us. He was smart and facile with words. But, crucially, he was unambitious. His smile may have dazzled my mother, but his lack of attention to her, and to his career, infuriated her.

In this fraught union, my parents sizzled together.

Following World War II and my father's discharge, my parents lived in a small, dark-red brick house on 14th East and 13th South with Sandy, born in 1942, a willful and independent child. I was next in 1944, a cheerful, happy baby. Lucy was born in 1947, a quiet, thoughtful, and sad-eyed girl. Clark entered the family in 1949, an afterthought who became the invisible child.

Eric came much later, when I was ten, from a different father.

———◆———

Unable to avoid the day any longer, I sipped the last of my coffee at Starbucks and headed for the Dark House, where we lived until I was six. The drive would take a mere ten minutes if I went straight. Which I didn't.

The Prophet Brigham Young designed Salt Lake City for easy accessibility. The streets, wide enough to allow wagons pulled by teams of horses to turn around, were laid out in well-platted, waffled grids, numbered from the Temple in all four directions: 1st South, 2nd South, and so forth; 1st West, 2nd West, and so forth; and North and East the same. In the northeast residential quadrant, however, the streets were called the Avenues and labeled 1st, 2nd, 3rd Avenue, on up, and the cross streets were A to V Streets. Beyond them, Federal Heights nestled in the foothills.

Our first house was fourteen blocks east and thirteen blocks south of the Temple. The one-story home was small but respectable: two bedrooms, a bath, a utilitarian kitchen, a matchbox-size yard out back, and a thin front porch.

As young as three, I walked these safe Salt Lake City streets or rode my tricycle, and then my bicycle, to escape the noise and tension of my house, and to act out stories I invented. After Daddy left the family when I was nine and until I married, I wandered my city alone and unsupervised. Ninyah issued my only warning: "Never go west! The bad people live there—the coloreds and hoodlums." So I ventured south, east, and north, into the Avenues and through the rich neighborhoods, sometimes walking for hours, often hiking into the foothills. I felt safe, protected by the mountains.

Now, driving slowly toward the 14th East house, I approached the turn and then purposely detoured. I was nervous, steering with one hand, biting my nails on the other. I drove past the corner where Sandy had set up her Girl Scout cookie stand and then past another corner, where Mr. Paulsen had given me lollipops from behind his store counter. Then I headed to my elementary school, Uintah, where I pulled to the curb and stared, remembering that in kindergarten the teachers had insisted that every day I remove my shoes and leave them at the door of the classroom because I kicked the other children. Even so, I went on kicking in my stockinged feet. I looked back and was dismayed that I was so angry when so young.

Parents defended themselves in my courtroom, claiming that their parental fights and excessive discipline couldn't possibly harm the children because they were "only two" or "only four." But I understood that children are deeply affected by domestic violence, including screaming and verbal abuse, and they often exhibit aggressive or frightened behavior as a result. Though I knew this intellectually from textbooks and expert testimony, I realized as my hands gripped the steering wheel that day and the backs of my legs began to sweat on the leather seat that I also knew it on a much more visceral level.

I took a deep breath, pulled away from the school, and drove to the place where I began the life I would now revisit. I parked across the street from the 14th East house, which still looked small and bleak. I stared at it, wanting to knock but not wanting to be let in.

Sandy always called it the Dark House. She remembered our father sexually abusing her there, but she was uncertain whether this was recovered or invented memory. She won't discuss it anymore. "I've been in counseling for years," she said. "I'm done talking about our childhood." It was true that in this personal silence she was a far more cheerful adult than I was. She explained that she saw enough sorrow in her work as a Child Protective Services caseworker, rescuing children from danger.

The 14th East house *was* dark. Low-watt unshaded light bulbs hung from the ceilings; dark, heavy furniture crowded the rooms; little light penetrated through the small, opaque windows, even in the bright Utah summertime.

At first there were happy times. Mom and Dad were playful. She was flat chested and wore padded bras to appear larger breasted. When Daddy felt mischievous, he stole the pads and hid them in unusual places, like the freezer. If she was in a good mood, she laughed.

"Hank, you give me back my falsies!" She would chase him around the house until he succumbed.

"Here they are," he would say, handing her the frozen orbs.

She kept an extra store of them on hand, and when the foam began to crumble as the pads aged, she gave them to Sandy and me. We banged on the hilly half globes with wooden spoons to see whether they would bounce. Daddy didn't seem to mind her pancake breasts. "You're beautiful without big breasts," he would croon. "Your nipples are succulent raspberries."

"Hank!" she would giggle. "Not in front of the children."

"Daddy thinks your boobies are pretty," I told her once when she was bathing. She tossed water on me and shooed me away. "Little pitchers have big ears," she sniffed, but I could tell she was pleased.

Naturally slim, Mom never lost her figure or her power to appear taller and more fluid than her five feet, three inches. She wore a tight girdle, straps hanging down. Sandy and I sat at her feet and watched her wrestle into it, and then we clipped her nylon stockings to the straps. I thought her daring and gorgeous, and at those moments I wanted to be her. But I inherited my father's features—dark hair, short and square stature, and a very large bum. I looked like a giant boulder. I didn't mind too much, though. Daddy was steady.

Roughened by a life of chain-smoking, Mom's deep alto voice was her most appealing feature. Our house never lacked for a piano, no matter how little of everything else we had, and on rare quiet evenings, or after fights, or unaccountably in the middle of the night, the hushed notes of the piano and her velvety voice wafted luxuriously into the turmoil of our home. This silk scarf of music weaving through the house softened the strain and comforted us, wrapping us in a film of family togetherness.

Daddy could be loud and raucous, singing Baptist hymns and songs of hope at full volume: "The Lord's Prayer" and "I Believe." He tossed me in the air, squealed with me as I fell back into his arms, and chased me around the house with fierce growls of "Gonna getcha!" My mother frolicked with her children, too, in those early days. She dressed us in costumes, made up skits, and taught us how to playact.

On some hot summer days, the family piled into the Studebaker and went to swim in the landlocked Great Salt Lake. Saltier than the ocean, we could actually float in it! Mom suntanned while Daddy dashed into the salty water with us. We floated with the seagulls, emerging covered by a thin film of salt that captured the heat of the sun like a hug. In the car on the way home, we'd fall asleep, legs and arms akimbo, grains of sand in our hair.

Sometimes our parents left us home and took a train to Saltair, where they danced to big-band music under glittering chandeliers in the Great Hall. Mom was giddy with happiness the morning after such nights. She whirled around the kitchen, laughing and singing, "I was born to dance."

But as years went on, the atmosphere became heavy, thick with criticism, confusion, and worry, filling me with an undefined anxiety. I think now that my father must have loved my mother and wanted to please her, but he was not ambitious, did not care if he was rich, and was frustrated by her demands for more money, better status, a bigger house.

Mom had been raised with high-class tastes and told me, young as I was, how disappointed she was in Daddy. "I want more!" she cried. More of this and more of that—clothes, trips, a maid. And tuition so she could go to college, start a career. She had once dreamed of being a concert pianist; she had not envisioned herself as a housewife, saddled with three children and no nanny. It took me years to understand all of her complaints; as a small girl, I was simply alarmed by the tone of her voice. Mom and Daddy stopped laughing, stopped going out. She began to nag, pout, and yell at him, and we began to irritate her more and more.

By the time I was five, fights almost always erupted at the dinner table, often with little provocation. One night Daddy teased Mom, saying, "A wife who loved her husband would bring him a second serving of pie." He winked at me, a promise to share.

Mom slammed the pans into the dishwater and came storming back into the dining room. "You think I married you to wait on your stinking needs? You think I married you because I loved you?" She scorched Daddy with her eyes.

"I do," he said mildly. "The latter."

"Well, let me set you straight, Buster. I married you because Mother and Father told me not to."

"That's not so, darlin'. You loved me then, and you still do. And you love the children, who don't need to be hearing this." He stood, moved over to her, tried to take her in his arms.

Shoving him, she jumped back. "Don't touch me. I'm sick of having children. They're little brats." She turned. I was watching, wide eyed. "Do you hear me?" She was very loud. "Brats. That's what you are. Little, shitty brats."

"Stop it right now. That's enough." Daddy took me by the hand and lifted Lucy from her high chair. "Come on, honeys." Sandy climbed down from her chair. "Let's go for a walk."

"That's right," Mom cracked. "Take the girls away. Why don't you take them for a long walk off a short pier?" She picked up the ladle from the table and threw it at us. It hit Daddy's arm, and cold gravy splashed onto my sleeve.

Daddy turned to go. Over his shoulder, I saw Mom put her head down on the table. "Why don't you ever take *me* anywhere?" she yelled into the cloth. She began to cry, but we were out the door.

CHAPTER 6

RUNNING AWAY

———◆———

IN THAT SMALL HOUSE ON 14th East, the chaos tumbled down on us. The noise increased, abrading our lives, pocking them like hailstones— my mother's high-pitched wailing; her long, windy sighs; her snarls of frustration, buzzing behind her clenched teeth. My father's grunts, sibilant hisses, and electric silences filled me with trepidation. Their arguments sent me into a dark, hollow interior: my eyes closed with my hands slapped over my ears, or my head covered with a blanket and my knees hugged to my chest.

My mother's dark disappointments must have sullied her life. They certainly stained ours. She had wanted to be rich, as in her childhood, but could see it was not to be. She was furious at her parents' rejection of her husband and hence of her. She had not wanted children but felt it was her Mormon duty. We had been an interruption in her pursuit of happiness, and she let us know it.

She began to hit us. Occasionally, then often.

But my father adored me. I began to cleave to him.

In my earliest memory of terror, I had been abandoned. I wasn't yet four. It was night and too quiet in the house. I climbed out from under my star-studded blankie and slid to the floor. Lucy slept in her crib; Sandy, in the upper bunk. I half walked, half crawled to Daddy and Mom's bedroom. It was empty. I looked in the dimly lit kitchen. Empty. In the dining room, I steadied myself on the wooden leg of the table chair and stared into the dark place beneath the table. I often hid there, closed in by the hanging tablecloth. I was frightened by an urgent need to know where Daddy was.

Alarmed by the silence of a house usually filled with rancor and pandemonium, I hurried awkwardly toward the living room. Something was wrong. The scary space between the too-tall ceiling and me was frighteningly high. From here to the front door was darkness. I began to gulp in little half gasps of fear. I couldn't form clear words yet, only the skeletons of words. The one word I could wail, however, was perfectly clear to me as I spread it through the room in a wail: "Daddy!"

Harold leaped off of the couch where he had been lying next to Molly. Like all my babysitters' boyfriends, he was not allowed to come over while she sat. But like all of them, he sneaked over anyway.

"God, I'd better get out of here." He tucked in his shirt and hurriedly left.

Molly awakened from a soft sleep and reluctantly came to cradle me. "It's OK, Kathy, for Heaven's sake. I'm right here. Your mom'll be home soon."

"No Mom," I cried out. "I want Daddy!"

This would be my cry for years to come.

———

Our family lived together in the 14th East house, but not in harmony. Sandy became sullen and belligerent. I had thought things would be better after Lucy was born. Bald at first, her head soon feathered with white fluffs of hair. She was a beautiful baby who never cried or gave trouble. Still, Mom and Daddy fought about the children, about money, about her parents, and sometimes about nothing I could understand. Mom hurled accusations and objects—lamps, dishes, and books. Daddy growled sarcasm, spit insults, and fell into long silences.

Mom got a job. She worked as a secretary and was exhausted much of the time. We were watched by a series of ladies who came to the house. Molly sat sometimes, until my mother came home and found her on the couch with yet another new boyfriend. Mom wouldn't give him his trousers and made him leave without them.

We knew when Mom arrived home after work because she always slammed the door. "OK," she'd demand, "give me a report on the children." Each babysitter was required to snitch on our bad behavior, after which Mom spanked us with the back of the hairbrush. If the crime committed had been especially horrendous, she threatened, "Wait till your father hears about this."

My parents did not beat each other up, but they were wounded nonetheless. The bruises fell on us as well, like stones falling on a talus slope, over and over until, exhausted, they settled. Though I detested my mother's vitriol, I was acutely hurt by my father's passivity. I couldn't understand why he didn't save us from my mother's wrath.

But I never doubted his love.

At night, when I cried in the dark, Daddy had low, hard words with Mom, and then he came into my room and turned my night-light back on. He read to me until I fell asleep. If, in the middle of the night, their harsh words woke me up, he'd come in and sing to me. Sometimes I tried to wake myself up to call out, "Daddy, I'm scared," so he would tell me another story, sing me another song, and let me hold his hand until it fell from my own in slumber.

On days when Mom was in a foul mood, Daddy took me outside, in the light. He pushed me up and down the sidewalk on a tiny toy car with wheels. He pulled me in the wooden red wagon two blocks down to the corner store for a piece of penny candy. He sat on the lawn, rolling a ball back and forth with me. We made lemonade and served it to each other in teacups on the lawn.

From my swing, I could see the mountains. Daddy told me stories about the trolls and kind giants who lived there. "The tall peaks are the fathers," he explained. "They have many wives, who are shorter and rounder. Can you see?" We found them in the crevices and shadows of the peaks, or when the sun struck them. Some were skinny, some plump, some smiled, some scowled.

"Henry!" Mom scolded from the porch. "There are no multiple wives." Daddy just chuckled.

Of course there were hundreds of children, little elves and trolls turning hilly somersaults. Juniper bushes and Ponderosa pines played on the slopes until dusk enveloped them and the mothers called them in.

The Wasatch Mountains could be seen from almost any house in the city. I knelt on the couch as a child, my chin on my arms, and looked out, watching those friendly and gentle giants, talking to them in my babble. When I ran away, it was always toward the mountains.

Throughout my childhood and adolescence, a sense of calm enveloped me when I looked to the east at the granite peaks, or strolled through the sandstone foothills, or gazed west to the sun setting over the milder sister mountains. In a profound way I knew, even when very young, that the mountains were safety, reliability, and predictability to me in a world that was consumed by conflict and contempt.

What pulled me in, what bound me, was my certainty that the mountains were always there. They were there when I left. And when I returned. They were there when I was born. They would be there when I died. I believed that they would never leave me.

"Oh, yeah?" Mom snickered. "Have you ever heard of earthquakes?" I looked confused. "That's a metaphor." She smiled, but not kindly. Bitterly.

———◆———

I learned what to do. When Mom shouted, threw a tantrum, hit me, or heaved a cup or a bar of soap or an ashtray at me, I simply faded into the mountains: deep in powder snow, lit by a sharp summer sun, or muted in a copper sunset on the Great Salt Lake, where gulls and cranes soared and settled in the marshes. There, in the kitchen, dishes flying all around, Mom's voice strident and the other children cringing, I escaped, disappearing into my imagination. I let my mind take a walk in the foothills, a hike up the red buttes, a foot soak in City Creek as it tumbled through the cliffs. My eyes were open, but I saw nothing of the flying forks, the mashed potatoes on the floor, or the broken porcelain sink, cracked by the heavy pan. I rested in my own glade of pine on the mountain ridge. From the glaciated peak, I looked out over the valley, and I became part of the Indian tribes, the trapper camps, and the pioneer Mormon families.

Any family but mine.

One day, when I was three or four, Mom threw a glass at me and cut my arm. "I'm leaving!" I shouted.

"If you are," Daddy said, "first put a Band-Aid on your cut and drink some juice." I did. "Don't cross the streets," he said sternly.

I mounted my tricycle and ran away for the first time. I wanted to run to the mountains, but first I would try to find Mr. Paulsen's candy store, where I could sit in his sunlit front window sucking Neccos. If I was tired when I got there, I would rest on a nappy rug he spread between the cupboards, which were stocked with jars of peppermint sticks, wax lips, boxes of jawbreakers, sunflower seeds, and peanuts in crinkly plastic bags.

I liked Mr. Paulsen, and he liked me. He had a corrugated face, all hills and valleys, sloped, like the wind had whipped through him and eroded his head. Bumps and holes spread over his nose, which was red like a sunset. Always cheerful, he flapped his arms at me like tree branches, soughing, "Here she is! Here's my dumpling." He was glad to see me.

Off I went. I pedaled and pedaled, going south. I saw the mountains off to the east. I was happy; I had a plan. I would live with Mr. Paulsen when I returned from the mountains, because I didn't want to live in the Dark House anymore. A Brownie selling Girl Scout cookies offered to help me across 10th South, but I didn't want to make Daddy mad, so I turned the corner, away from the mountains, and kept pedaling.

The block was very long. I was heading west now, and in the distance I could see the Oquirrh Mountains, which were softer, like blankets thrown in a bundle on the floor, forming yet another range circling the valley.

I came to another corner, so I turned north. I imagined pedaling to Antelope Island in the middle of the Great Salt Lake, where herds of antelope roamed. But I was getting tired and thirsty. So when I came to a corner again and a wiener dog sniffed at me and wagged his tail, I slid off my tricycle and sat on the lawn to pet him. I looked back and thought I saw a man hiding behind a tree. But I didn't have time to play hide-and-seek, so I climbed back on my trike, turned the corner, and pedaled off.

Now I was headed east, getting lonely. I couldn't see the store. I wondered, "Where are my people?" My Sunday-school teacher told us we always had our people, but I couldn't see anyone at all. I had lost track of where I was. I pedaled to the corner. I couldn't cross the street, so I had to turn a corner again. By now I was hot, worn out, and scared.

And then I saw my house up ahead. Hooray. I was relieved and sure that Daddy would be missing me by now. My legs pumped the pedals faster, round and round. And then, a miracle. Daddy came right up behind me. Where did he come from?

"Well, well, well!" he exclaimed in surprise, his voice loud and happy, his hands on his hips. "Look at the little traveler!" He picked me up and gave me a big scratchy-faced hug. I smelled his Brylcreemed hair and his sour sweat. His cheek was warm like mine.

He nuzzled me and then confided, "Little darlin', shall I tell you a secret?" He looked straight at me with his blackberry eyes. "You can't run away from home when you're angry," he said, "or you'll always come back."

I complained, "But I want to go to the mountains."

"The mountains are right there, honey," he said, tapping my chest. "Whenever you want the mountains, just close your eyes and go to them in your heart."

Of course, my father had followed me around the block, watching to make sure I was safe. But I believed he was a miracle man and that whenever I got lost, or was tired and hungry, he would save me. Later, I realized it was much more complicated than that.

———

Over the next seventeen years, I ran away many more times. Usually I went on foot. Even when I was very young, I walked miles through the downtown streets. Once, when I was ten, I stopped to rest at the city library and spent the hot summer night curled up on the doorstep. The next morning, the librarian's long, honeysuckled hair tickled my cheek as she bent over to wake me. "What are you doing here, little girl?"

"I want to check out *Through the Looking Glass*," I lied. She gave me the book, some hot chocolate, and a bus token. I rode the bus home. My mother had not known I was gone.

When I was twelve, I took a Greyhound bus through the mountains to the east. I made it to Evanston, Wyoming, where a fat sheriff's deputy, smoking a cigar and carrying a clipboard, boarded the bus and roared, "Is there a short, squat little girl on this bus? Name of Kathy?" Other passengers quickly pointed me out. The fleshy man squeezed his way to me, grabbed me under the arm, and pulled me down the aisle. I was scarlet, shamed with the double humiliations of being both caught and squat. He led me into a stuffy office in a nondescript building, where he sat me on a folding chair that was missing a rubber tip on one foot, so it tipped back and forth. I was both scared and angry, and I rocked the chair nervously. I could see there was a jail in the back room.

"Now, little gal," he started.

"Am I under arrest?" I asked loudly. "Because my daddy's a lawyer, you know."

"Well, from what your mama says, he's not at home anymore," the deputy said. "And you've been a little pistol, haven't you? Givin' your poor mama all kinds of trouble."

What did he know of trouble? What did the librarian know? Both of them telling me to go home. If that deputy had been nice to me, I would have broken down in tears and told him all about trouble. I would have begged him to adopt me.

"You're a lucky little girl, though," he said, "'cause your mama has agreed to come and get you and take you home. Do you appreciate that?"

I refused to answer. He leaned back in his chair and put his feet up on the desk. "But she can't come 'til mornin'," he said, smiling. "So I guess you'll just have to sit there till then." He put his hands behind his head. "You could do a little thinkin' about whether you'll be runnin' away again anytime soon."

After a while he fell asleep at his desk. I quit being so angry, but I was still scared—and tired, but I didn't dare sleep. I slumped down in the chair. Then I sat backward on the chair and rested my head on my arms. I pulled my coat over my head and rubbed my feet, but I was still cold. And hungry. Then I was lonely. I thought about leaving, but where could I go?

I waited all night and most of the next morning until my mother came to pick me up in that hot little town. "You made me miss work," she scolded. "I hope you've learned your lesson." She thanked the deputy, and we drove home, Mom listening to the radio and singing along, me just silent. She didn't stop for food, so I stayed hungry. Wyoming stretched out, barren and dry—how could a person run away and hide on such a flat plain?

As we came down the pass from Evanston to Park City, the mountains came toward me like friends, saying, "Welcome back, Kathy. We missed you." I was so glad to see them, I almost cried. But Mom would have misinterpreted my tears as an apology, and I didn't want to give her the pleasure.

———◆———

When I was sixteen, I stole my mother's car and drove up Parley's Canyon, headed for New York, where I intended to become a famous stage actress, earning my keep as a singing waitress. This time I made it to Cheyenne, where the Utoco gas station man rejected my mother's Beeline credit card and told me, "It's no good here or clear out to the Atlantic Ocean, little lady. No one takes Beeline in the civilized world." He filled up my tank and gave me ten dollars on the promise I'd turn around and "Go back now to your ma, honey." I turned around and went back, though I fell asleep twice at the wheel and wished I hadn't wakened. When I saw the mountains this time, I was happy to see them, but in a different way, like when you have tried to escape, have been caught, and are delivered back into the hands of a sympathetic jailer.

When I couldn't use my feet, I used my mind to run. And I ran with my heart. I was Tintin and his little white dog racing through the sandstone spires of Bryce Canyon. I was Alice falling through a deep chasm on Mount Olympus into Wonderland. When I was older, I secretly read my grandmother's *National Geographic* magazines, and my mind took me to Africa, where I plowed up and down the desert dunes on a camel, and to Oahu's majestic Ko'olau Mountains, which I climbed with my bare hands. I became beloved, admired, and world famous, as the first woman to climb the craggy, ice-laced peaks of Annapurna, and the only woman to dare to dive down into the underwater mountains of the Baltic Sea.

I lived everywhere but home.

CHAPTER 7

NINYAH AND BABA

—◆—

OFTEN, WHEN HER FIGHTS WITH my father were prolonged, my mother called Ninyah to come and fetch the children from the 14th East house.

"Have a good time, little darlin's," Daddy said, giving hugs, while Ninyah stood stiff and ready to take us, ignoring my father.

She gave Mom an icy nod. "Call me when you've resolved your difficulties."

Off we went. In the car, I settled into a quiet calm in the front seat, leaning into my adored grandmother, looking out the window at the mountains. "See the mountains, Ninyah? They are so big and beautiful. Every time I look at them, they look at me back."

She took her hand from the wheel and put her arm around me. "Of course, dear. They love you."

Ninyah's parents, wealthy San Francisco aristocrats, had unfortunately been Episcopalians. At her parents' insistence, Ninyah had married Baba in San Francisco in the Episcopalian Church. However, Baba's mother would not speak to Ninyah until she converted to the Mormon Church. As with many converts, Ninyah became a fervent believer. Because of the Mormon belief that civil marriages end at death, Ninyah and Baba married again in the Mormon Temple, where they were sealed together for all eternity.

No one told me then, or ever, what the fiercely secret marriage ceremony entailed. The rumors were that the man and woman stepped through magic curtains, were called by secret names, and were given holy underwear, called garments, to wear forever after. Ninyah simply explained that from then on my grandparents were building a home for our family in Heaven, where we would all be together, eternally happy.

"But what if I don't like my family?" I asked. "And what if the sister is good, but the brother is a brat? And what about the bad people who live on the west side of town?"

"God will see to it." Ninyah concluded the conversation with her usual answer to difficult questions.

Baba became the city attorney for Salt Lake City; thereafter, he and his eldest son opened a respected private law office, though Baba hardly needed the income. Both Ninyah and he had inherited a substantial amount of money—although hers became his, as was the custom then. They were both oblivious to poverty. When I was in college, I asked Ninyah what she and Baba had experienced during the Great Depression. She responded, "Oh heavens, dear, I think that was long before our time." It wasn't, of course. My mother was fourteen in 1932, when the Depression was at its worst. My grandmother was simply so rich that she hadn't noticed it.

Because of her parents' profound wealth, my mother wanted for nothing as a child, though her professional dreams of becoming a classical pianist, or a lawyer like Baba, were derided and denied.

"You will marry an independently wealthy or prominent professional Mormon man within your class, young lady," Ninyah directed. "Begin a family and employ, as we do, maids, cooks, and other servants."

Baba agreed. "We want you to manage a large home and a large Mormon family, dear. This is the dictate of the Church."

To that end, they sent her to a New York City finishing school, where she learned comportment, style, etiquette, and her place: how to walk straight, dress properly, and set a fine table with proper silverware. In addition, in to order be capable of volunteering for the Church and social clubs, she learned to type, take shorthand, and balance accounting books. Unbeknownst to Baba and Ninyah, she also sneaked out to Harlem, danced at the nightclubs, learned to love jazz, and mixed with colored people, whom she envied for what she perceived as their joie de vivre, freedom, and reckless abandon.

Mom's graduation elicited rare praise from her parents. "You are now competent to serve as a secretary or treasurer for the Church," they applauded. "And you'll make an excellent wife."

She resented her parents' dreams for her; she wanted her own.

Ninyah had stayed home and raised her own four children. My mother was the eldest child and Ninyah's only daughter. Even though my mother was not allowed to pursue a higher education, Ninyah did so. She returned to school when the children were raised, earned a master's degree in textiles, and became the oldest person in the University of Utah's history at that time to complete graduate school.

She put her education to use organizing a children's theatre, making puppets, producing plays, designing costumes, and teaching drama at Rowland Hall, a private boarding school. Enormously talented, she became the director of the costume department at the University of Utah, where she designed and executed wardrobes for the school's theatre, opera, and ballet productions for thirty-five years. She often whisked me away to the costume department in the basement of Kingsbury Hall.

So why had Ninyah, so ambitious in her own right, spurned my mother's ambitions?

"She's hateful, that's why," Mom whined. "She's jealous of me."

I was Ninyah's defender then. "Why?" I mocked. "You're a secretary, and she's a costume mistress."

Mom complained that Ninyah disliked her from babyhood. Baba, on the other hand, doted on his little princess and gave in to everything she wanted, except her ambitions. My three uncles, her brothers, grew up resenting her and accused her of being a spoiled brat.

As I learned over the years, my mother was right. Though Ninyah adored me and I adored her, she disliked Mom. I didn't understand until I was an adult that she had a dark side: she resented Baba's attention to my mother, punished her unreasonably, and then competed with her as an adult and eventually turned her back on her. She discouraged my mother's aspirations and derided her talents, her marital choice, and her parenting.

She stole the children's love.

I tried to accept that Ninyah was cold and disdainful to my mother while being warm and encouraging to me at the same time. But as hard as I try now to recall some affection, I never saw Ninyah embrace my mother, never heard her give Mom praise.

"Ninyah," I asked her once, against all hope, "do you love Mom?"

"She's my daughter, isn't she?" Ninyah answered. That was all.

Most important to me, however—as to any child—Ninyah loved me unconditionally. And she rescued me from peril.

Ironically, my father, who had every reason to disparage Ninyah and Baba, would not allow me to complain about them. "People are two-sided coins," he said.

I have carried that wisdom into my judicial work.

———◆———

In September 1939, Germany invaded Poland; soldiers were stationed at Fort Douglas in Salt Lake City in 1940. At a dance there, my mother, twenty-two years old, met and fell in love with my father, Henry, a handsome and good-spirited man, an army lawyer waiting to be deployed overseas, and a Southern Baptist from Selma, Alabama.

All hell broke loose. Because Ninyah and Baba were highly regarded in Utah society and in the Church, they were deeply embarrassed by my mother's choice of a potential husband. In fact, they were appalled and prohibited the marriage. They scorned my father's heritage, his class, and his religion.

"He is out of your class, young lady, and headed for no good," Ninyah scoffed.

"He's a lawyer, Mother," Mom defended.

"The army only employs second-rate lawyers," Baba argued.

"He's just a poor boy from the Deep South, educated in inferior schools," Ninyah joined in.

"He's good natured," Mom countered.

"That just shows he's ineffectual, undirected, and dull. Definitely lower class."

"There are few Christians lower than the Southern Baptists," scoffed Ninyah.

That ended the conversation.

How did I know so young that they hated Daddy? Did my mother tell me? If so, I blush for my mother's inappropriateness, for her efforts to ally me against Ninyah and Baba, for telling me more than a child should know at a young age. But it must be so, for I remember sitting on the couch in the 14th East house living room, listening to Mom tell me the story I would hear many times over the years and feeling sick at heart.

"When I introduced him to your grandparents," she related, "he reached out and grabbed Baba's hand, and shook it way too hard."

It made me wince. Poor Baba. Poor Daddy.

"I was so embarrassed." Mom tapped her cigarette ashes into the bowl of an ashtray, reached out as though shaking hands, and mimicked Daddy's "awful Southern drawl," as she called it. "He'd said, much too loudly, 'Whah, ah'll be! Ah'm mahty pleased tah meechoo.' Your grandparents were shocked and scandalized."

She paused. "Do you know what 'scandalized' means?" she asked. "It means they thought that everyone would look down on them if I married your dad. And they were right, I can tell you. Huh!" The smoke from her cigarette puffed out in a large cloud. "Your dad's a lazy, no-good lawyer. A wimp."

I didn't know what a wimp was. Someone cruel, I imagined. It sounded awful. I wanted to run out of the room. But I was frozen in silence.

"So they forbade me from marrying him," she went on. "Hah! Like they could stop me." She rose and said, "Time for another drink," and headed to the kitchen.

When she returned, she pulled me into her lap and sloppily continued the story. I hated the story, but I loved her lap.

She and my grandparents had reached an impasse. Ninyah, fiercely displeased, had taken a deep offended breath, clasped her hands to her chest, and commanded, "We will not have you marrying beneath your class, young lady."

"I will if I wish," Mom retorted.

"You'll have no help from us, then." Baba ended the conversation.

When she married Daddy against Baba's wishes, Baba kept his promise. "They cut me off," she said. "Just like that."

Baba, as well, turned his back on his princess. He stuck to his threat. Mother's support from her parents dribbled down in small, begrudging dollops. Any help came with conditions. They refused to help my father in any way, tied strings to any help for my mother, and doted on their grandchildren, giving us much of what our parents could not. In this way, my grandparents attempted to control her, as they had done when she was a child.

Baba refused to take Daddy into his successful law firm. After all, they were Mormon, and Daddy was Baptist. They were elite; he was common. They were moneyed; he was poor. Rather, Baba secured a job for him as a low-level clerk at the state capitol building, where he had no panache. They humiliated my father at every turn.

This was my Baba, who called me "little Kathleen Mavourneen" and treated me like a queen. This was my Ninyah, who kissed and hugged me, and was my salvation as a child.

"Poor me." Mom slid me off her lap, splashing her drink. She reached down to rub her bunions. "Poor me."

———◆———

While my family lived in our small, gloomy house on 14th East, my grandparents lived in the posh Federal Heights neighborhood, on a high hill, in a tall house that seemed to me to be a mansion. They had servants, only three whose names I recall. Mrs. Adair was a plump, gushy woman who smelled like lemon polish and mothballs. She took care of the house. I saw her kiss the butler once—unless it was the iceman bringing a block of ice, or the milkman bringing the jug of milk with cream on top. The cook was called Cook, and she was a robust woman, especially her bosoms, which swung back and forth when she beat the meringue. Her hair was bronzy orange and wiry, like a Chore Girl scouring pad, barely contained by a tight and constant black net. She befriended me and let me lick the gravy spoon and stir the brownie batter. A Chinese man was the gardener; we called him Chink. He grew herbs and dried them for Cook.

I loved going to my grandparents' house. I rummaged in their closets, which held tailored dresses and suits from expensive stores: ZCMI (Zion Cooperative Mercantile Institution, the first of Brigham Young's cooperative efforts to establish a communal commercial system for the Mormon pioneers, where Mormons would sell to and buy from other Mormons) and an elegant store named Makoff Design, both expensive stores where my grandmother shopped. Ninyah possessed long gowns of satin and lace. Baba had several tuxedoes and winter suits that smelled rich and dense like strong coffee. Sometimes Mrs. Adair let me help fold the laundry and hold Ninyah and Baba's silky Mormon underwear—high-necked T-shirts and squared panties—to my cheek.

"Do they wear these all the time?" I asked her.

"Yes, dear, except when they bathe and swim," she answered.

I delightedly realized I had someone who would answer my questions, so I forged ahead. "But why?"

"Because it reminds them of the promises they made to God in the Temple."

"Are they magic?"

"Well," sighed Mrs. Adair, "not exactly. But the garments protect them from evil and harm, and make them less likely to give in to the temptations of the world."

"What temptations?" I perked up. Did they want to steal, like I did?

"Not so many questions, dear." Mrs. Adair reached out and took the underwear from me.

"They are kind of ugly," I mused. "Especially Baba's."

"Now run along," she said, kissing the top of my head.

"Ninyah," I asked my grandmother one day. "Do you wear your underwear all night long?"

"Some things, dear," she said sharply, "are none of your concern."

I roamed from the huge bedrooms, to Ninyah's sitting room and Baba's den, to the sunroom and music room, to the maid's bathroom, to the kitchen, where bread was baking, and to the breakfast nook, where I sat and drank hot chocolate Cook made for me. If I felt brave, I crept down to the dark basement where we would live when I was ten and Daddy divorced Mom.

I hated our little house.

So did my mother. "Why can't you provide?" she hissed at Daddy.

"I would if you weren't so damned spoiled," he spit back.

"We ought to have a bigger house," she complained.

"Be patient, for God's sake!" he pleaded.

"My parents would help us if you'd work harder."

"I doubt it."

"I hate these damn children!" she barked. "They cost us everything we have."

"They *are* everything we have," he said. "Of value, anyway."

He loved us that way.

I did not know all this history of parental dissatisfaction as a child, except in snatches heard from the porch, or during the night when it slipped in under my bedroom door. I did know the noise, the sizzle of Mom's seething, the scuffles and slaps, the crack of the belt on my legs, Mom never getting what she wanted, Daddy never able to give it.

But I knew my devoted grandmother loved me, cuddled and caressed me, and my grandfather paid attention to me, patted my head and told me tales. They were rescue and sanctuary.

———◆———

Now on this trip back to Salt Lake City as an adult, I marveled that I had dared to come. I sat in the car outside the Dark House. I walked around the block, and I saw the place where Mr. Paulsen had his store. I lost track of time and could see the sun lowering in the cloud-shifting, afternoon sky. The evening would present one of the glorious crimson sunsets for which Salt Lake City is known.

I remembered my quest. From this place, this house, I needed to select a token. I knocked on the door and hoped no one would answer. When no one came, I walked around the house to the backyard.

How had my mother done it? How had she given up all her dreams of artistic and legal accomplishment, married a man her family treated like a loser, lived in a house in her parents' name, suffered scorn by her Church of origin, and raised three girls who already disliked her and two boys yet to come?

But I puzzled these thoughts with a flush of anger. I was a small child. She hit me. She yelled at me. She threw things at me. She was an alcoholic. She made me feel terrible about myself. I smiled at the coup de grace: she subjected me to secondhand smoke, for god's sake.

"You'll get it when your father comes home," Mom had often warned, irritated but oddly triumphant.

"Go cut a switch for your father," she would order us when he arrived home. "Not too thin. And strip the leaves."

I would go fearfully to the backyard and try to pick a twig that wouldn't hurt too bad and hand it to my father.

"Sereta," he'd protest, "I'd rather not."

"Do it, Hank," she would spit. "Don't make a fool out of me. I told this child you'd switch her, and I meant it. Now do it."

Then he'd whip me. It had hurt a lot.

The aspen was gone. But others had sprouted up and grown tall, as aspens do, birthing and dying, coming and leaving. The leaves clacked together softly in the breeze, like castanets. Thin branches reached out low on the trunks. I twisted a long sucker from a tree, stripped it of its leaves, and placed the knobby switch in my nylon bag.

CHAPTER 8

ON A MISSION

We moved to a larger white clapboard house on Laird Avenue in 1950, when I was six. The house was pretty, with green shutters and trim. Large windows let in more light, and the light made the house seem airy and hopeful. When Clark was born, he was given the smallest bedroom, and we three girls shared a slightly larger one, our beds sandwiched together. I didn't mind, because the window looked out on the cottonwood tree in the backyard, and at night I could hear the crickets in the field next door.

Best of all, I loved the half-finished basement, where Daddy set up a table and a typewriter, encouraging me to write stories and plays. I began to write and direct neighborhood productions, most of which dramatized Church doctrine.

My new Sunday-school teacher was Sister Mallow. She was about Mom's age, but very huge, a large, cheerful woman who, every week, wore a white tent frock covered with blue stars. Sister Mallow seemed to get bigger every week. She bumped down the stairs to our classroom like a giant cloud, rolling back and forth, back and forth. I always wondered whether she would make it through the door. But once she was on solid ground, she floated into the classroom, an enormous white cotton ball across the sky.

Over our heads and around our shoulders she glided, waving and hugging us up in pillows of white. I smelled her soft bosom as it pressed against my cheek, a powdery, sweet scent. I imagined I was suspended in the sky with her, sitting on her fluffy cushiness, eating biscuits and honey. I closed my eyes and believed everything she told me.

"What are those big white clouds called?" I asked Baba on one of our Sunday drives. Ahead of us, in a clear blue sky, huge cotton balls bundled together, coming toward us, ready to enfold us.

"Those are called cumulus clouds," he said, taking a long puff on his pipe.

"Do they get all black and cause thunder?" I leaned up over the front seat and talked in his ear, where soft little hairs waved back and forth like thin blades of grass in a breeze. The nappy texture of the seat top scratched my arms in a good way. The deep sweetness of his tobacco curled around his answer.

"No, honey, thunderclouds are called cumulonimbus clouds." He sucked at his pipe, took it out, and held it in his steering hand. He leaned forward and looked out the front window, up toward where I was pointing. "Those pretty white ones are good clouds. Gentle clouds. They won't harm you."

"Sister Mallow is a cumulus," I said, satisfied, and sat back. I decided she could be believed, trusted.

This was not the only image Sister Mallow called up for me. She was a goose-down quilt bundled on an unmade bed, with ten queen-sized pillows piled on top. In winter she was whipped cream on top of hot chocolate. In summer, she was white water, and I was her raft. Then she became a white-sheeted bed, and I folded into her. She was my first passionate crush.

One Sunday morning, she shepherded us into a circle. All the children sat in little chairs. Sister Mallow pulled up her cottony bulk. Her arms fluttered like vapory scarves, and she sang out in her whispery, musical voice, "Children, children, I have something wonderful to teach you today! Come closer now."

We lifted our chair bottoms and scooted nearer together and farther forward. Janice clapped her hands. Camille grabbed my hand—I squeezed her chubby fingers. Bobby picked his nose, as usual.

Sometimes Sister Mallow strode over to Bobby while she was talking, reached down, and without it seeming to bother her at all, gently pulled his finger from his nose. She gave him her white, blue-flowered hanky. "Here, Bobby dear, use this to clear out your nose. Blow into it, that's right. That's a very good boy." She'd then give him a hug, muss his hair, and squeeze his shoulder—what a lucky boy! I tried picking my nose one Sunday. I did it all through class. But Sister Mallow just looked at me sweetly, straight into my eyes, until I got embarrassed and stopped.

When we were finally quiet, she stood above us, so large she covered our view of anything else. "Man is that he might have joy," she announced, and her blue eyes shone like Bear Lake glittering in sunlight. Her arms shot up to the sky like lightning bolts coming out of the earth. She said it again, "Did you hear me, little ones? Man...is...that...he... might...have...joy!" I pulled in a breath, and my mouth opened to let out a gasp of delight. It flew out into the air.

But then my eyebrows lifted, and I frowned in confusion. My upper lip wrinkled and pushed up my nose. My hand shot up in the air. This could not wait for Baba and a Sunday drive.

"But I'm a girl," I blurted before she called on me.

Sister Mallow's substantial arms fell down to her hillsides, and her body shook with her chuckles. "Oh, honey," she said, sweeping them back up in circles round and round. "You're included in 'Man.' Man is everybody, girls and boys."

Is it animals?" Camille asked. When Sister Mallow said no, just people, Camille got very quiet. I squeezed her hand again. I guessed what she was thinking: she liked cats, dogs, and all animals. She even tried not to step on ants on the sidewalk when we marched from Sunday school to the chapel for the closing hymn. She wanted them to have joy, too. When we played "One Wish," she wished to be a grasshopper, because they have such long, beautiful legs and can leap away from things. We looked for grasshoppers in the field on our corner. I caught them in a mason jar. She set them free. We did this over and over.

"Man holds woman." Sister Mallow arced her arms in front of her, the hands clasping the elbows. "See? This is Man, and you are in his circle."

The lesson was my first memory of knowing that men and women were treated differently in the Mormon Church. Women were included in the label "Man," but they were not equal. Mom had said it was so, but now I believed it. Now I knew it. The boys could bless the sacrament, preach, and be priests, deacons, and bishops. Not me.

Mom had often complained to me. "The boys can grow up to be priests and give you the Holy Ghost by laying their hands on your head," she told me, lighting one cigarette from another. I shuddered. I actually didn't want strange men to put their hands on my head, and I wasn't too sure I wanted to put my hands in anyone else's hair. "And they can be high priests, like a bishop," she continued, "and give blessings to the wives and children, and heal the sick."

She took a long drag on her smoke. She blew out circles and watched them curl up over her head. "But girls can't." Then she looked straight at me and arched her eyebrows. "Is that fair?" she asked. How was I to know? "You know what else?" She was in a bad mood, I could tell. "Boys get to go on missions. And girls don't."

Everyone talked about the boys and their missions, how they went to exotic places for two years to proselytize and bring converts to the Church. The boys huddled in groups and guessed where they would be sent. Brazil? France? To me, a child who liked to get out of the house, this meant travel! Why couldn't the girls go to faraway places and preach the Gospel and have boxes of cookies sent to them and letters with pictures pasted on them? Everyone loved the missionaries.

One Sunday I pestered Sister Mallow. "What if I don't want to get married or be a wife or have children? Can I go on a mission then? What if I grow up to be like you and be all alone and not married? Can I go?" Sister Mallow sighed. She seemed overcast that Sunday. She was somber during the lesson, which was about Jesus's Last Supper. I hadn't liked that lesson, either—only men had been invited to the dinner.

"If you are a spinster, perhaps you can be a ward missionary and bring the Gospel to the people in your neighborhood," she said cheerfully, taking my hand and giving it a quick squeeze. She drifted away for a moment and looked out the window. I willed her back to me, and she smiled as she turned. "You know, Kathy—" She stopped, but then seemed to decide to go on. "A few years ago, when I was twenty-five, I went on a mission to Idaho." She smoothed her skirt with her ample hand. "Would that make you happy? A mission to Idaho?"

No, thank you; I had *no* interest in Idaho. I'd been there. Bear Lake is half in Utah and half in Idaho. Ninyah and Baba's summer cabin was on the Utah side. When we needed to go shopping, Ninyah would let me ride with her on the drive to Paris, Idaho, or on a big trip, clear to Montpelier. In my mind, this was not true travel. This was just driving through lots of sagebrush to a run-down grocery store for a bag of potatoes, or to Sears Roebuck for a new nightgown, or to Abbers to get the coal bucket fixed. I wanted to go to Africa, maybe. Or California.

I was confused. Still, Sister Mallow could be trusted.

But I was bitterly disappointed.

So I began to steal.

In a daring first theft, I stole gum from the corner market. The following week, I stole a jawbreaker. This was not difficult. Camille and I had gone to the store to buy jacks for her sister's birthday. Mr. Talbert was at the cash register ringing up the sale. He reached down under the counter to pull out a small brown bag for the jacks, and as he did so, I took the turquoise ball, wrapped in shiny plastic, and slipped it into my sweater pocket.

Mr. Talbert looked right at me and said, "And what for you, little lady?"

A grand thrill of fear and pleasure ran from my throat to my knees. "Nothing. Thank you, sir." I smiled.

I made Camille walk clear to the park with me before I dared to pull the candy from my pocket. "This is for you." I held my breath, waiting for her glee. Maybe she would hug me, kiss my cheek.

There was a silence. "Kathy!" Suddenly I was alarmed. She wasn't smiling. She looked like Mom did when her sums didn't add up on the adding machine.

"What's wrong?" I held my hands out, palms up.

"Did you steal this?" Her eyes turned me over in a question, and my stomach twisted. I would leap into the pond and drown if Camille didn't like me anymore.

"No!" I lied. "No! I bought it for you yesterday."

"Ooooh," she crooned. Her singsong voice went up and down. "Oh! Thank you!" She hugged me and offered to push me on the swing. I felt her warm hands as she pressed my back. I pumped my knees and lifted higher and higher. Camille pushed harder and harder. I could touch the sky.

"Nope. Sister Mallow's wrong," Mom argued. "Girls do not go on missions."

Years later, I discovered this was not true: a girl could go, as Sister Mallow did, on a stateside mission if, when she got older, she had not fulfilled her duty to marry and have children. But girls were not encouraged. I never knew a girl who was a missionary, yet boys were expected to go as their duty to God. And most went.

Mom leaned into me and said sarcastically, "But you can marry a missionary when he comes home from his mission." Her voice sang, each note climbing the scale a little higher than the last. "Won't that be good enough for you?" She stubbed out her cigarette with vigor. "To be a loving, supportive missionary's wife?"

When I told Sister Mallow what Mom had said, she told me that even though the Lord loved my mom, my mom was not close to Him, so she couldn't hear His true messages.

"So what *can* girls do?" I asked.

"Honey, what the Lord really wants you to do is to be a faithful wife, have lots of Mormon children, and be a devoted mother." She told me to prepare myself. She was sure I would be very good at it.

Instead, I became very good at stealing.

Usually I stole alone, but I learned to steal when I was with Camille at Mr. T's, or with Mom at the grocery store, or with Ninyah at the fabric store. I roamed away from Camille and snatched a coloring book and stuffed it in my coat. I left Ninyah fingering fabric and slipped a thimble in my pocket for her birthday. Without Mom noticing, I grabbed a candy bar for myself. I gave Lucy the stolen coloring book to do my chores, I ate the candy bar hidden behind the garage, and when Ninyah opened the thimble on her birthday, she hugged me tight. "What a sweet, sweet gift." She was all smiles, and I basked in the glow.

I stole several of the miniature wax juice bottles from Mr. Talbert's shelf. I bit off the cap and drank the juice inside. Then I chewed and sucked on the wax until my jaw hurt. One day I nabbed two of them right from under his nose. I leaned down to pretend to tie my shoes and slipped the treats down into my socks.

When I stood up, Mr. Talbert looked at me all friendly and said, as usual, "And what for you, little miss?"

"Nothing. Thank you, sir," I said, smiling. I looked right into his eyes. I was safe. The world was mine.

"Are you sure?" he said.

"Oh, yes. I'm just looking."

"Is that so?" He crossed his arms and held my look.

Those crossed arms. I knew what that meant. It meant, "I'm waiting for the truth." Mom waited for me to confess that I was the one who hit Lucy first. Sandy waited for me to tell her where I hid her doll. Teachers waited for me to admit cheating. The usual thrill of stealing iced up in my stomach and stuck in my mouth. Silence stopped me, its hands around my throat. I thought fast.

"Oh, for goodness' sake," I said, like Ninyah always said when she dropped the saltshaker or forgot her purse on the backseat. That "Oh, I've made such a silly mistake" tone with her hands up in the air.

I leaned over and retrieved the bottles. "Oops. I dropped these wax bottles, and they landed in my socks."

"So they did." Mr. Talbert leaned over the counter to look. "How about that?"

I pulled them out and put them back on the counter. "You should move the display box back a bit so they won't fall out anymore."

I suppose if I hadn't blamed him, Mr. Talbert might have patted me on the head and given me a good moral lesson. As it was, he called Mom.

Mom came to get me and apologized for my bad behavior. "She's such a problem," Mom sighed. She paid for the candy.

In the car, she smoked her cigarette quietly and didn't talk for a while. I waited for her to yell at me.

"Silly man," she puffed. "Every child shoplifts. It's not *that* big of a deal. I don't know why he had to chew on *me*."

"I won't do it anymore, Mom. I promise," I pleaded, chasing away the possibility of a spanking.

"Please don't," she said, her irritation still sizzling. "You embarrassed me to death."

CHAPTER 9

BELIEVING

———◆———

LIFE BECAME INCREASINGLY UNPREDICTABLE AT the Laird Avenue house. Mom was cheerful and nurturing; then, in a flash, she growled, and her face gnarled up like a gingerroot. Her pitiable complaints took the form of loud weeping, slurred and guttering diatribes against the Church, resentments against women's lots, excoriations of her parents for their neglect and bigotry, and condemnations of her children for their worthlessness. She pitied herself, complaining of her burdens, sobbing and shrieking. She crushed our spirits with insults and withered our self-confidence. She shattered any hard-won peace with my father or in the house.

We began to hate her.

Sandy hated her because she berated us, hit us, and began to refuse to feed us as well. Lucy was afraid of her and began to suck her fist. Clark became oddly quiet as a toddler and often walked on his tiptoes. I resented her for her decay—her thinning hair, her shamefully flat breasts, and her false teeth, which I thought gross, sitting at her bedside in a glass of water. More problematic, I also loved her, longed for her care.

But she was a sinner. She smoked and drank, which was against Church doctrine, and she did so publicly and without shame. More and more she chain-smoked. She drank vodka and orange juice, a glass always in her hand, her tongue slipping over her words, eyes gauzy and red veined. She didn't go to Church. She did not pay her required 10 percent tithing. Ninyah told me, and I believed it, that God abhorred her.

I still believed in the Church faithfully and with dramatic devotion, although I began to suffer doubts. So even though I scorned my mother in what I saw as her abject state, I opened my arms to her, as I believed Christ would, and sought to save her from damnation.

I exerted childish efforts, trying to open her eyes to her sins. I nagged her to repent. She just laughed and said, "Do you really think He will turn his back on me? That good man?"

I prayed for her. I promised her I would dedicate my life to her salvation. "Are you sure?" She arched her eyebrows. "Really, *really* sure?" She didn't see the light. She just smiled. "Don't you think you might have better things to do?"

I loved the Church. Though I continued to steal for pleasure and power, I usually tried to guide my life by many Church principles, and when I failed, I felt tremendous guilt. I wanted to be good, to be chaste, to be clean and tidy, to believe in family as the foundation of life on earth, and to serve others.

What thrilled me most, however, was the history of how the Church came to be, a story I now doubt as improbable and fantastical. But when I first heard it, I was a young child full of spit and vinegar, already eager to live anybody's life but my own, inventing peaceful and welcoming worlds.

I learned the story little by little. Sister Mallow taught me that Joseph Smith, the founder of Mormonism, was born in Vermont in 1805. When he was in his early teens, he became deeply concerned about his salvation. He sought Divine guidance, and in answer to his prayers, he was visited by two Heavenly Beings, who told him not to join any of the existing churches, but to wait, *wait!* And he would be given the secret to the True Church.

In Mom's sober moments, she loved to expound. "Sure enough," she said, "he waited until he was twenty-two. And then, in the autumn of 1827, a Heavenly messenger, the Angel Moroni, appeared to him." At this point she would stand, spread her arms, and fly back and forth across the room. "Moroni led him to the ancient proof of the True Church. It was all written on golden plates—*golden! like dental crowns*—and buried in a hill named Cumorah, near Manchester, New York." I thought "Come Over" was a perfect name for a hill in which to bury golden plates that bore the truth of our salvation.

"These plates held an ancient account of the full Gospel of Christ," Mom continued, "which Christ had taught to the Nephites."

"Who are the Nephites?" I asked.

According to Ninyah and Baba, the Nephites were a lost tribe from the House of Israel. Lehi was the leader. His tribe had been told by God to leave Jerusalem and go to the Americas and become a big civilization. They did, long before Columbus, and called it the New World. How thrilling! I imagined the Nephites in the ship, the untouched world rising up green, pillowed in clouds on the horizon.

After Christ was resurrected, He came to the Nephites and taught them the True Gospel. But they lost it because they fell into sin. I was shocked. How could you lose such a valuable thing?

"But fortunately," Mom went on, "a Nephite prophet named Mormon had written the True Gospel down on golden plates. So it wasn't lost after all." She shrugged.

Dad, reading the newspaper, looked up. "Surprise!" he snickered.

Sister Mallow told me the best part. Mormon's son, Moroni, later became an angel and flew to New York to lead Joseph Smith to the plates. Imagine! An angel! What an adventure!

As a child, I believed Christ had appeared right in the center of America, which is in Utah, of course. Possibly he'd been in my very own backyard. I dug up the yard in several places, looking for footprints, a sandal, a dead cat—anything that would reveal Jesus's presence long ago. Mom corrected me; he had appeared in *South* America.

"Where's the evidence?" Daddy asked. "None," he answered himself.

Over and over, I begged Mom to tell me about the golden plates.

"OK, here's the drift," she said. And I snuggled into the couch with her in a moment of sober camaraderie, with Dad reading his paper and a fire burning in the fireplace, fed by coal from the brass bucket. "Joseph

Smith unburied the plates and put them in a big box. Moroni told him not to show anyone the plates, so he just let folks hold the box. But Joseph got to take a good look at those plates. And when he did, he cried out, 'Oh my goodness! These plates are written in ancient Egyptian. How will I ever translate them?'" Mom clapped her hands to her cheeks.

"Right. Here comes the good part." Dad snorted from behind the paper.

Mom ignored him. She made fun of the Church, unless Daddy did. Then she defended it.

"Joseph looked closer in the box, and guess what he found," she said in a low, suspense-filled voice.

I was all ears.

Daddy dropped his newspaper and leaned forward. "Rocks! Two rocks. They must have fallen out of his head."

"Hank, stop it," Mom spit.

Daddy picked up the newspaper again and pretended to read, but I could tell he was itching to scratch. He tapped his toe and rolled his eyes impatiently.

"In the bottom of the box were two seer stones, which were named Urim and Thummim. Joseph put the stones in a hat and held the hat to his face; then he could miraculously see the ancient script in English. This is how he deciphered what became the Book of Mormon, which he published in 1830."

Daddy scoffed. "Ha! Now we know the words weren't in any known language. Just gobbledygook."

Mom stood up, swept the newspaper from Daddy's hands, and tossed it on the floor. "Let it be, for god's sake, Hank." She stomped out of the room and into the kitchen. Daddy winked at me, though I crossed my arms and pouted. I believed the Mormons' conviction that Joseph Smith's Book of Mormon, along with later supplemental revelations, was the only True Gospel of the Lord on this earth.

But Daddy wouldn't let it be. He turned to me. "From then on ol' Joseph could preach, baptize folks, heal the sick, give blessings, and receive revelations from God." Daddy paused and then whispered conspiratorially. "And he could give the Holy Ghost to all his followers." Here he stood, raised his hands over his head, and went, "Wooooo," like a supernatural being. He sat down by me and uncrossed my arms, held my hands. "And now all the men in the Church can do that. Just the men, mind you, little darlin'."

"Hank," my mother said sharply, coming back into the room with a drink. "Don't confuse the girl."

"Not to mention the good news about polygamy," my father said, and laughed. "Joseph got himself thirty-some wives. That boy was shrewd."

I pulled my hands from his. "So where are the golden plates now?" I asked Mom.

"Disappeared," answered Daddy. "Rather conveniently."

"Joseph gave them back to God," Mom said, but not very convincingly.

Every Sunday, Sister Mallow told us part of this story, illustrated on a large easel containing a nappy board with felt cutouts we moved about as she recited. This week, the cutout of Joseph moved here and there, the felt Angel Moroni came down from Heaven, and the golden plates were dug out of a cave. Sister Mallow drew eyes and a mouth on the two seer stones that were placed in a hat. Each of us read a scripture while pointing at the hat.

With the Book of Mormon as his Bible, Joseph Smith set up the Church of Jesus Christ of *Latter Day* Saints, to distinguish us from the *ancient* Saints. Joseph showed the translated book to everyone, preached his heart out, and made converts by the dozens. Everyone who became a Mormon was saved, he said. God kept talking to Joseph, and when Joseph died, God talked to the next Prophet, Brigham Young, and God talked to every Mormon Prophet thereafter to tell him how to lead the Church.

What a magical tale! For a long time after I heard this story, I asked to set the table for dinner, no matter whose turn it was, because I thought God might send me messages on our plates.

———◆———

That night, Eric and I talked about the day's activities over takeout food from the Chinese restaurant and then talked on in the motel hot tub. I told him my stories of the 14th East house, where I had lived before he was born.

Eric described his visit to his foster home earlier that day. It had evoked both fond and painful memories. He recalled how after I married and left home at twenty-one, when Eric was eleven, Mom briefly "placed him out" to a military-type school for troubled youth. He failed there, so returned home. But when he was fourteen, he couldn't get along with Mom's third husband's kids, so she placed him through the Church's social services for respite care into another Church family.

"They were good to me," Eric recalled, "but I felt abandoned and lonely, betrayed by Mom." He attempted suicide by trying to hang himself in the basement.

"The pipe broke," Eric reminisced, looking vaguely past me.

He panicked after this failed suicide attempt, afraid to return home. So he called me and begged to come live with my then-husband and me in Oregon. We took him in. And he thrived.

Eric stepped out of the hot tub, went to his duffel bag, and pulled out a rusty length of pipe. "I found this. I'll use it as my token." When he returned to the hot tub, I sat by his side and put my arm around him.

By midnight, we had talked enough. We made cocoa and buttered toast, a favorite that Ninyah used to prepare for us. We then settled in for the night. I sank once again into a miasma of muddy dreams.

Soon the sun curled over the tips of the Wasatch Mountains, light furling over the valley floor. Over breakfast, we decided that day would be "Ward Day." We planned to visit our Mormon neighborhood ward buildings, which housed offices, recreational halls, and chapels.

From the time we moved to Laird Avenue until I went to college, the Mormon Church became my family. And what a big family it was. In the world there are over thirteen million Mormons. Of Utah's three million people, over 60 percent are Mormons. I didn't have a family tree—I had a forest. Yet I tried to chart it on butcher paper anyway.

The LDS Church is ruled over by Apostles of Christ, called the General Authorities. The highest of the Apostles is the Prophet, chosen by God—like Joseph Smith and then Brigham Young. When the ruling Prophet dies, a new Prophet is chosen and remains so until he dies. The Prophet—also called the President, the Seer, and the Revelator— lives in Salt Lake City. He is the supreme authority, the one who re- ceives revelations from God and passes them down. He and two other Apostles are called the First Presidency; below them are twelve men— the Quorum of the Twelve Apostles. The Apostles are special witnesses who are called by the Lord to testify to the world of His divinity. The Quorum delegates power down through the General Authorities, who delegate down to the ward bishops. All members of Mormon leadership are white males.

Grampa Penrose was an Apostle in the First Presidency. As a child, I didn't know that only the Prophet actually talked to God. It gave me a thrill to act out long conversations I imagined Apostle Grampa had with Heavenly Father. I played both parts.

In recent years, when it became clear that there were circumstances in which the Prophet was sometimes too old or disabled to function well, the doctrine was changed to allow Apostles to receive revelations in his stead.

A revelation can change the Church's doctrine and does so, some- times rather conveniently. For example, only men who had no African lineage were allowed to be priests. Then, in 1978, the current Prophet received a revelation allowing African American men to now "hold the priesthood." Even with this advancement, however, the higher authori- ties are all white men. African Americans have never been called by the Lord to serve in the Quorum.

All of this rankled Mom, of course. In her most cynical moods, she refuted the 1978 vision. "Ha!" she said. "The Church did it when the NBA wouldn't allow the Brigham Young University basketball team in because it discriminated against blacks." A puff on her cigarette. A sip on her drink.

Mom never let up on the issue of women in the Church. "You know what?" she sneered. "No revelation has ever been received that gives women the power to be priests. Or homosexuals the right to marry." Sometimes my mother shocked me. This was the first I had heard of "homosexuals" from her. All I knew about were poofs, fairies, faggots, and lezzies. Because the leaders were all over seventy years old and served clear into their nineties, my mother called them "the Quorum of the Dead."

Every state is divided geographically into sections called stakes. Each stake is ruled by a man, called the stake president. Each stake is divided into wards, and each ward has a bishop and a neighborhood boundary, which residents within it must attend. And then, in the ward…

Whew! Try charting that! I gave up.

The administrative bureaucracy of it all confused me as a child. What I loved was the ward building itself, beautifully designed and well landscaped, housing a chapel, offices, classrooms, and a recreation hall for dances, where chaperones made certain there was enough room between the dancing boy and girl for a train to pass through. For the support of all the buildings and functions of the Church, each Mormon tithes 10 percent of all gross income to the Church. When I made thirty-five cents an hour ironing, I gave the Church four cents.

"It's a voluntary tithe," I insisted to Mom.

"Is it now?" she said. "Try not paying it."

The Mormon ward is ruled over by a man called by the Lord to be a bishop. Not every man is called to be a bishop, but every man in the Church can be called by the Lord to become a lay priest and perform ecclesiastical acts of service in the name of God. These acts, particularly the ones called ordinances (like baptism and marriage), are recognized by God and are binding on earth and in Heaven, on earth and in the afterlife.

"Hold on, there's more." Mom was my main source of information, other than Sister Mallow. "All the boys become priests. They start as deacons, then become teachers, and then an elder. Got it?"

No, I didn't get it. I was a Brownie Scout. That's all.

"Now, here's the good part," Mom continued. She stood and got up on the chair. "After that, they rise to an even higher level of priesthood, with higher powers." She raised her arms and lowered them onto my head. It gave me chills.

"It's a lot of work, though." Mom got down, sat, and lit another cigarette. "And no one gets paid." She paused. "Ha! That's why the Church is so rich—slaves!"

Men donate their time. Women, too, donate their time. Women are not allowed to be priests; they are called instead to teach Sunday school, complete administrative tasks, and engage in social-service projects. They hold office in these service branches of the Church.

When I was a girl, I cared only that there was an overstructured ladder of privilege that was totally unattainable to me. I asked my mother why women couldn't be powerful priests, and she said, "Because the Church thinks women are inferior."

Not believing, and not satisfied, I asked Sister Mallow. She said, "Because God doesn't want us to." I always thought I would get a better explanation when I grew up, something that made intelligent sense to me. I didn't.

In this same "because God said so" type of answer, the recent President and Prophet, Gordon P. Hinckley, explains, "Women do not hold the priesthood because the Lord has decided it that way. It is part of His program." Women have an equally prominent place in the Church, he says. They run the auxiliary programs, such as the Relief Society. Under the direction of the Church authorities, women support the men, plan activities, bring food to the hungry, visit the sick, and are their husbands' companions. Thus, rather disingenuously, the Church claims that women are "coequals in this great enterprise" of salvation. As a child, it seemed that the women were little more than servants.

——◆——

Daddy quit his clerk job to hang out his own shingle. It didn't go well. Because of my father's nascent and sputtering law practice, Mom worked two jobs as a secretary and bookkeeper. She constantly complained, job after job, that she was paid less than the men who performed the same work. She railed about the lack of women's equality in the workplace.

Although she bristled when Daddy scorned Church doctrine, she deeply resented the Church's mandate that women "marry, have children, and be a good wife." She harangued further about Church doctrines with which she disagreed. Perturbed and angry, she sent embittered pronouncements into the turgid religious air that held Salt Lake City in its insular, self-absorbed grip. She mocked what she viewed as the Church's hypocrisy and denigrated the Gospel as fantasy and unproven dogma. When she refused to quit complaining, she was asked not to attend. She fell away and became a Jack Mormon, believing in some, but not others, of the many Church doctrines. She simply practiced what she believed and ignored the rest.

Eventually, she told me bitterly, she was excommunicated. Though I have tried to discover when and why, the Church authorities will not tell me.

Ironically, she continued to raise her children in the Church. I used to think it was because she believed in her deepest heart that the Church was true, but now I think it was more complicated. She believed Christ was a good teacher, and she wanted us to learn Christian values. But she also simply wanted to get us out of the house so she could have some quiet time, be alone, and drink.

My father continued in his personal, quiet Baptist ways. Clark, who was born in the Laird Avenue house and became a Baptist as an adult, tells me Daddy went to church on Sundays. But my father was usually home when I left for church, and he was home when I returned. So if he went, I never saw him go or went with him. I did see him sit with the Bible in his lap, gazing at it but not reading. I thought he looked sad then.

I look back now and I know my father was shamed, undermined in his efforts to be the head of the household. He and my mother fought about it constantly. She called him names: lazy, good-for-nothing, sloth.

I decided that I didn't want to be anything like my mother. I became repulsed by her deterioration. Her fingers were yellowing from cigarette stains. Sometimes she drooled when she drank; sometimes she passed out. She had a colliding cough, hacking at unreachable phlegm until people turned to look at her, their eyes falling to the child at her side. I was embarrassed by her and was glad when she stopped going to church.

Now, decades later, I parked across the street from my favorite ward chapel. The old bricks of the church radiated warmth and were colored crimson by shadow and sun. There was no cross. There isn't one on any Mormon church or temple.

"That's because Mormons focus on the resurrection, not Christ's torture and death," Ninyah told me.

"Not so," Daddy contradicted her. "It's because Mormons worship Old Joe Smith. He's the head honcho, not Jesus."

As with all of the Mormon properties, the grounds were tidily manicured; the grass was a deep green, though the foothills above were browning in the desert heat. Since Mormons are taught to keep their bodies and spirits clean and orderly, most of their streets and houses are clean and orderly as well. I got out of the car and sat on the lawn, the scent of mowed grass warm and pungent.

Inside the church, we went to Sunday school in the classrooms and after-school activities in the recreation hall. In the soft-lit chapel, we heard sermons about our Only True Church and about the path to salvation and Heaven.

In the similarly comforting living rooms of members' homes, we gathered on regularly scheduled nights for Fireside Chats, which were radio sermons for adolescents: lessons on chastity, marriage, family duties, women's roles, and Church obligations. I enjoyed these evenings. The sonorous voice of a High Authority boomed out from the radio. The teenagers sat on the floor, our bodies close, touching—which thrilled me because such touching was forbidden. The woman of the house served us cookies. We nodded our heads in agreement with the sermon, pledged to obey, and then walked home together, once again committed to perfection.

In addition, each individual family gathered together on Monday evenings for Family Home Evening: to pray, read scriptures together, and enjoy one another's company. Not my family.

My father rarely instructed me in religion, and he told me to make up my own mind. My mother didn't resolve my questions, either. She even confused me when I asked her about Church riddles, answering sarcastically sometimes, seriously other times. Though I sensed she approved of my inquiries, she simply would not make up my mind for me.

But she sent us regularly to every meeting and gathering. Church happened several times a week. At Sacrament meeting, men blessed the bread and water, and boys passed it to the congregation. Girls and women were never allowed to bless or pass the sacrament. As usual, my mother stewed about this sexism, which she viewed as a violation of everything fair and right and just. "Jesus would be shocked," she said.

My earliest memories of Church were of Fast Sunday, the first Sunday of every month. We fasted two meals and gave the Church the money we saved by not eating. I hated fasting. "We're supposed to starve and die of thirst all day?" I complained. "And for what?"

What I did love about Fast Sunday was testimony meeting. Everyone was encouraged to bear their testimonies, to tell the entire congregation how their faith had been formed and improved. Old ladies and men stood up and went on and on, disclosing electrifying stories, sometimes about miracles that had happened to them. I listened to people weep and say how the Prophet was in their souls, which excited me. I didn't want the Holy Ghost in me, lecturing me and tattling on me to Jesus, but the Prophet! He could come in anytime. People told how the Church had saved them and how they knew that this was the Only True Church, and I figured I would know this when I was their age, too.

Children were encouraged to stand and give their testimonies as well. I didn't care for this part. "I know that this is the Only True Church," they recited. This alarmed me. I felt left out. Kids younger than me stood up in testimony meeting and said, "I know that Joseph Smith is a true Prophet," while their parents beamed from the pews. I thought they were lying little brats. How did they know when I didn't?

On Tuesdays I went to Primary, where I learned about my Heavenly Father's plan, about baptism and about how to be a righteous woman when I grew up to serve others. Later, as a teenager, I went to MIA (short for Mutual Improvement Association meetings), where I learned to strengthen my faith and do good works, like visiting old people, taking dinners to shut-ins, and babysitting members' children for free. I learned that my body was sacred and how I must keep myself pure and chaste. We joined the boys to have supervised good fun: hayrides, square dances, and once a ride on a reindeer-driven sleigh. I joined the Girl Scouts, where I was a Brownie, and became an Intermediate, working hard for merit badges, patches to sew onto my bandalo (a sash draped over my shoulder, connected at the hip), which were awards for cooking and sewing and serving others. I dropped out, however, eventually tired of the lessons on knitting and cleaning and other "girl stuff."

Parents gathered little children in their arms and carried them to the Sunday services and activities mornings and evenings. I don't recall ever being in anyone's arms. We walked, or were dropped off at church. I mostly sat side by side with my two sisters, and then, after they were born and could be trundled or toddled to church, with my two brothers.

The Church folded itself around the children and teenagers, welcoming us, organizing ambitious activities, and always teaching us: be nice, be clean, be helpful, be prayerful, be grateful, be truthful, be obedient, serve the Lord, and thus be saved. I thought I'd finally discovered the right road to salvation. Although it was hard, I tried to obey.

Thereafter, I thought Mom's certain doom was what made her so mean. My Church leaders urged us to bring the Church to everyone, so I set out to save her. If I could do that, God would praise me and Mom would love me.

From then on, I also nurtured a deep desire to be saved myself, living in constant fear that I would be damned along with my father and my mother.

I tried to teach Mom. "You're headed for Hell," I warned her.

She snickered. "At least I'm in the driver's seat."

She contradicted me, saying it wasn't true that she was damned, and even if she was, it wasn't her fault. "I wanted to head for a courtroom to be a lawyer like your Baba," she defended herself. "Or to a performance hall to be a concert pianist." I had heard this excuse before. "I could have been either, you know."

She blamed Baba and Ninyah, and the Church.

"No, no, that wasn't to be," she scoffed. Her sarcasm buzzed. "A woman's highest calling is to be a good wife, a prolific mother, and a perfect hostess." She smiled then. "Do you know what 'prolific' means?" I didn't. She didn't tell me.

She waddled around pretending to be pregnant, prancing with a drink in her hand, pretending to set a table. "Doesn't this look fun?" She sat and was quiet for a moment. "I'm damned angry about all that," she sighed. But she looked sad, not mad.

"Now *you*." She grabbed my arm too tightly. "*You* can be anything you want."

Her breath smelled like cigarettes and booze. I turned away.

Every church building had a recreation hall, and each ward planned healthy activities for the children. Boys and girls participated together in plays and musicals, and attended carefully chaperoned dances, but most of our activities (homemaking lessons for the girls, horseback riding for the boys) were determined and segregated by sex. As I grew older, I began to believe that Mormon restrictions on women were unfair and controlling. I didn't know then the words "sexist" and "oppressive," but I did know that I, like my mother, smarted under the prohibitions and resisted the life that had been sculpted for me. I couldn't find in the Bible where Jesus said I couldn't play basketball and Mom couldn't be a concert pianist.

Mormon doctrine today still sets out as the highest role for women: marry, have children, and raise a family prepared to take a place in God's three-tiered Kingdom of Heaven, the husband and wife sealed together in the bosom of this eternal family. Doctrine dictates that a woman's primary job is "devotion to God, Church, husband, and children."

My mother bristled with resentment and ineffectual rebellion. It's not my mother's devotion to feminism I primarily recall, however, but her anger—a buzzing hostility. I learned to avoid it like an electric fence. And then I learned that anger myself.

CHAPTER 10

THE BOWLINE KNOT

——◆——

As I sat reminiscing on the lawn in front of the East 27th Ward chapel, I noticed two young boys sitting on the steps, fiddling with some rope. Mormon children often came to the church building to do community-service work, to join activities, or to congregate with friends. I listened to the boys' vague murmurs.

As a child, I had been happy in my Church family and at church. I shuffled into the smooth, shiny oak pews. When I was a toddler, my legs stretched straight out on the pew, my heels barely reaching the edge. As I grew older and bigger, my knees reached the edge and my legs dangled over. I swung them forward to kick the slatted pocket holding the hymnbook. I could see my best white shoes, my round white laces threaded carefully through every hole, and my double-knotted bows.

Sweet-chorded music, always resolving at the end, soothed me. I memorized the hymns and fancied myself a star. Children were allowed to sing; members smiled on me as if I were a little angel whose spirit was soaring. I sat there with my heavy hymnbook held in both hands, singing my heart out to "O Ye Mountains High," written by Grampa Penrose, singing loudly, making up words if I forgot them or just singing "Jesus" over and over to fill in the gaps. I kicked the seat in front of me in time to the music.

By the time I was nine, however, my friend Camille and I sang lyrics we changed surreptitiously in the hymnbook. Instead of "We thank Thee, oh God, for a Prophet," we sang, "We thank Thee, oh God, for a profit," thinking ourselves hilarious. The women sang, "I stand all amazed at the love Jesus proffers me"; instead, Camille and I sang, "I stand all amused at the lunch Jesus offers me." We laughed until snot ran out Camille's nose or I choked on a breath. We were frowned silent.

We made fun of the giant downtown statue of Brigham Young. His back was to the Temple, and he was supposedly beckoning pioneers and newcomers, but his outstretched arm reached out to Zion's Bank on the opposite corner.

By my early teens I tried to be a proper Mormon girl, singing politely. I laid my hands elegantly in my lap, the back of one hand resting in the palm of the other. I crossed my legs at the ankle. I lowered my head and looked up from under my eyes, to appear demure. But it was all so uncomfortable that within months I stopped.

Older still, I sang discreetly with Bruce, whom I chastely and dutifully loved until my heart dropped dead from aching, and whom I let sing louder than me, which I thought was right and just for a woman to do. We tried to hold hands while we sang, but our hands dampened, bathed in sweat. Hadn't we been warned that such touching would lead to kissing?

Today, whenever I meet an ex-Mormon, an uncanny thing happens: before five minutes pass, we break into song. "Remember this?" one of us will say. "Put your shoulder to the wheel, Push alo-ong. Do your duty with a heart full of so-ong." We sing several hymns, each of us knowing any hymn chosen, until we break down in laughter, agreeing, "Oh, the music was so grand."

Camille and I sang vigorously, adoringly. It was in church that I began to think of myself as talented, that I might really *be* somebody and might someday become famous or important. It wasn't just the music; it was the power of singing it so passionately, undeterred.

The men and boys gave two-and-a-half-minute talks at the lectern. Sometimes the women and girls did, too. Mom told me to pay close attention to the lessons but to make up my own mind. I rapturously listened. The speakers almost always urged us to bring others into the fold, which I thought, since I was learning how to iron, was an excellent way to put it. Elder Martin had a scratchy voice like an avalanche of gravelly rocks. Young Hyrum Larson stood on a stool and spit on the mike when he talked. Brother Cochran thundered. And Thayne mumbled into his shirt. "That was shirty," Camille said; hysterical, we shook the pew.

Sometimes Sister Grant gave a little talk. "Ladies," she crooned, and I sat up proudly. "You are blessed by God and sent forth to be a devoted mother and have children." Of course, I didn't think too much of this idea. I didn't like changing my doll's diaper; my favorite dolls were those I could stuff in my pocket. Besides, Mom said she hated being a mother.

Sister Madsen instructed the girls to "Do your duty and replenish the earth." When I first heard this instruction, I liked it, because it meant food. Mom would holler, "It's time to replenish the orange juice!" as she flung herself out the door to the grocery store. "Let me come," I'd plead, but she would yell over her shoulder, "No! I have another little stop to make."

Every orator delivered a must-do message that I took cleanly to heart and, for a day or so, tried to follow. "Go forth and be good." So I shared my stolen gumballs with Camille. "Pay your tithing!" So I went around the neighborhood pretending to collect for the eye bank and got enough money to pay all my tithing in arrears. "Bring our glorious message to those who've not heard the word." So I gave Church lessons to the neighborhood kids until Jacob's mom called my mother and told her she had to put a stop to it.

Mom just chuckled. "You go ahead," she advised me. "Just don't invite the Bernsteins anymore."

———◆———

Some Sundays I didn't want to go to church, but Mom made me go. "Rain or shine," she insisted. "Sick or dying."

I usually looked forward to joining the singing, throwing my head back and opening my mouth wide in song, but I was in a bad mood one

Sunday. Sister MacDonald was conducting the congregation, waving so hard the skin bags under her arms flapped back and forth. Her thick gray hair stood out all over her head. Camille said mice lived in her bangs. I didn't sing at all. Instead, I began to kick the pew.

Elder Hayes preached a ringing speech. He told us to take the Gospel to unbelievers, and I knew he was talking about Mom. "Bring the sheep into the fold," he commanded, and I wondered whether he knew how hard it would be to force Mom to come to church. He continued on and on like that. I thought he was looking straight at me, so I looked down. I was plenty irritated. I felt my face get hot. I kicked the pew a little harder.

Then Brother Dalton talked. "Be a helpmate to your husband and a protector to your wife." What was I to do with that? I didn't have either. "And children—" He paused. "You must obey your parents and your Heavenly Father." How could I do both at the same time? I tried to figure it out. God told me to pray for sinners; Mom told me to shut up when I did. God told me to pay tithing; Daddy told me to keep my hard-earned cash. I supposed I could be a more obedient daughter by tucking Mom's sheets in with hospital folds next time, by not getting grounds in her coffee anymore, or by doing my chores more cheerfully. But I was tired of all my chores—I never did them to Mom's happiness, so she always added more.

I began to kick the pew even harder, until Brother Bradley turned around and told me to be still. I wouldn't. I knew what I was doing. What did all these people know, anyway? I thrust my legs back again under the pew to gain momentum for another forward crash into the hymnal shelf. I kicked as hard as I could, and the slats holding the hymnbook split.

I knew trouble was coming.

Sister Edwards, who had been sitting beside me, swept me up under her arm and dragged me kicking and whining up the stairs at the back of the chapel to the Quiet Room. I was mortified. This was the room where noisy babies and little children were taken when their shouts and crying interrupted the service. The room was soundproofed, sealed off with a pane of glass that looked down to the altar. Sound was piped in through speakers in the wall, so the adults could still hear the lessons and the hymns, but no one downstairs could hear the children. Furious, I continued to kick and started to yell. I yelled until I grew tired of yelling.

Pressing my nose to the pane of the Quiet Room, I looked down and saw the tops of everyone's heads. I saw that Brother Borman had a bald circle I hadn't been tall enough to see before. I laughed and turned to Sister Edwards, who had stayed to supervise me. "He's sinned!" I yelled. "That's what happens to sinners. They lose their hair. My mom wears wigs."

"Listen to the lesson, dear," Sister Edwards said.

I held my hands over my ears to stop the lessons. I chanted, "Nah ne nah ne nah nah," to shut out the sound. I kicked the walls. I pounded on the glass. I looked out and saw the bishop standing at the lectern, his hands waving and his mouth moving. "We're all going to Hell," I shouted as loud as I could. Sister Edwards sat quietly in her chair, her hands folded in her lap, listening above my screams to the bishop's lesson.

Exhausted, I sat down in a clump. The congregation stood and began to sing. Sister Edwards pulled my hands from my ears gently.

"Are we ready to sing, Kathy?" she said. "You have such a lovely voice."

"What's the point?" I said angrily. "No one can hear me."

"God can hear you, dear." She smiled.

I broke away and shouted in my loudest possible voice. "Well, then, listen up, God. I wanna go back downstairs, OK?" I paused, and then with all my power, I shouted, "Get me outta here!"

But God wasn't listening.

My prayers often went unanswered, and I felt neglected, ignored, and unjustly treated. Explanations that God was busy, that God had more important things to do, that God was testing me, mollified but did not satisfy me.

I had thought my pleas were reasonable: make my mother quit yelling, don't let Daddy switch me, and save them both. God's failure to respond perplexed me when I was sad and angered me when I felt feisty. Mother called God "lazy fair," and I agreed. I resented His being lazy and didn't think He was fair on my account.

Yet I loved the Church. My chapel was washed in light. From the stained-glass windows, color fell and floated like feathers. The chapel hummed with goodwill, the ladies chirping and chattering, the men reverent and authoritative. No one yelled at me in church or slapped my hand if I took a handful of bread from the sacrament bowl instead of just one piece. The adults were affable and merciful, even when I was being reprimanded.

"Now, Kathy," crooned Sister Brown, "you really mustn't put gum in the hymnal, dear. Let's go upstairs to the Quiet Room and see if we can pry these pages apart, hmmm?"

The placid ladies and the gracious men embraced me. The Brothers chucked my chin and patted my head. The Sisters plucked me to their abundant bosoms. Sister Whitman kissed my cheek and tickled it with her thin moustache. Brother Armstrong shook my hand firmly with his good arm each time we met. Children played together with little rancor. I was surely loved.

Now as I sat on the church grass that July morning decades later, listening to the boys chattering on the chapel steps, I felt strangely wrapped up in the warmth of the Church, calm and centered. Even though I had fallen away from the Church, I felt an accepting air about me, as though this was a family welcoming home a prodigal daughter. I was actually tempted to go in and look around for some companionship. But another part of me sensed a danger, a fear that I would be seduced by the ambiance and aura that awaited me inside.

I was so disconcerted by these feelings that I walked away, a block north, to the old City Cemetery, where I wandered for a while to distract myself. Many of the Prophets were buried there, as were my ancestors, including Ninyah and Baba. I didn't seek out their gravestones. My excuse was that the cemetery was quite large, and it would take too much time to visit their graves. But I knew I wasn't ready. Something was missing. My remembrance of Ninyah and Baba as perfect beings was cracking. Were they good? Were they bad? Who had they really been? I knew there were questions still to be answered.

Reading headstones, I noted graves as old as the days of the pioneers. Several graves held children who had died at birth or as toddlers; there were the graves of a mother who died in childbirth, leaving eleven other children, and a father hailed as a patriarch. Religious messages were inscribed on most stones: "Gone home to Our Heavenly Father," or "Now in the Celestial Sphere." A husband and wife had been "Sealed in the Temple in 1904, now Together for Eternity."

One inscription reminded me of a childhood perplexity: "She has her Perfect Body now," it affirmed. Mormons are buried facing east because that's the direction from which the Lord will come when He returns to earth. At that time, He will give each Mormon his or her perfect body back for eternity. "Which body?" I always puzzled. "What age?" The answer was always unsatisfactory: "God will decide."

The boundaries of the cemetery were certain, as were the boundaries of the Mormon Church. I was encircled in both as I walked among the graves. It was as difficult to pry answers from the dead as it had been from my childhood mentors.

Questioning of Church doctrine is not encouraged. Church leaders suggest that members expose themselves only to faith-affirming materials: films, programs, books, and music. A Mormon relative of mine will watch only G-rated movies; an LDS friend asked me not to renew a gift subscription to *The New Yorker*, saying she would prefer to read Church magazines; another returned a copy of *Grimms' Fairy Tales* as too grim. The Church prefers its members to read the Gospels (the Book of Mormon, the Doctrine and Covenants, the Pearl of Great Price), the Church's magazines (*The Ensign* and others), and family-rated classical literature (certainly not *Madame Bovary* or *Lolita*.)

When I was a child and members were stumped by my questions, the usual and utterly frustrating answer was, "We cannot know all things, dear. We only know, and believe, what our Prophets tell us—it is the will of God. You must have faith."

Was this why Mormons seemed so content? Joyous, even? Unquestioning faith?

I turned and went back to the ward. I glanced at the recreation hall and remembered the Halloween slumber party in the basement, when Camille and I climbed through the window and spent the night in the cemetery, fearing the Holy Ghost was crouched behind a tombstone. I thought of the crepe-trimmed ballroom, where I learned to waltz primly and where I sang and acted in Church musicals. And I recalled the welcoming classroom, where teachers had opened up Heaven and let its peculiar complications rain down on me.

I became confused, muddled by these fond memories of the Sisters and Brothers, Sister Mallow's beatific face, and the saving embrace of the Church. All these I held up against the dark of my mother's disappointments in the Church, my father's scorn of the Church's judgments, and the discriminatory doctrines on women, blacks, and Jews. I had soaked up my Church's moral and ethical teachings, and blossomed in the help and compassion I, a believer, received. I held this up against the Church's self-righteous belief in itself as the only true church and its rigid rules and judgments against nonbelievers.

I knew that all these paradoxical memories were worth keeping. I looked for a token. I approached the two boys still sitting on the steps. They were still twisting pieces of rope.

"Hi," said the older of the two.

I smiled. Mormon children are taught to be respectful of their elders.

"Hello," I said. "What are you doing?"

"We're practicing knots for Boy Scouts. I'm teaching my friend."

"I see." I watched for a moment as he looped the rope. "Do the girls learn to make knots?" I asked.

"Nah," he answered. After a pause, he said, "Well, my sister is in Young Women's."

"And what is she learning there?"

"They're crocheting doilies for the old folks' home," he said, rolling his eyes.

I looked down. "Say, that's a good bowline knot. Looks like it'll anchor real nice."

"How'd you know it was a bowline?" the younger boy asked, surprised.

"I learned to tie knots when I went sailing in the San Juans," I answered. "With three other women," I added. I picked up a knot at his feet. "You have to be careful, though. This one's faulty. See? You tied your loop backward at the start of the rabbit hole, so it'll slip when you grab the end." I showed him how to do it right. "You want to tie your rope to someone or something and be sure it holds, no matter how strong the tension on it is."

He nodded. "Thanks."

"I'd like to learn to sail," said the older boy.

"Well, maybe you will someday. It's hard work." He looked interested. "But boys can do it, too," I said, and smiled.

"You been to San Juan, then?"

"No, the San Juans are islands."

He stopped knotting. I sat down, and we talked about geography, travel, sailing, boats, nuclear subs in the Puget Sound, his dreams of going to space.

Eventually, I asked, "Would you mind letting me have one of your knots?"

He thought a moment, debating. "Oh, sure, that's OK," he said, handing me one of the several pieces of rope at his feet.

"Thanks," I said.

I put the rope in my sack. I had a token for the Church.

CHAPTER 11

THE THREE KINGDOMS OF HEAVEN

———◆———

I WAS FIERCELY INTERESTED IN the concept of salvation. The Church taught me to believe that if I obeyed my Mormon principles, the Lord would save me for eternal life in the Kingdom of Heaven.

"That's terrific," Mom said. "I'd like you to be a little darling." She leaned over her ledgers. "But let me tell you this. There isn't anyone who's going to save you but yourself. *You* are the savior, and the sooner you figure that one out, the better."

One Sunday, Sister Mallow taught us about Jesus's Plan for Salvation. She said salvation meant "saved." That confused me some, because we saved food at my house, and in my opinion, that was not a good thing. It was better to eat it.

"No, honey, it doesn't mean saving food." Sister Mallow flapped her hands toward me and chuckled. She turned her head, her chins bobbling, to take us all in. Last Sunday I had sat right next to her and leaned into her, my cheek against her arm. I could hear her stories on my skin. But this Sunday I sat across from her so I could look at her pinked-up cheeks and bouncing bosoms. She smoothed her skirt to make a spot for her knobbed pie-tin hands. "Stop your fidgeting now, children." She leaned forward into us. "I have something wonderful to tell you."

We sat still and looked up.

Almost every Sunday there was a moment like this, when Sister Mallow told us a secret. Usually it was something grand, like last Sunday when she had taught us how to pray properly.

"First, do this," she had instructed as she placed her palms together in front of her. "Now make a pyramid with your hands." She moved her wrists out so that only her thumb and fingertips were touching. "Fingers pointing toward Heaven." We put our hands together.

"Not quite so wide, Kathy." She pushed my wrists in a bit. "Be moderate."

She pointed to our hands. "Those hands are your telephone line to God. You can talk to God on it anytime you want! Now bow your heads to pray."

Everyone else leaned over his or her pyramid to pray, but I figured out that if I lifted the pyramid up toward my forehead, thumbs touching my nose, and spoke into the base of it, my head wouldn't get in the way of the message shooting out through my fingertips. I could aim my prayer wherever God might be sitting. I poked my new best friend Camille with my elbow so she could look and see how to do it right.

I sent God many messages this way. Once, in the grocery store, I stood by the candy, put my hands together, and spoke right up in my best loud voice, "Dear God, please give me a candy bar." The big-toothed grocery clerk smiled and gave me a Sugar Daddy. "God won't always answer you so quick," she said, "but He hears you, honey. Don't you worry."

God may have heard me then, s the only time He answered me. I figured He must be pretty busy.

Sister Mallow took up again the next Sunday when we were settled down. In a hushed voice that we strained to hear, she hummed, "Salvation means that God has saved all of us from our sins and we will go to live with God in God's Kingdoms of Glory." We sat quietly, and she repeated her message in a louder voice, "Jesus has saved you, and you will go to live in God's mansion."

This set me off in a daydream. I would rather live in a mansion. In our Laird Avenue house, if the bathroom door was left wide open, it caught on our bedroom doorknob and held the door shut.

Once I got stuck inside the bedroom. "Let me out!" I hollered. I pulled and pulled, and it didn't budge. Lucy just looked at me and went on playing with her doll.

"You're such a baby," Sandy sniggered, but she got off the bed and came to forcefully yank the door open.

"What if you're not here to help me?" I whined.

"You'll have to drink your pee." Sandy huffed back to the bed and her book.

Suddenly, Sister Mallow's voice was loud in my ear, startling me. "Will you, Kathy?"

I didn't even pause. "No!" I shouted, absolutely certain. "I won't ever, ever drink my pee!"

The class was quiet. Then kids began to laugh. I knew I'd said the wrong thing.

"Dear," she said smoothly, silencing the giggles. "I asked you if you'll go *here*." With a long, round stick she was pointing to a flip chart she had placed in front of the half circle of our Sunday-school class. On a large white sheet of paper, she had drawn a big house with three floors. On the top floor where she was pointing, she had written "Celestial Kingdom." The middle floor was "Terrestrial Kingdom," and the bottom floor was "Telestial Kingdom."

"This is God's mansion, Kathy, where we will live after we die and God takes us home to Heaven." She tapped the floors top to bottom and then again bottom to top with her pointer. "Do you know which floor you will live on?"

I was looking hard at the chart. I was looking for the kitchen.

Camille asked whether there were dogs in the house. Sister Mallow said no, dogs didn't go to Heaven. I squeezed Camille's hand so that she wouldn't cry. I didn't think she should have to leave Buster.

"God's mansion is just for humans." Sister Mallow's arms went up and around in a circle. She swept us in. "All of God's children."

All of them? I was concerned that it would be too crowded, more crowded than at our house. What was the point of having a big house if you jammed it full of kids?

"When do we go there?" Sean waved his hand in the air.

"Christ is going to come back to earth someday," Sister Mallow said, and beamed. But I thought this was a very bad idea. The last time I'd seen Him, He was nailed on a cross, all bloody and gray. Unless His dad had cleaned Him up, this would scare the younger children, though I thought I could handle it.

"When? Will it be tomorrow?" Bobby asked. He was sitting right next to her.

"That's such a good question," she said, holding Bobby's picking hand in her lap while she talked. I wished she would hold *my* hand.

"No one knows when this visit will happen, but if we are good, we will be prepared to meet God." I knew about this preparation stuff, because all Mormon families were supposed to keep two years' worth of food in their basements or storage sheds so we would be ready. "He will be here for a thousand years. These years are called the Millennium."

"A thousand years!" I cried out. Over went my chair as I leaped up. "How can we make two years of food last a thousand years?" I spread out my arms to the other kids, lifted my shoulders, asked them the same question with my voice rising. "Well?"

"Let's pick up your chair, Kathy dear." She glided over and leaned past me to reach my chair. I could smell her lavender perfume and feel the warm cotton of her shift. She sat the chair upright and sat me in it. "This is not about food, honey. Let's sit down now." She moved back across the circle to her seat and cushioned herself down. "Let's move on."

———◆———

Mormons still keep stores of food. I remember being told it was for the Millennium, but I can find little authoritative information about what the Church instructed in the 1950s. Today, the stores are for emergencies, with the time cut from two years to seventy-two hours. But the lesson, along with our lack of food at home, stuck.

"Mom, we're supposed to have two years' worth of food in the basement," I complained one day after Sunday school.

"Ha!" she scoffed. "We can't afford two *weeks'* worth."

"Well, what are we going to do when the Millennium comes?"

Mom laughed a dry, coughing laugh. Usually when I came home from Sunday school, she was lying on the couch, resting up. Today she sat at the dining-room table, her ledger books spread out, the adding machine propped close to her right hand. Beside it, her glass of orange juice sat on a paper coaster, water beading down the side. The ashtray was full of cigarette butts. She tapped the pack on her hand. *Tap-tap*, a new cigarette fell out. She caught it in her fingers and reached for the matches.

"We'll go to Camille's house. They have plenty of food."

"But they have seven kids. And not much room."

She struck a match on the closed cover of the matchbook. "They won't turn us away, Kathy." She lit the cigarette, and I moved closer to inhale the sweet sulfur of the match, the fragrant first scent of fresh-lit tobacco. She spoke through the exhaling smoke. "That wouldn't be Christlike." The smoke blew out with her words. She cocked her head at me. "Now, would it?" Smiling, she scratched her nose with her little finger, and then she sat up and went back to her ledgers. I could tell she was done talking about it.

I felt better. We'd get in at Camille's. But where would we sleep? There were six of us: Mom, Dad, Sandy, me, Lucy, and by then, Clark. That would make fourteen people. We would let Buster in, no matter what. In my mind, I worked my way through Camille's cellar storage room, laid out sleeping bags, and divided the crackers and Cheez Whiz. Camille and I could sleep in the same sleeping bag and scratch each other's backs. Buster could sleep with us. That wouldn't be so bad.

"Besides"—Mom startled me out of my reverie—"what good is two years of food going to do us in a thousand-years-long Millennium?"

I clapped my hands. "Ha! That's what *I* wanted to know, too!"

"Well, aren't you the smart little girl?" She laughed and mussed my hair. "Now get lost. I have twice as much work to do since your bum father isn't making enough."

I was giddy with pride at how smart Mom and I were. I went out behind the shed and ate seven of my stolen cookies.

———◆———

Sister Mallow shifted back into her seat, her large lap covering the entire chair. "Here's what happens after Christ comes back to earth. He rules the earth for the one thousand years during the Millennium, and we live in peace and harmony. Then we go to his Kingdoms of Glory to live forever."

This was hard for me to imagine. Between Thanksgiving and Christmas was a forever time. How could I wait a thousand years? Would I stay alive? Would I get old like Mrs. Jespersen, with my face all cracked and wrinkled like dry earth and my nose pocked like a peanut? Would everyone use a cane? Would we outgrow our clothes? I waved my hand in the air, but Sister Mallow didn't see me. I kept my hand up.

"During those thousand years, girls and boys, each person will be a missionary," she continued. This was news to me! I had questions. I waved my hand more vigorously.

"We Mormons will bring the Gospel to all non-Mormons during the Millennium." She pointed out the window to the world. "Everybody who isn't a Mormon gets the chance to become one." Clasping her hands, she threw back her head and looked down her chin at us. "Are we happy about that?"

"Yes, Sister Mallow!" we said.

"Let's say it now, children." Sister Mallow stood up and led us. "This is the Only True Church. I know that Joseph Smith was a true Prophet." We all said it with her.

"I know that David O. McKay is a true Prophet of God," we chanted about our current Prophet.

All this time, I had my hand raised. But my arm was tired by then, so I finally put it down.

I know now, of course, that Sister Mallow was ignoring my waving hand. I must have been a troublesome child with all my questions. Oddly enough, as a judge I am endlessly patient with inquiring litigants in my courtroom, answering all their questions, explaining complicated procedures until I believe they understand. It is one of the justifiable complaints about me as a judge—that I take too long, giving ear to everyone who wants to speak or ask questions. I admit that given the length of the docket and the press on judicial time, I am not good at managing my caseload. But I seem incapable of cutting people off.

"When the Millennium is over, all the Mormons will climb the stairs to Heaven," Sister Mallow explained, pointing to the mansion on the chart. She tapped the highest floor. "This is the Celestial Kingdom," she said, pointing her stick at the top floor again and tapping it vigorously. "This is where God and Jesus live. This is the highest Kingdom of Glory."

Sometimes Sister Mallow looked radiant, and this was one of those times. Through the basement window, the morning light hit the glass-topped table, bounced up, and shone on her face as she looked down on us. Her chins lit up as she looked to God in the ceiling, her eyes closed.

"Ohhh," said the twins in unison. "That's where angels are."

"That's right, children. Only the very best Mormons go to the Celestial Kingdom." I was pretty sure I would not be on the top floor.

"My mom says you have to be married to live with God on the top floor," blubbered Camille, "and that I'm ugly and won't ever."

"I'll marry Camille!" I shouted. I didn't think that would be so bad, because she was my best friend and I liked her house better than mine. She had a dad, a mom, a dog, and a hamster in a cage.

"No, Kathy, you won't," said Sister Mallow. "Girls can't marry girls. Only boys can marry girls."

Here we go again, I thought. I rolled my eyes and gave a big sigh. Sister Mallow didn't look at me, so I did it again, louder. But she still didn't look.

"Here's what your mommy means, Camille." *Tap-tap.* "The Celestial Kingdom has three rooms in it." She took her black marker and divided the top floor into three rooms, each one bigger than the next. She pointed to the biggest room. "This is the best room of all. To live in this room, you must be married in the Temple and sealed together for time and eternity. If you do that, you can live here with your whole family."

Now I was decided. First, even if it was the biggest room on the third floor, it was still smaller than the whole middle floor. Second, who wanted to be with their whole family? Daddy, yes, and maybe Mom, Lucy, and Clark. But not Sandy. Was I the only one who understood all this?

Sister Mallow moved her stick down a floor. "This is the middle floor. This is called the Terrestrial Kingdom." We repeated it with her. She tapped again. "Jesus can come down from the Celestial Kingdom and visit the Mormons who live here, but they can't go up to see Him." I could see this was getting complicated.

"The Mormons on the middle floor haven't believed strongly enough in our Church or been good enough. So they'll be here. Also living here will be people who had a chance to be Mormons on earth and said no but who now say yes in the Millennium."

Like Grace's family next door. They were Catholics. No matter how hard I tried, I couldn't make them be Mormons. *Too bad for them*, I thought. But if I got to be a real missionary in the Millennium, maybe I could change their minds and they'd become Mormon. Or I could baptize them when they were dead. Middle floor for them.

"And people who are basically good but have been blinded by the craftiness of men will live here, too." Her pointer tap-tapped the middle floor. I looked hard. Gerald Tate was blinded in one eye by a firecracker last Fourth of July. I wondered whether having just one eye was enough to put him there. It was getting crowded.

I decided that stopping at the middle floor might be OK. I didn't care much for God, because He let His son get killed, so I didn't much want to live on the top floor with Him. But I liked Jesus, and He could come down and visit me if I was on the middle floor.

I had to point something out to Sister Mallow. I shouted, "I'm already a Mormon! Why do I have to wait a thousand years? Why can't I just go on up to my floor?"

"You must wait to be judged by the Lord," she answered. "He will assign you to your Kingdom."

She went back to her chart. *Tap-tap.* "To get assigned to this middle floor, you have to live a good life, be baptized, and try hard to follow all of the Prophet's rules." Well, that was a shock. That definitely left me out of the middle floor.

All the other children had been baptized for themselves at eight years old, but I wasn't going to. I didn't mind being baptized for the dead, but I didn't want the Holy Ghost entering into *me.* Ninyah said the Ghost stayed with you forever and always, to tell you whether you were doing right or wrong. Then he would report it to Jesus! That seemed icky to me, like having a spy crawling around inside your body all the time. He wouldn't get any light or air, and he must go all damp and smelly, so he'd be mean. No, I wouldn't do it. The bottom floor was the place for me.

Now Sister Mallow tapped the bottom floor. "The Telestial Kingdom," she said sadly. "Here is where all the poor souls go who do not accept Mormonism in the Millennium."

Wait a minute! That was not me! I accepted. Something was missing. I didn't fit anywhere. Would I not be saved?

I finally decided that I would be cast to the bottom floor. But what about Mom? I'd heard that God had a basement under the house. It was called Limbo, and all the lost souls floated there. I admitted that Mom would be thrown into God's basement. It upset me terribly, and I worried about it night and day. It seemed I was the only one who cared enough to try to save her.

I begged her again to come to church and to quit smoking and drinking like the Word of Wisdom required. "Quit nagging me," she said grumpily. "It's called the Word of Wisdom because it's just advice."

I corrected her. I told her what I remembered from my lessons, that the advice had been turned into law when Prophet Heber Grant had received a revelation from God.

"Well, I don't see how a man who illegally had several wives in secret can be telling *me* not to smoke and drink. Do you?"

"He talks to God, Mom."

"Get lost," she said, and turned back to her books.

I told Sister Mallow the next Sunday morning.

"Your mother is the lost one," soothed Sister Mallow. "She has disobeyed the Lord." Sister Mallow looked down sadly at me, hefted me onto her lap, and gave me a big, warm hug, crushing me into her layers of waist. She rocked me back and forth. "The Word of Wisdom is a law now," Sister Mallow told the class. "Heavenly Father tells us it is against Church law to smoke cigarettes or drink alcohol, coffee, or tea."

"Why?" I asked from within her folds. I needed to know. In my family, Baba and Mom smoked. Everyone drank.

"Because it is very bad for your body."

"My mother says it's bad to be fat," said Camille, who was sitting beside us.

Sister Mallow flushed, reached down, and patted Camille on the head, "Now, let's not say mean things, Camille."

She addressed the children. "Kathy's mother smokes and drinks." Everyone looked at me. "Those are sins. Let's all say a little prayer for Kathy's mother to repent and be saved."

Sister Mallow's white shift burned into my cheek. I buried my head in the dark, cool canyon between her bosoms. My forehead became a cliff; I felt its sharp edges. A lake of tears began to form. Sister Mallow turned me around and took my hands to form a pyramid pointing upward. I imagined a blue sky, seagulls soaring above the cliff. The lake stayed calm. We all bowed our heads. We prayed, "Dear Heavenly Father, save Kathy's mother from sin so she can enter your Kingdoms of Glory."

I tilted back my head, lifted my pyramid to my face, and prayed the loudest. But it was no use. I knew it was true. Mom would be down in the damp, dark cellar with her cigarettes and drinks. Tears puddled out of my closed eyes. I had to stop praying to wipe them away.

Would I ever see my mom in the salvation? If I was on a floor above her, she couldn't come up to see me. Could I go down to Limbo to visit her? Or was it forbidden to visit people so low in the basement?

One night, I dreamed of Mom in Basement Perdition. She wandered in a wet-dog-smelly cellar under God's house. No light came in. She had learned to see in the dark and crawled on all fours like a cat. Water collected on the damp-earth ceiling and dripped into her hair. Spiders crawled up her legs. Slimy, sharp-toothed bats hung down, hissing.

Food was passed in through a thin slat in the cellar door. It was slop, creamed corn mixed with grape juice and chunks of pork fat. I couldn't bring myself to go down to visit.

I woke up crying and needing to pee. The door jammed, so I woke Sandy up. I told her Mom's fate. She unjammed the door for me and said, "Mom can rot there. That's where she belongs." Not only would I miss Mom, but I would also be stuck on the bottom floor with Sandy. That made me cry harder.

Sister Mallow finished her lesson. "This grand scheme is called God's Great Plan of Salvation." She folded her hands in her lap and smiled. "It will be glorious, children." She stood, prepared to lead us in song.

I asked, "What about food? What will we eat at God's house?"

She chuckled, shaking her head back and forth. "Manna," she said softly. The word trailed out like a stream of whipped cream curling around and around. "You'll eat manna."

This left no room for more questions. Manna sounded good, like bananas, or dinner at Ninyah's, or ice-cream sauce. I could believe in that.

Everything else troubled me.

CHAPTER 12

TEACHING

———————

I THREW MYSELF INTO MY writing, hidden away in my basement cubby, where Daddy had set up my writing table, typewriter, and lamp.

I wrote original plays and musicals, which we rehearsed in the other corner and which I produced for the neighborhood children.

I wrote Saturday sermons, using what I learned on Sunday as my guide.

I wrote about the pioneers, who often starved or froze to death in the end, which made the little kids cry. But I resurrected myself to cheer them up. In my best story, Camille played a cat that loved me, even though I was a dog that had been cursed by a witch. Because of her love, I turned back into a queen and she turned into a queen, and we got married and lived happily ever after. Camille did "meows" very well, and the audience clapped wildly. We ate the gingersnaps Emily had brought. Nobody told us queens couldn't marry.

Usually Lucy played a part, and sometimes Sandy did, too. Clark was the baby, so I made him be a pet or a tree. Otherwise, I played all the parts myself. I acted out fairy tales. I put on revues with dances and jokes. I sang songs from musicals like *Oklahoma* and *Showboat*, changing the lyrics to "Oh, what a beautiful Mormon" and, as a joke, "Ol' dammed river," which shocked the Mormon kids until I told them it meant to block up a stream.

I posted flyers on telephone poles and dropped them into mailboxes, inviting: "Come one, come all, especially kids."

The week after I learned about the Kingdoms of Glory, I decided I should bring the story of God's mansion to the neighborhood children. Sandy crossed her arms, told me it was silly, and refused to help. Lucy passed out my flyers advertising the upcoming event.

Ten kids came. Twelve-year-old Grace, whose family was Catholic, brought her twin brothers, Peter and Paul. They all sat on the lawn with animal crackers and lemonade, and I began my presentation.

I demonstrated the exciting story on a long piece of butcher paper I nailed to the cottonwood tree—my hand-drawn and colored version of Sister Mallow's chart.

"The Mormons who have been Saints and never been bad go to the highest floor possible. That's the Celestial Kingdom," I said, pointing a stick at the top floor, which I had outlined in red. "This is the floor God and Jesus live on. The food gets sent up on this little teeny elevator here." I tapped the dumbwaiter I had drawn in the wall, modeled after the one at my grandparents' house. "You have to be a perfect Mormon to get to live on the third floor with God and Jesus."

Then I pointed to the middle floor. "This is the Terrestrial Kingdom. Let's all say it together." We all recited it, except Grace, who sat with her arms crossed. "This is the floor with the kitchen, where the food is cooked." I announced. I had drawn in a kitchen, quite large and bordered in green. I waited for this to sink in, sure that the kids would pick this floor to live on.

"Jesus comes down here to visit his friends on the middle floor." I pointed to the stairs, little lines I had cleverly inserted. "But he mostly lives upstairs with God and the Saints." My stick climbed the stairs.

Now I lowered the boom. "But you have to be baptized. And you have to be really good. And I mean really, really good!" I looked straight at Paul.

He burst into tears. This alarmed and thrilled me. I must be doing a good job.

"I'm a bad boy," he cried. "Dad says so."

I wanted to make him feel better. So I grabbed a wad of cottonwood fluff floating down from the tree. I took it to Paul. "This is you, Paul," I said in my most comforting voice. He held out his hand for the airy, wispy ball. "You are just a child, not even eight years old. So God thinks you are just a little thing, all innocent, and not a sinner, even though you're Catholic." Paul's nose was running. Everyone was watching. I went on. "He thinks you don't even know what sin is." I patted him on the head.

I knew what sin was, but I was pretty sure Paul didn't. I'd never seen him pocket a gumball, or step on a beetle just to hear it crunch, or carve something in a tree trunk with a knife.

"If you die before you're eight, Paul, you get to go up to the Celestial Kingdom anyway. Even if you've been bad, it doesn't matter, because God thinks you don't know what you're doing."

Paul wiped his nose and stopped crying, but Peter began to whimper. "I don't want Paul to die."

Uh oh. I turned to Peter. "No. It's OK, Peter. He won't die."

Paul cried out, "Then if I don't die, I won't go to Heaven."

"No, wait, Paul. Just if you *do* die, you will."

"No!" sobbed Peter. "Please don't kill Paul."

"Stop this, boys!" Grace smacked both boys on the knees. "I want to hear the rest of this. Go on, Kathy. Convince me."

"Let's see." I had lost my place. "Well, when you boys become Mormons, you can get to be a high priest and have a head start!" None of us knew exactly what a high priest was. I thought quickly and pointed to the top of the cottonwood tree. They looked. They stopped sniffling.

"Can girls?" asked Grace.

"Well, no, they can't." This difference still upset me, but I was being the teacher, so I had to make it be OK. "But if you get married in the Temple, you can go with your husband wherever he goes. That's because you get sealed together for time and eternity. You can get to the top floor that way."

"What about girls who never get married?" Grace flipped a stone with her toe. It landed by my foot.

"Well..." I was becoming confused. I wasn't as good at this as Sister Mallow was. I'd forgotten her answer.

"And what if your husband is bad and goes to the lower floor? Where do you go if you've been good, but you're stuck to him?"

This was a question I hadn't thought about. Mormons who got married in the Temple got sealed to each other for eternity. I had a lot of questions about this. How did they walk around afterward? Were they just sealed at the hands or all over? How many people could you get sealed to and still function? But it was a secret, and no one would explain it to me.

The lesson was scrabbling out of control. "You go with him, I guess." This didn't seem fair, I thought. But he couldn't go up to the top floor with her, and women had to follow the men. What other choice was there, anyway?

"That's stupid, Kathy." Grace flicked another stone. "Your whole Church is stupid." Paul poked Peter with a twig. I was losing my audience. I didn't really want to talk about it anymore.

But Grace wouldn't let it go. "What about your mom? Where will *she* go?"

I poked my stick into the ground. I twisted it around in the dirt while I thought. Maybe Mom would climb out of the cellar to the bottom floor. Or maybe even to the middle Kingdom of Glory. She was honorable, just not as good as she should have been. But she'd had her chance on earth to be a good Mormon and refused it. In the Millennium, she'd be given a last-chance offer to be a faithful follower, but I was pretty sure she'd refuse that, too. This meant she couldn't go up to the middle floor, either. I was hopelessly confused.

I knew she wouldn't make it out of Perdition. But I didn't say so.

"She'll be on the bottom floor, I guess," I said miserably. I looked at my chart. It wasn't white after all. It was flimsy, a dull yellow, stained a little on the edge. I'd walked to the Emigration Market and begged it from the butcher. On the way home it had dragged twice. I'd worked most of the night on it, but now, as I looked at it, the house looked crooked and leaning. The floors weren't straight, and the lower Kingdom was too narrow, like it had been squashed by the weight of the top two. I hadn't really considered assigning anyone there today. I started to tap it hard. Maybe I should rip it down.

I turned to the kids. One said, "Hey, let's play hopscotch." I brightened.

"No, she won't," said Grace. She walked up to me, her eyes all black and evil, staring. I looked up at her face, which was bright with triumph. I wanted to pull her pigtails, which stood right out from her head. If she came closer, I would poke her eyes out. "She won't go to any Kingdom at all."

Grace stood right in front of me and put her hands on her hips. "My mom tells me your mom is going to the Mormon Hell. That's where sinners go after the Devil gets them and makes them not go to church." My dark fear had been revealed!

"Will not!"

"Will so!" With her shoe, she scuffed dirt up at me. "The Devil makes your mother scream and chase you and hit you all the time. We can hear her at night."

"Cannot!"

"Can so!"

Grace lifted her arms above her head and shook them. Her voice rose as she imitated Mom, each shout as shrill as the pile driver at the sand and gravel pit—*clang, clang,* endless. "'You goddamned sons of bitches,'" she mimicked. "'I'm gonna beat the living daylights out of you. You're gonna get it. You are nothing but little shits.'" Grace came close, put her face up to mine. "Your mom's disgusting! We can hear her all over the neighborhood."

I had little hammers in my cheeks, and they beat out against my skin. The shame of discovery burned my head, and I could smell an awful defeat like Mom's charred toast. I raised my stick and lashed out at Grace, but I was too close, and she moved quickly out of the way. She ran back, took the switch from me, and slashed it into my chart. "Didn't your fat Sister Marshmallow tell you there's a basement under the house? It's the Mormon Limbo. Your mom's going to Hell. That's where she belongs."

I reached up and punched Grace in the face, and then I pounded her with both fists. Paul and Peter screamed and ran away, but Grace stayed and grabbed me by the hair, twisted me to the ground, and kicked dust in my face. I began to cry. The dust stuck to my cheeks.

I ran into the house and sat weeping on the couch until it was almost time for Mom to come home for lunch. I turned on the oven to cook her usual grilled cheese sandwich. I put the potato chips and cookie on her plate, folded the napkin, and poured iced tea into her glass. Then I sat at the table and began to cry again.

"Oh, for Heaven's sake, what's the matter?" Mom said as she flung her purse on the counter. She snapped the radio on to *Fibber McGee and Molly.*

When I told her what had happened, she sat there eating for a while. "I don't want to deal with this," she said. "I'm having a bad day." She ate and listened to her program. I just sat there miserably.

Finally, she sighed. "You can't invite Grace anymore," she said. "She's a bad influence on you." She turned again to her show, listened, and laughed at a joke.

When I first heard about Limbo, I thought it was a tree, like a big maple, broad and umbrella-like. But Sister Mallow had made it sound like Hell. Now I wondered whether it was actually true. Would a good God really have a basement?

"Mom," I finally asked, "is it the truth?" I silently willed her to make it not so.

"No one knows what the truth is," she said, and scowled. "It moves around."

This gave me hope.

"So how do I find it?" I asked. "Where do I look?"

She paused so long I thought she wasn't paying attention anymore. She sipped her iced tea, and then she looked sharply at me.

"Make it up," she said. "Whatever suits."

We didn't talk for a minute. She pushed her plate over. "Here, have half my cookie." She let me pour myself a half glass of milk, and we sat quietly eating, listening to the radio.

———•———

Eric and I had promised to meet for a late lunch at a restaurant close by the Laird Avenue house. I had time to pick up a token.

I drove to the Emigration Market, though I couldn't bring myself to go to the butcher's counter. I sadly moved up and down the aisles. I picked up a can of frozen orange juice. Would it matter if it thawed and spoiled before I made it to Bear Lake? At the checkout stand I also bought a pack of Marlboros.

With time still left, I asked directions to the nearest liquor store. I bought a pint of vodka. Mom's favorite brand, Smirnoff. It sounded desultory and foul, and I experienced a flash of shame.

I put these sins in my sack.

CHAPTER 13

HAPPINESS

———◆———

ONE SUNDAY, SISTER MALLOW BEGAN her lesson. "Remember when I taught you that Man is that he might have joy?" she asked after we had scooted our chairs into a tight circle, giddy with expectation.

She pulled her straight-backed chair into our circle and plopped her capaciousness down. Once she sat, I couldn't see the chair, not a single grain of wood. Her mountainous chest and shoulders covered the back of it, her enormous bust fell through a crevice into the valley of her lap, and her magnificent thighs and legs rolled and draped over the chair legs.

"Yes, Sister Mallow," we all said in unison.

"Do you know what 'joy' means, children?" Her voice was a loud whisper, filled with excitement. I heard a mystery. She tilted her head toward the center of our circle of chairs. We all leaned in, too. She inhaled deeply, raising her shoulders. I condensed myself to let her breathe me in.

"What?" we cried out. "What? Tell us!" Bobby had quit picking his nose. Camille was squeezing my hand. Sister Mallow looked each of us in the eye, nodded her head sagely, and placed her hands on her knees.

"Well..." She exhaled a soft wind.

We all leaned forward. Every child was rapt.

"What it means is that every one of you is meant to be happy. That's what joy is." She let this sink in.

"Happiness." She moved back slightly, letting each of us go softly into our own place. "Happiness," she repeated.

I was thrilled. I looked around to see whether anyone could possibly be as excited as I was. I knew what happiness was! Happiness was taking the bus downtown to the library all by myself and spending the day in the children's room. It was popcorn popped on the stove by our favorite babysitter. It was standing on a bench watching the neighbor's new TV through his picture window. It was a whole bag of marshmallows eaten in secret behind the garage. It was Daddy lying on the grass with me at night, looking up at the stars and listening to the crickets. Once in a rare while, it was Mom stroking my head, absentmindedly giving me a kiss.

But my greatest happiness was stealing. I had a pile of stolen things stored in hiding places in my room or behind the garage—peppermint sticks, candy-button punch cards, Pez fillers, gum, and sourballs. And not just food—gloves, books, small toys, and trinkets. I ate the sweets in secret until my stomach hurt. But I gave my prizes away, and the people I chose to bless with my gifts blessed me back and treated me with affection and kindness. This was happiness.

My latest great joy was a frog clicker I'd slipped into my pocket at the T-Street Market. Two small bowl-shaped pieces of metal were soldered together in a V. One cup was painted on the outside to look like the back and head of a frog, the other like the belly. I held it between my fingers and pressed the little cups together. They clicked! *Ah-rah! Ah-rah!* I planned to give the frog clicker to Camille. I wanted her to love me; once I gave her the frog clicker, she'd be mine forever.

"Jesus wants you to be happy." Sister Mallow glided around the room. "To have joy." I rocked back and forth in my chair. Jesus and I were one. We both wanted the same thing for me.

"The Lord wants us to be happy," the cloud said, shifting trancelike in the sky. "That is the whole design of His plan." Her eyes looked like stars.

"I know! I know!" I yelled out. I wanted to tell her about the buttered popcorn and offer to bring her some. I wanted to invite the children over to watch the test pattern on the TV between programs. I wanted to bring my stash of stolen candy to Sunday school and show them how I stole it—we could all begin to steal and eat together.

"Here's how to be happy," I wanted to say. But Sister Mallow was waltzing with her eyes closed.

———————

ZCMI had started out with all Mormons doing business only with other Mormons. Now anyone could shop there. Ninyah took me with her to buy linens and fashionable dresses and drink hot chocolate in the tearoom, where I had to wear white gloves and sit like a lady.

One day I took the city bus downtown. I had two dollars to spend on my mother's birthday present. I was headed for Kress, which sold things for a nickel, but was distracted by the window display at ZCMI. Nothing in there would fit my budget; still, I liked wandering through the store, so I went in.

I rode up and down the elevator until the man pulling the lever made me get off. I stopped at the second floor and wandered into the jewelry section. A woman in a mink coat was trying on a spangled silver bracelet.

"I want a mink coat," Mom had answered when I asked her what she would like for her birthday. "And a gold necklace, thank you very much."

"Mom, be serious," I begged, determined to please her this time.

"Oh, anything," she said, brushing me off. "Just don't draw me another picture."

I pressed my nose against the display case. An emerald ring, a bracelet shaped like a snake, waterfall earrings, a cranberry-red ruby pendant—all these gems sparkled out at me from the glass case. On a low table across from the cash register, a shiny gold necklace hung on a rotating rack with several other chains, all reflected in the light from an elegant stained-glass lamp. The necklace was made of small links, each clasping the next, a row of sunbeams holding hands and dancing. This was my mother's necklace. I could feel it in my heart.

I took two chains down and turned back to the counter. As I moved, I closed my palm over one and slipped it into my pocket. The saleslady turned to look at me. I stood on my toes and held the other chain up to the counter.

"How much is this chain?" I asked.

"More than you can afford, my dear," she said, taking it gently from me. "Were you looking for something for your mother?" I marveled at the kindness in her voice. She seemed to like me and think I was a good girl to be thinking of my mother.

"Well, yes," I said, alert to the necklace touching my thigh through my pocket, "but I have only two dollars."

She came out from behind the counter. "What a sweet child," she said, bending down to take my hand, "Come with me, and we will find you something." She smelled faintly of Chanel No. 5, and her pleated skirt brushed against me as we walked.

The saleslady had called me a sweet child. In that defining moment, I felt the blush of shame. I wanted to put the necklace back, but how? And then I didn't want to put it back—if I was such a sweet girl, didn't I deserve to have it?

"Does your mother like dogs?" she asked.

No, she didn't.

"Yes, she does," I said politely, feeling awkward and criminal. She led me to a small square stand at the front of the store. CLOSEOUT SALE—$2, read a sign.

"How about this?" She plucked a thumb-size porcelain dog from the items—a white-and-brown cocker spaniel, curled up, its nose resting on its front legs. "If I had a darling little girl like you, I would love to get a treasure like this."

I bought the little dog and gave it to Sandy in exchange for her doing my chores. When she received it, she gave me hugs and kisses, and did my chores for me without complaint. It sat on Sandy's vanity table until one day when we were fighting and destroying one another's things, and I smashed it to pieces.

———

That was the first day I stole something expensive. I came home and was wrapped in a cold sweat of fear because I'd been taught that being dishonest would make me feel bad and would make my friends and family treat me differently. But nobody had. In fact, when I gave Mom the necklace, she kissed me and held me close in a long embrace.

"Oh, you little angel!" she exclaimed. "I'll bet you saved your allowance for a long time to buy this."

"Yes," I lied. She gave me a kiss.

I decided I could live with that.

———

When the Sunday-school lesson was over, Sister Mallow led us in "Jesus Wants Me for a Sunbeam," my favorite song. She stood up and, looking right into my eyes, warmly said, "Kathy, dear, you have the loveliest voice of us all. Children, if you lose your tone, follow Kathy." I blushed with pride.

Sister Mallow beckoned us to rise. The baton in her hand became a long wooden spoon, ready to mix up her little pupils into spiritual dough. We held hands on the final verse. She held my hand; I held Camille's. She stirred us round and round in a circle while we sang. She nodded and bobbed her head; her knees flexed down and up. We nodded and bobbed, bent and flexed with her. I was quite joyous; I shone. Jesus wanted me to be happy, and I was. No matter what else happened, I was to shine with happiness.

Sister Mallow was so many things to me then. She was physically affectionate: snuggle and hug, embrace and kiss, a tender touch. She was my teacher: a scholar and a guide, my moral model and mentor. She needed me: to help her straighten the chairs, to put felt cutouts on the storyboard at her direction. She believed in me.

Under her tutelage and in the embrace of her trust, I thrived.

Maybe I would give the precious frog clicker to Sister Mallow. Maybe she would give it to Jesus.

He would love me.

Even though I was a thief.

———◆———

When I served on the juvenile-court bench, a child eleven or older could be charged with theft for shoplifting. These cases touched me in a very particular way, of course, because as a child I had stolen continuously and with greater and greater acumen. I knew the thrill of successful thieving and the rewards for doing so. I also knew the reasons I had thieved. I had shoplifted for love and power. So I was deeply interested in these children, in each child's story.

In one case, a boy denied stealing necklaces from a store.

"Boys don't wear necklaces," his own lawyer defended.

The boy contradicted her. "That's not true. I have a lot of necklaces. See?" He pulled several out of his shirt. They all still had the price tags on.

In another case, a girl claimed she hadn't "stolen" her friend Angela's purse. "'Theft' means I was going to 'deprive' it away from her forever," the girl said, quoting her lawyer, no doubt. She looked at me as though that settled the case. "I was going to give the purse back when Angela quit flirting with Deshawn."

In one case, the only evidence of a young African American girl's theft was the eyewitness account of a Caucasian floorwalker, whose testimony persuaded me the girl had indeed stolen a watch. When I said so, the girl yelled at me. "What does that white honky know? Every black person looks the same to you all. My mama was right—nobody's fair here."

After the courtroom was cleared, the girl's lawyer asked me to describe his client. I couldn't. He asked whether I thought I could now pick the girl out of a lineup of black girls, and I realized that I probably couldn't. Shaken, I realized that though I had struggled to overcome and unlearn my racism, I was tainted still.

In another case, I warned a boy, "If you don't abide by the conditions of probation, you'll spend the weekend in detention."

The child kept looking at his hands stretched out on the counsel table. "That's OK, Your Honor. That'd be better than home."

At the time I presided, a popular theory held that some children are simply "invulnerable" to bad circumstances, while others have a predisposition to suffer and collapse. Researchers asserted that some children who live in abject poverty, who are beaten and abused, demeaned and discouraged at every turn, nevertheless rise above their circumstances to succeed, while others, the "vulnerable" children, even though born into comfort and nurture, nevertheless fail. This theory encompasses the proposition that the *nature* of the child will prevail no matter how the child is *nurtured*.

This theory may be true, in part, but I am unconvinced that the origins of success or failure are simply genetic. While nurtured children may fail, I believe that *all* children—particularly bereft, hopeless, and confused children, trapped in the terror of their own depression and defeat—can be guided, even saved, by a person who unconditionally loves them with a resolute belief in their goodness and who inspires an ability to trust in others and in one's self.

Once I determined that a child did, indeed, steal, I set the time and terms of probation. I asked the probation officer to look for one person in the child's life who gave unconditional love and could be a mentor. Did the boy have a devoted grandfather? Did the girl have a teacher who paid special attention to her? Was there an aunt, a Big Brother or Big Sister, who could take a role? Could that love and attention lead the child out of a life of crime and circumstance?

I came to believe that every child, not just delinquent children, deserves at least one doting, involved adult in her or his life. A grandparent, a schoolteacher, a religious leader, a friend, a camp counselor—someone who recognizes and encourages the child's potential, a person who looks to the origins of the child's being, a person who understands that the child's behavior is deeply rooted in the life she or he leads and that those roots, like tubers, must be dug up, separated, composted in richer soil, and watered and fed consistently. When tended and harvested with love, the child blooms.

Looking back, I see Sister Mallow as a woman who had patience and goodness in her heart. She tried mightily to turn my head toward the happiness she was convinced I deserved.

Still, I stole.

I knew that stealing was wrong. I knew I had to stop, but it had become a deeply ingrained habit. Even when theft no longer gleaned the rewards of affection and friendship, I stole for the thrill and power.

"I deserve it," I would say when I kept what I stole.

Please love me, I would think as I gave it away.

For my childhood efforts, I received physical affection and praise from my mother. I stole more and more elaborate gifts for her, and she hugged me tighter and longer. Then I began to use my thefts to allay her violence—she was a cumulonimbus cloud, full of dark and ominous threat.

"Mom!" I hollered out when her storm began to gather. "I forgot to tell you. I spent my ironing money and bought you a gift."

The clouds began to scatter.

She subsided. "Oh?" she smiled, pleased. "And what might that be?"

CHAPTER 14

GIVE, SAID THE LITTLE STREAM

———◆———

WE WENT TO CHURCH EVERY Sunday.

"Bye-bye, children," Mom called out from her bed if she was still "resting up." Though Mom didn't go to church anymore, she continued to send us to Sunday school, rain or snow, whether we were sick or well. "Pay attention."

We trundled off to church: Lucy reached up to pull the door shut with the knob; Sandy tied Lucy's hood over her flyaway white hair and boosted her onto her back; Clark sucked his thumb and climbed into the wagon, which I pulled. In winter, I tucked blankets snug around him. My mittens were connected with string that was strung through the arms of my coat, but the string was too short, so I could wear only one mitten. I pulled the wagon with my mittened hand; the other mitten was stuck inside my coat at the wrist. I blew hot breath into my curled fist.

Sandy grumbled, but I was content to go to church. Mom knew we needed the devotion. It made me happy that she cared.

"Where's Mommy?" Clark asked.

"She needs some time alone," I answered, "to have breakfast and read and have some quiet to pay bills and stuff."

"Ha!" scoffed Sandy.

When we got home, Mom was lying on the couch reading her latest *Reader's Digest Condensed Book* with a glass of orange juice by her side. Daddy was in the chair, his Bible on his lap.

"Welcome home, children," Mom chirped. "All your sins forgiven now?" I told her yes, they were, and asked whether she would like me to sing the latest song I learned.

"That would be just lovely," she crooned. "You, too, Sandy. You know it, I'll bet." Sandy begrudgingly complied so Mom wouldn't get angry.

Mom sat up on the couch and smoothed her bathrobe. Daddy took Clark onto his knees. Whenever we were to perform—dances, songs, and recitations of poems—Mom made a big show of it, clapping her hands, aheming to the invisible crowd for their attention, announcing our upcoming theatricals.

"La-dies and gen-tle-men," she lilted, "turn your attention, please, to the little ladies on the stage here. They are about to perform a sacred piece for your edification."

She threw out her arm toward us, and we took a low bow from the waist. Sandy's hair flowed to touch the floor; mine simply flew around my face. We stood up tall. I warmed to the occasion and gave it my best, singing with great gusto:

"Give," said the little stream,
"Give, oh give,
Give, oh give.
Give," said the little stream,
As it hurried down the hill.
"You're little, I know, but wherever you go,
The grass grows greener still."

While I sang this song, I imagined Grampa Penrose plodding wearily down the mountain, trudging through the tall grasses and pussy willows, and dragging his oxen through mud and rock beds. Gramma Lucetta wept inside the wagon, holding her dead baby. Jessie comforted her. "It's OK, Momma, you'll have another." Grampa followed Emigration Creek, a rippling, hopeful stream that came to be a canyon, which came to be a valley, which came to have *me* in it, my mother's talented daughter.

I radiated in Mom's praise.

"Enough!" Sandy snarled, sullen as usual. She went to our room, but I stayed, bowing and bowing, as Mom's smile broadened and her eyes were merry.

"That's an excellent lesson," she slurred. "Give, oh give, oh give and give and give and give!" She broke out laughing. I was pleased to see her so cheerful.

She leaned over and picked up her glass. "Here, Kathy. Give, oh give, a little more orange juice for your mother."

I took her glass to the kitchen and poured in the vodka and then the rest of the orange juice from the pitcher.

"I can give you more lessons if you want, Mom," I said, returning.

But she'd gone into a funk. "I'm tired of those stupid lessons." She sighed. "Bother your father. He likes your stories."

But Daddy had gone back to his Bible.

———◆———

The story of Mormonism was rich, exotic, and just my style—full of adventure and magic. Sister Mallow thrilled me with its truths: the return of the True Church to an illiterate young boy; the fact that we had lived forever and always would; the idea that God has a three-story mansion on the Heavenly planet, Kolob. I was eager to share these stories. So I continued my weekly Saturday sermons for the neighborhood kids.

My marketing expanded. I posted a big sign in our front yard: "Come All Ye Kids on Saturday at 1:00 p.m. for a Secret! Free Admission." I issued invitations while we were playing in the streets at dusk, or chalking the sidewalks, or riding our bicycles up and down the road. They came, sometimes two or three of them, sometimes eight or nine.

In the summer, I continued to hold my meetings in the backyard under the cottonwood tree. Daddy bought me folding chairs. In the winter, we met in our basement, where Daddy put up the chairs, washed the high windows for light, and hung a thick blanket for the curtain.

I taught the children about how we all had lived forever. "Before I came to earth," I instructed, "I was my Heavenly Father's spirit child, living my Heavenly life in Heaven, waiting for my earthly body. You were, too." The children were all ears, as Mom would say.

"All stand," I told them, and they did. "We are spirits!"

Premortal Heaven was what I imagined to be a cloudy, harp-filled spirit world, the children running around happily playing (I made my audience run around happily), eating whatever they wanted whenever they wanted it (we pretended to eat our favorite foods). Our Heavenly Parents kissed and hugged us (we kissed our hands and hugged ourselves and each other).

"They swirled us up in their Heavenly arms." I picked up my doll and swung her around. "Our parents read us ghost stories at night," I continued. "The spirits sang and leaped from cloud to cloud." (We leaped.)

Premortal life was incandescent. I imagined being alive in God's Heaven before I came to earth. I pictured myself glowing with good health and vitality. I wiggled deep into the spiritual embrace of my Heavenly Father.

"But God decided this spirit life was too easy," I continued. "So he decided to set up a test for all his spirit children." I pointed to Sam, Edith, and Sarah. "He decided that each of us should go to earth, receive a body, and be tested by troubles." I waited a moment. No one was nodding, so I leaned in toward Sarah.

"Don't you have troubles, Sarah?" I asked.

"Yes," she said meekly.

"See?" I was triumphant.

———◆———

"That's why you're here on earth, Kathy," Sister Mallow had soothed. "You must use this brief time in your physical body to follow your Heavenly Father's will and pass His tests."

She counted her fingers, one by one, nodding her head each time. "If you are faithful to Him"—one finger—"follow His instruction"—second finger—"and live an excellent Mormon life"—third finger—"then when you die, you will go to live in one of His Heavenly Kingdoms." She lifted and spread her arms out like an opening heart. We were silent in awe.

"Wait!" I raised both hands high so she would not miss seeing me.

Sister Mallow made the expression she had just for me, a little smile I took as intimate and approving. "Yes, dear?"

"Camille says we will get our body when we go to Heaven."

"That's right, honey. You get your perfect body back."

"But which body?" This seemed a very important piece of information. "Will Sister Ruby get her dead body all shriveled and pale?"

I stood up and turned to Harold. "Will you get the body you had when you were an ugly little baby?" He frowned.

Now I addressed the whole class. "What if you only have one leg? What about if you're murdered and your body has blood all coming out of your nose?" I was on a roll. "What if—"

"That's enough, Kathy. Sit down, please, dear." I thought I had made my point. But she just said again, "You get your perfect body." She thought that explained it.

"But—" I insisted.

"Now children," she said, ignoring me, "let's continue the glorious lesson."

———————

I continued the backyard sermon.

"When God's plan was announced, two of Heavenly Dad's children offered to go to earth first. Jesus was the good guy. But Lucifer was the bad one, so when he came to earth, he didn't get a body."

I lowered my voice and moved stealthily among the children, my shoulders bent, my face twisted, so I could look ominous and dangerous.

"He and his pals are just spirits, roaming around, trying to get us to do bad things." I hunched farther down, limped, stuck out my arms, and curled my fingers like hooks. I went around poking them and growling. Sarah started to caterwaul, and Eleanor started to cry. Thrilled, I began to cackle and moan, "I am the Devil Lucifer, haa haaa haaaaa, and I'm coming to get you."

We all started running and hiding. Tucked in between the garage and the fence, I was safe. Suddenly Sean jumped from the roof and terrified me. "*I* am Lucifer," he whispered. "Lucifer sucks blood." He came at me. I shrieked and ran into the house.

I believed the story. I was frightened of every dark place—under my bed, inside the stove, Ninyah's basement. When I refused to put a casserole in the oven because Lucifer was there and would drag me in, Mom laughed and said, "Don't be silly, honey. Satan's after bigger game than you. Like that asshole Carrone, who fired me. And your father, who doesn't earn enough to support us."

That did, and didn't, comfort me. I was glad I wasn't in Satan's sights, but I didn't want him to go after Daddy.

"The other special spirit child was Jesus," Sister Mallow told us. But I was shocked at what she said next. Jesus had agreed to come to be bodied and earthed, and then He died on a cross, all nailed up! I mean, how gruesome, exciting, yucky, and fabulous was that! I made Sister Mallow tell it over. She told it with even more enthusiasm.

"Jesus did that for *you*," she told us.

Me! And not just for me, for everyone.

"He did it to pay for your sins." This was great information, because I had definitely sinned a lot by then: lying, stealing, hiding food from Mom, teasing Lucy, breaking the tusks off Sandy's glass elephant. If Jesus had already died for my sins, I wouldn't get punished. This was very good news.

But Sister Mallow had a condition. Jesus would pay for our sins only if—and this was a big if—"you are really sorry about them, and repent, and promise to do better and follow the Prophet's commands. If you do that," she said, glowing, "you will pass the test and go up to one of the three Kingdoms of Heaven."

I was convinced.

For years I tried to get into a Kingdom of Heaven by obeying most of the rules I was taught. I was helpful, I wrote thank-you notes, I was clean and tidy. I fixed up my room, and I weeded the garden.

Even when I began to fall away from the Church in my late teens, I abided by the rules Sister Mallow taught us about love and virtue, kindness and charity, sacrifice and salvation. These became a part of who I was. Though I came to disbelieve much of the doctrine—the place of women, the original rejection of African Americans, the homophobia and the current anti gay marriage stance, the belief that only Mormons will enter the Kingdom—I never forgot the rules that reflected Christ's morality and compassion. And I obeyed other Mormon rules in my own way.

———

I ran home and told Mom the good news. "Mom! Guess what? Jesus died for our sins to be forgiven!" She looked up, smiling. I had her attention. "When you apologize for smoking and drinking and cursing and hitting us, you'll go to Heaven with me."

I hoped she would clap her hands; we could sing the joyful praises of the Lord.

Instead, she lit a cigarette and said, "Well, then, if that's so, I think I'll wait to repent until just before I die. Then I don't have to give anything up too soon."

I hadn't thought of that.

I tried another tack. "You can go live with God on the planet Kolob, you know."

"And where is that, pray tell?" she asked.

"Well, no one exactly knows," I answered, deflated.

"Point taken," Mom replied, as though she'd won the argument.

I took another approach. "If we're good enough, we can even become Gods and have our own planets."

She was still unconvinced.

"I like this planet," she said, inhaling. Her voice squeaked as she held the smoke in. "Besides"—she blew it all out in one big exhale, her cheeks popping out—"only men get planets of their own."

I was shocked. I hadn't heard that. "What happens to us? Do we just float around?"

"The women become the multiple wives of the men." She leaned into me, grinning. "Goody-goody, no?"

Whenever I asked anyone about Kolob, they changed the subject. Even today, there is little information about it anywhere, and most Mormons I know demur when asked to discuss it. No one will tell me where it is, what shape it is, or who really lives there. But as a child, I believed it was there somewhere. I looked and looked for it in the night sky.

I knew Daddy didn't believe in Kolob and thought it was hooey, but to help me find it, he made a rotating star chart. On one big cardboard circle, he drew all the stars and constellations. Then he made a second circle and cut four pie wedges out of it. He clipped the little circle to the big one. It rotated around to show what was in the night sky during a certain season.

He put Kolob in all the triangles. "Because," he said, "if there *is* a Kolob, it will be there for you all the time."

I made him promise that the shooting stars we see are not Kolob, no matter what! I thought that would be terrible, all those Kingdoms of Heaven falling from the sky, gone just like that, Jesus all nailed up for nothing.

Mom's grumpiness continued for as long as we lived at Laird Avenue. But it did not erode my faith. Every Sunday I said sorry for the things I'd done wrong the week before. I had committed a lot of sins—put gum in

Clark's hair, wrote my name in the new cement in front of the Bennions' house, and tried to "step on a crack to break my mother's back." But more and more, I came to doubt the wisdom of some of the unbendable rules: don't drink beer or smoke, don't do anything fun on Sundays, give 10 percent of all your income to the Church, don't kiss on the lips until you're married. I didn't see why God cared.

Pray—I liked this rule. I felt like it gave me a special connection to my Heavenly Father. But when I found out that He had let His spirit child be nailed up and bloodied, I prayed to Jesus instead. Jesus told me to forgive His Dad, but I was slow at it.

Increasingly, I wondered about my Church. How did all the other Mormons know theirs was the only true church when there were so many things *I* didn't understand?

Sister Mallow told me to have faith. "Without faith, you can't believe the story," she said. *Well, yes,* I thought. But didn't I have to believe the story to have faith? And shouldn't it make sense for me to be able to believe it?

I asked both my parents over and over again what was true or not. They said I had to figure it out for myself.

Neither of my parents bullied me into believing one way or another. But I needed more guidance. Children can't figure things like God out for themselves without some yardstick to go by, some hand that encourages their progress. I was living with "on the other hands." I was too confused to know how to ask all the questions, much less figure out the answers.

When I was eight, Daddy bought me a small diary with a red vinyl cover and a key that locked it. He told me it would help to make a list in my diary of all my beliefs. I wrote:

What I believe:
Jesus is good;
So is everybody in their deep down;
Everybody wants to love other people;

Everybody wants to have everybody else love them;
No one should be angry and hit and hurt other people;
I believe in good food and lots of it.

I wrote this list when I was eight; I transferred it to my journal when I was ten. I copied it again every time we moved, into each new journal, and many times after that.

I later printed and framed this, and still keep in on my judicial bench. When I am hearing a particularly tragic case—parents chained a child to a sink in a basement washroom, teenage skinheads brutally beat a Chinese man, a child hacked his aunt and cousins to death with a hatchet—I look at my list and try to believe in everyone's deep-down goodness.

Sometimes when I am out with colleagues or friends who want to hear about my tough cases, they exclaim over the horrendous facts, asking, "How could a parent do such a thing?"

"You know," I say, "I believe that every child *wants* to be a good child and that every parent *wants* to be a good parent. But things go wrong. People make terrible mistakes, and if all we do is excoriate them and tell them how awful they are, they will close up and freeze us out. They will never learn what to do with their sense of failure. Except more harm."

Sometimes these speeches lead my listeners to eye rolling and a quick change of subject. Sometimes, however, they lead to a compassionate discussion of how to give sanity and competence back to the lives of these families.

"Your list is ridiculous," Mom warned me. "You'll set yourself up for disappointment."

I haughtily defended it.

"You know what Anne Frank wrote in her diary while she was cooped up in that attic?" I lectured. "She wrote, 'I still believe that people are really good at heart.'"

"Yeah," Mom replied, "but that was before Auschwitz."

Eric and I wanted to learn what other people had thought about our parents and grandparents. So we set up interviews with our mother's only living brother, Uncle Thurston, his wife Aunt Rose, and our Aunt Elaine, the widow of Mother's youngest brother. For one of the interviews, we met our aunts at a family restaurant, where we could linger without interruption. Eric and I each had a list of questions to spur on the conversation if it flagged. We were nervous, anxious that we might trigger long-held resentments or unearth shocking facts. But our aunts were as dear and sweet as we recalled, and they talked to us for several hours, through two meals, confirming what we remembered.

Aunt Rose described my mother's eventual antipathy toward my father. She was sympathetic. "Your mother hadn't felt that way at first," Rose told us. "I think she truly loved your father, Katharine. But Ninyah and Baba were so hard on him, called him a rough hick from poor pedigree."

She recalled Ninyah's demeaning of the Baptists and recounted a scene during the first year of their marriage.

"Your Uncle Thurston and I were having dinner at the Alta Club with Ninyah, Baba, and your mom," Rose began. "Ninyah expressed relief that your Baptist dad wasn't there. Your mom protested. 'There's nothing so wrong with Baptists,' she said. 'They are no stranger than the Mormons.'"

Rose laughed. "I thought that was a terrific retort."

"Your mother had a very sharp wit," said Aunt Elaine.

"Sarcastic," said Rose, agreeing, "and very funny at times."

Hearing them talk about her, I realized that I hadn't understood my mother's sarcasm or appreciated her wit.

"Well, anyway," Rose continued, "your Baba barked at your mom. He complained that the Southern Baptists believe they can walk and talk with Jesus personally. Members don't have to do anything but interpret the Bible as they see fit; they each have their own special relationship with the Lord. Baba thought this was ludicrous! Well, your mom was cool as a cucumber. 'So?' she countered. 'Sounds a whole lot easier than Mormonism.' Boy, that rankled your grandfather."

Rose took on Baba's voice: "'Salvation does not come so easily,' he said in that preachy tone he could get, 'nor should it. The Prophet has given us the path upon which we must struggle to arrive at Celestial glory.'"

We laughed at her accurate impression of Baba.

"He sucked on that pipe of his like he was reeling in a fish." Rose sipped her iced tea. "Then Baba slapped the table that way he used to do, remember? He said, rather loudly, 'The Southern Baptists have no... rules.' Well, people began to look at us."

Rose smiled and leaned in. "Do you see the irony? Baba was puffing away on his pipe while he was huffing at your mom. Smoking tobacco is against the Word of Wisdom, but Baba didn't like that rule. So he just didn't follow it. He drank, too. Too much."

Aunt Elaine furrowed her brow at Rose and quickly interrupted. "You see, Baba and Ninyah thought that for the Baptists, finding Jesus and God was just a personal experience: they could read the Bible any old way they wanted to, and that was that. Baba stewed about that sacrilege. He thought your father believed he didn't have to work hard at salvation like the Mormons did. Called him a shiftless, good-for-nothing apostate."

Aunt Rose went on. "Well, we knew a conflict was brewing. It always did around this subject. Your mom got snide."

Here, Rose imitated Mom. "'How is the Baptist belief any stranger than Mormons believing God lives on the planet Kolob and talks to our Prophet?'" She sounded eerily like Mom. "Oh, my, your mom was getting all heated up, went on raising her voice." Rose's voice rose as well. "'A Prophet who then tells us secondhand all the mumbo-jumbo hoops we have to jump through before men can get to be Gods and have their own planets, with a lot of us wives sitting at their feet and still having babies like rabbits.' Well, Baba just erupted. 'Sereta!' he yelled. 'I'll not have this kind of blasphemy! You were raised better than that.'"

I was mesmerized. Rose enacted the scene exactly as I could see it my imagination: Baba all fury, Mom all belligerence. Rose continued, "Your mom just seethed. 'Really?' she scoffed. 'To hate niggers and spics and queers? In a Church that won't let them in?'" Rose turned to us, flushed. "Sorry for the *N*-word, kids," she apologized.

Now Rose took on Ninyah's voice. "Your Ninyah stepped in and said, 'Now, dears...'—you know, the way she did—but Baba was furious. He got up and stormed out of the club."

Rose paused, then said soberly, "Ninyah was awfully mean to your mom then. 'Well, now look what you've done,' she accused your mom. And your mom just sat there, looking kind of defeated. 'Hank,' Ninyah then grumbled. 'What kind of a name is that?' Ninyah rolled that name around on her tongue. 'Sounds like a clump of hair.'"

The disdain in Rose's voice, so like Ninyah's, unsettled me. I wanted the story to end.

"Well, your mom didn't say a word. Just got up quietly, folded her napkin, put it on the table, and left. Ninyah, Thurston, and I went on like nothing had happened. That's how they did it in that family."

The waiter brought dessert for Rose and Elaine. We all sat in silence.

I felt a terrible sadness for my mother, which I had never felt before and which I had never expected to feel. There she was, in Salt Lake City's Alta Club—a fancy, men-only membership club, with women attending by invitation only—surrounded by her parents' high-society lady and gentleman friends, defending a man who by then she probably didn't much like anymore, defending a church she didn't actually believe in anymore, disputing with a mother who scorned her and a father whom she had idolized and whose love was now denied her. Four children. A divorce on the horizon. No money. Trapped.

I couldn't eat anymore.

Men left their children, as my father left me and as Eric's father left him. Back then, even women abandoned their children, though less often. Mom could have left. She had education and skills. She had a car. She had a checkbook. She had a reason.

But she didn't go.

Then Eric spoke up. "Did she love *my* father?" he asked.

Elaine turned to him. "Oh, my dear boy," she said. "*Your* father was the love of her life."

Rose added, "When Mort left her, she was devastated. I don't think she ever recovered."

They talked for a long time about Eric's father. Mort had been devastatingly handsome—tall, a slim rectangle of a man, with a bush of salt-and-pepper hair—and rich. He had invented a new and better sealing wax for canning, called Seal-Tight. Mom had been his secretary. He left his wife and four children to marry her.

"I wasn't a very cute baby, huh?" Eric said wryly.

"Oh, lovey," Elaine consoled, "you were a little button. Your dad was a scoundrel, leaving your mother like that, stealing Baba's—"

Rose put her hand on Elaine's arm. Elaine then dabbed her lips with her napkin. She caught herself. "I'm sure he loved you."

When Elaine and Rose had exhausted the subject of Mort, we still sat in the booth, quiet and thoughtful.

I asked, "Was Mom a racist?"

"Oh my, no!" Elaine and Rose spoke up together.

"She was a bit wild, loved jazz and the music of Harlem," said Elaine. "She'd gone to New York as a young woman to that finishing school. I think she met Negroes there. Baba said that's what ruined her."

Though my mother tried to tell me differently, when I was little I believed Ninyah and Baba when they told me people of color were inferior to white people. Church doctrine enforced this belief. Sister Mallow, my Sunday-school teacher, confirmed it. She told me that black skin was what marked a person who had sided with Satan in the Prelife, rather than with Jesus. She said that's why "blackies" couldn't become lay priests and hold the priesthood.

Because I rebelled against my mother, I adopted my Church's and grandparents' racism and homophobia. African Americans were "niggers," and "queers" were disgusting perverts, though I don't recall where

I first heard that word. And while I loved my first best friend Olive and we slept together at slumber parties with our arms entwined and tried sucking on each other's breasts and looked at our vaginas, this behavior never translated for me into the idea that we were "lezzies," the name Baba had for lesbians.

Though they didn't know a single one, my grandparents called black people useless "coons," even though Ninyah's great-grandmother had owned black slaves and her mother had used blacks as servants. A favorite restaurant in Salt Lake City was named Coon Chicken Inn. The specialty of the restaurant was "coon-fried chicken." We entered it through the red-lipped, laughing mouth of a giant facade bearing the face of a black minstrel—the doors were his bottom front teeth. With bulging white-lined eyes and his monstrous face several feet wide, he terrified me.

My grandparents admonished me not to mix with "those kinds of people" and told me that if I ever met one, I should spit. I was alert and cautious, but I never saw an African American person until the ninth grade, when I went to live with my father in Alabama.

I would change.

CHAPTER 15

FISHING

———◆———

I THOUGHT OF THE DARKEST secrets I had, the secrets I'd never told. I tried not to think about them ever, and yet they both came to me in the marrow of my bones, in bumps on my skin, and in unaccountable chills. They lay in wait to spook me at the least likely moments. They continued to take on color and texture that I would deny. I remembered, and I didn't remember.

At the Laird Avenue house, my first dark secret began.

But still I resisted going back there.

I jumped at Eric's suggestion that we do research instead. We spent the morning at the county courthouse and government office buildings, documenting dates and addresses, looking up deeds to our houses, and researching transfers of property titles.

We made a surprising discovery. At the deeds department we found microfiche deeds to the 14th East and Laird Avenue houses. We studied them for a long time, puzzled.

Eric finally said, "My god, they didn't even own the houses. Ninyah and Baba did."

My father could not afford to buy my mother a house. So Ninyah and Baba had done so, but they purchased minimally suitable houses in their own names, only allowing my family to live there. I didn't know whether rent passed hands. I imagined their intention was to control and punish my mother and humiliate my father, and I was sure they did.

I began to cry. Eric put his arm around me, and we sat there for a long time, staring at the machine.

We lunched at the Hires Root Beer drive-in, a favorite childhood haunt. I turned the conversation to pleasant things, told jokes, and analyzed current events. I wasn't fooling myself. I was building up my courage to go back to Laird Avenue.

Finally, we hugged, and I drove away. Four blocks east of the Laird Avenue house, near the ward chapel, I drove past the park where my father sat on his end of the seesaw while I hung, suspended in the sky, at my end.

I drove past the field on the corner. Here we caught grasshoppers in jars, took them home, and put them in a cardboard box with leaves and grass and dead potato bugs for food, where they promptly died, bashing their heads at the closed top, desperate for freedom.

One street down, I drove past the drugstore where my father taught me about root-beer floats: "The vanilla ice cream is a princess's castle, surrounded by a muddy moat," he'd explained conspiratorially. "If you eat the castle and drink the moat, the princess will live inside of you forever and tell you how to do good in this world."

His princess was far more appealing than the Mormon Holy Ghost, a spirit that would enter my body when I agreed to be baptized, on which day I would become subject to being judged for my sins forever after! *I'd rather have a princess than a ghost inside me,* I'd thought. The Holy Ghost had a direct line to God, and there were things I didn't care to have reported. So I avoided baptism. But my friends succumbed, in spite of my warnings. Camille even tried to stop sinning. She seemed sadder and more scared after that, and I fell out of love with her. But I outwitted the Ghost. Instead, I kept the princess close and appreciated her tolerance for my little sins. As far as I knew, she never told God.

I kept driving, past Warren's house, where I had watched him and Thayne throw the football in their front yard. I had wanted to play football in a way that made me ache. But girls didn't play football then. We played kickball at the church.

I drove past the ward, where there had been new frets. I'd had to wear a dress to Sunday school; I couldn't be a Cub Scout; I had to learn to cook and clean, as if I didn't do enough of that already at home. I may have been young, but I was figuring a few things out, and I didn't like them one bit.

I parked and wandered again inside the Emigration Market. I bought a pack of Neccos, my favorite childhood candy. Mom habitually had sent me there to buy supper food, which I carried home in a brown paper bag, steering my bicycle one-handed. Next door to the market lived my friend, Lewis, who, when I was ten, showed me his thingy and asked me to show him my stuff. I lifted my blouse and showed him my buttons, but I refused to show him my cave.

I was nine years old when my father taught me about my little buttons and my little cave. He left our family right after that. He packed and was gone. This memory began its slow climb up my spine.

I drove back to the Laird house, knowing that the time had come. I had known when Eric and I set out from Oregon to Zion that there were untold secrets I would need to tell, would need to speak out loud, if only to the air.

I stared at the small house and tidy yard. I felt a surprising and intoxicating childhood joy come over me. I put away whatever it was that had been frightening me. "In a while," I said.

There was the tree in which my kite tangled and my father had helped me climb way up to get it down. There was the backyard where I produced my neighborhood plays and taught Church lessons to the kids on the block. There was the garage that housed my red bicycle. My father pinned playing cards to the spokes so that when I rode up and down the street, my wheels clicked and spit and sounded like a race-car engine. He waved his cap at me and cheered, "You're a winner, darlin'!"

The houses on Laird Avenue were still working-class houses, small and close together, separated by a narrow driveway leading to a one-car garage. I looked for a place to sit and remember. The perfect place to sit as a child was in the backyard on a narrow rectangular patch of ground between the back wall of the garage and the border fence. This hideaway was covered by the eaves and shrouded by bushes. Here I had hidden my stolen goods. That secluded spot was not accessible to me now. Neither was the backyard giant cottonwood tree, where I might have sat imagining again gathering up the audience for my performances.

I contemplated sitting on the grass. But the square front lawns were tiny. As a small, wonder-eyed child, I used to think them copious and sprawling, but now I saw that they were little checkered patches up and down the block, some watered green, some weathering brown. Someone looking from a living-room window would surely notice a middle-age woman sitting on a front lawn. I drove back and forth.

I was aching to look at my Laird Avenue house, to gaze into the good memories—to feel the blankets and comforters on my old bed, smell the wood smoke from the fireplace, taste the peanut-butter-and-raspberry-jam sandwiches my father made for me until the divorce came and the food disappeared. I imagined I heard the clacks of the typewriter in the basement as I wrote and my father cheered me on. "Write, honey. Write me a story." I had plunked with two fingers until I became fast enough to pound out dozens of poems and stories, which he read with enthusiasm. "My little two-fingered typist," he called me.

Even today, as I write these memories, I am typing with two fingers; they fly across the keys.

I finally parked and walked to the house across from the Laird Avenue house. I knocked at the door, and when no one answered, I sat on the steps. I gazed straight across the street at my childhood house.

I felt how young I had been then, how cheerful, in spite of the muddle and tension. Life was good. I walked to school. I walked home after school. I stopped at the drugstore and spent the dime my father gave me for a root-beer float, or I stopped at the grocery store for dinner items. I went out to play until Mom came home from work: in the summer, playing jacks, jumping rope, and riding bicycles, and in the winter, sledding,

making forts and snowmen, and fencing with icicle swords. I was bliss-
fully unaware of how soon it would all fall apart.

Mom had two jobs now. She came and went, bringing home stacks
of long brown account books that she carried like a sleeping child cra-
dled in both arms. When she opened one of the long books, it took up
the whole width of the table. The pages were cream colored, fenced in
long columns of green and red lines stretched across the pages like a
stand of mountain ash in a forest thicketed with bitterbrush and bear-
berries, each square a clearing. You could get lost in these columns,
and she did.

Sometimes Mom would give me a sheet to draw on, and we would sit
companionably, she marking numbers, while I was creating a map of a
whole new world. Her hand-penned numbers laddered up and down on
the pages. She wrote carefully, punched her adding machine, and transferred numbers from the long white tape onto the columned pages. I
drew castles and moats.

"Get me another," she said, handing me her empty orange-juice
glass, "and empty this." She handed me the ashtray full of butts. She
worked and worked until it was time for bed. Sometimes we had no dinner, or we fixed ourselves something, or Daddy came home early and
fixed us sandwiches, which he ate with us, picnic-style, on the kitchen
floor, so as not to disturb Mom.

When bedtime came, Mom sometimes called for a hug. I climbed
up into her lap and smelled the pencil lead on her hands as she absentmindedly pushed back my hair. She held me with one arm while her
fingers flew on the adding machine and her pencil etched black lines of
numbers on the sheets of the ledgers. If she forgot I was there, I laid my
cheek on her chest, which moved in and out as she inhaled and exhaled,
the smoke curling into my nose. I rubbed my face on the weave of the
blouse she wore.

"Hand me my drink," she said, and I did, happy in this rare moment
of sharing.

Mostly, however, Mom was in a bad mood. "Get away," she snapped. "I have to work. Go bother your father; he's never busy." I avoided her then.

But I held on to Daddy.

One evening, Mom was working on her books. She and Daddy were fighting, but I had learned not to listen. I was reading The other kids were watching TV. Daddy came into the bedroom. He told me he wanted to educate me about the birds and the bees.

It was hard to pay him close attention because I was reading *The Princess and the Goblin*. Outside the bedroom window, crickets were beginning to hum, and I imagined they were leggy black dwarfs creeping toward my sill. My princess inside me was preparing for battle against the gross creatures.

But I was distracted from my reading. Daddy was stroking my hair and talking in a low voice that sounded different than usual. He talked and talked. He looked funny and wanted my attention, so I abandoned my book and listened to his lesson.

I didn't understand how what he was saying had anything to do with feathers and stingers, but I did what he told me to do. I took off my pajama top and let him show me the little raspberry bumps on my chest, which he called "buttons." I let him touch them, stroke them up and down. I was startled and felt like the goblins were coming closer.

I hoped Daddy would take me in his arms and slay the goblins. I felt the thrill of the coming rescue.

He wanted to show me my private part, which he told me was my "cave." I took off my pajama bottoms and spread my legs very wide, and he placed his chin on the bed so he could see. "Look here," he said. He pulled aside the small parentheses of skin to show me. I leaned over. Though I had put my head down to look, and though he was kissing the top of my head and guiding me with his hands, I couldn't see inside. My cave was dark and deep. I was airy and dizzy when I lifted my head.

He put his fingers in my cave and told me what he was touching. "This is the wall of the cave, honey," he explained, and he rubbed his fingers up and down. "Now I am going deeper into the cave." His longest finger moved over a hump on the top of my cave. "This is a pile of rocks from the ceiling," Daddy told me, "but see how we can slide under them and go clear into the tunnel at the back?" Daddy's fingers moved all around my cave, which was wet with seawater, he said.

"You have a little button in your cave, too." His fingers moved back toward the cave's entrance, and there, hanging from the ceiling, was a button he found with his finger. I could feel him push on it, moving it back and forth. Then he took it between his thumb and finger, and rubbed it gently.

"Do you want to touch it?" I didn't, but I didn't mind if Daddy did. I was caught up with the goblins, and Daddy was being wide and strong, and had moved so close to me that I was certain no wart-faced dwarf would be able to capture me. Daddy smelled of Old Spice, and his chin prickled my cheek. His breath was warm and damp in my ear, and his body moved as though he were running toward the goblins to wave them away.

He sat back a bit, and his fingers slid out of my cave; the goblins had skirted away and back into the forest.

"Now," Daddy said, "boys don't have caves." He unzipped his pants and pulled out his thingy, which looked like a fat fish, wiggling. "Here, touch it," he said.

"Daddy, that's gross," I said. "It looks like a fat fish."

"It does, doesn't it?" Daddy laughed. "Boys have thingy-fishies." His fingers moved quickly over his thingy-fishy. "Watch what happens when I try to catch this old fish. Got it! Let's give it a hug."

I watched as the fish grew bigger. "Now it's a big fish, swimming in the ocean." Daddy gasped. He was not really looking at me now, but his leg was on the bed, and it curled around me. I watched with fascination. I was filled with a strange wonder, not just at the ugly fish, but also at my time with Daddy. I knew that this was a secret time between us, and I felt strangely giddy. *Another wonderful time with Daddy*, I thought, *just us.*

"See, it's spitting a little," he said breathlessly. "Don't tell." He held me close with his arm.

Until Mom opened the door and said to his back, "What are you doing, Hank? Why isn't that girl dressed for bed?"

"We're getting there, Sereta," he said quickly, straightening up, which blocked my view of Mom. His fish wiggled away. He leaned over me and grabbed my pajamas and put them on his lap between us. "OK, squirt," he said loudly, roughly, "enough stories, let's put these on."

He looked back at Mom over his shoulder and snapped, "Go on, Sereta, I'll be out in a minute. For god's sake, quit nagging me."

"Well, hurry up," she growled, and she turned and left.

———◆———

When Daddy left the family soon after and went back to Alabama, I thought this was the reason: Mom was jealous of his time with me, because I was his special daughter and because he taught me about thingy-fishies and caves and buttons. He loved me more than her.

Secretly, I knew he did. I should have protected him. I should have told Mom to leave us alone.

I was sure his leaving was my fault.

I have scoured the courthouse files, delved into the archives, and read the microfilm records of my parents' petitions for divorce and their affidavits for custody, for child support, and for failure to pay. I have read the transcripts of their hearings. But I didn't find any reference to child sexual abuse.

Years later, I read the only personal papers Mom saved: carbon copies of letters sent, unsent letters, and poems and essays she wrote when she went to college as an older woman. But I didn't find any reference to sexual abuse.

I never confronted my mother to ask whether she had known.

Of course, sexual abuse was a dark and hidden subject in the 1950s.

As a child, I blamed myself, not my father and not my mother. Now, as an adult, I consider blaming my mother for not protecting me. Shouldn't she have known? Or was it not so easy to know? I think she did. And then I think she didn't.

This is the space sexual-abuse victims inhabit with their secrets. What happened? What didn't happen? And who is to blame?

As a judge hearing family sexual-abuse cases, I am asked to determine not just whether to take a child away from the offending father, but whether to take the child away from the mother as well for her failure to protect. I listen to the arguments of lawyers and the testimony of expert witnesses, who assert that the mother should have known what was going on and should have stood against the father if she did.

The prosecutor chides the mother, incredulous: "This was going on, and you didn't know?" Then the defense describes how secretive and clever the father had been, how trusting, absent minded, or distracted the mother was.

My father. My mother.

I take custody of the child away from both parents: the father for the abuse, the mother because she should have saved the child but didn't.

I stared at the Laird Avenue house. I imagined the hall to the back bedroom. I imagined I saw my mother.

I imagined she sat at the dining-room table, bent over her ledgers. Then, suddenly, that maternal part of her, that fright that rises from the deep well of mother love, that intuition born of caring, vibrated through her. She raised her head from the books. She heard the silence, felt an evil, and acted.

I imagined I saw her stand, her cigarette glowing unnoticed in the ashtray, her vodka and orange juice weeping on the glass. She pushed her chair back and moved hurriedly down the hall. "Henry?" she yelled on her way, though we were engaged in fishing and didn't hear. "Henry!" She picked up speed.

I imagined her throwing herself at the closed door, turning the doorknob, thrusting open the door. "Hank. What the hell are you doing?" she accused. I imagined that she knew, that she burst forward to the bed and grabbed at his hair. "Leave my daughter alone. Don't you touch her!" This would have been the angriest I ever saw her. She pounded on him with her fists. "Get out. Get out!" she shouted, yanking him by the shirt and shoving him out the door as he tried to close his pants. I imagined her coming over to me, covering my thighs with the blanket, and holding me in her arms. "You're safe now," she said.

———•———

I stared at the house from across the street. It didn't happen that way, of course, but I wanted to believe it did. I wanted her to have confronted my father later that week, in that loud and angry fight I recalled before he left. I wanted that knowledge to be the reason she made him go, the reason she wouldn't let him kiss me good-bye, there at the front door on the morning he left.

But I was torn. Because if it was true, if she knew, if she sent him away to protect me from him, then why did she send me to Alabama five years later to live with him for a whole year? Where so much happened, things she should have known would happen.

———•———

I knew what I wanted for my token. I drove to the Rexall Pharmacy, looking for a scenic card of Utah's deep and dark Timpanogos Cave. That was not the only card I found. Farther up the rack, I found a photograph of a fish. Not just any fish—the Bonneville Cisco, a fish found nowhere else in the world except in Utah, in Bear Lake.

I bought the postcards, and put them in my sack.

CHAPTER 16

MUSIC IN THE PROMISED VALLEY

———◆———

ERIC BROUGHT COPIES OF OUR parents' divorce decrees and the transcripts of our mother's child-support hearings for me to read that evening. "How ugly," I said. "They were so bitter toward each other."

"Yep. It's always the other one's fault." He looked at me. "Sound like anyone else we know?" I laughed.

All five of Mom's children are eager to blame and criticize. "Did you take my car keys?" "You forgot the list?" "I told you to remind me about Saturday."

In more important cases, as well. "It was your fault the marriage ended." "The children act up just like *you*."

We are certain others are out to get us. "She did it to spite me." "You wanted me to fail the licensing test!"

I know now my mother blamed my father, her parents, and us children for all her woes. As for everyone else, she was sure they were against her. We learned these habits thoroughly. I would later see this habit in others, repeated again and again in the cases I heard. I understood it well.

We sat in silence, reading the documents, disbelieving.

"My father never paid child support." I was astounded.

"Neither did mine," he said, and shrugged. "That's the way it was back then, I guess. No responsibility. No enforcement." He continued. "I remember Mom working constantly at her bookkeeping jobs. Always on the weekends. Most evenings."

"It's hard to believe Ninyah and Baba never helped her."

Eric sighed and shook his head.

How did she do it? Five kids. No unemployment or food stamps back then. No welfare. No money from her folks.

———

I often stayed with Ninyah and Baba when I was small, sometimes for several days. Ninyah would spirit me away if my parents were fighting. The other children stayed with them, too. While I hated the dark basement, the rest of the house was a haven.

I slept in the bedroom next to Ninyah's upstairs parlor. In winter, I was snuggled into flannel sheets on a feather bed so high I had to climb aboard using a stool. In spring, a tall lilac bush bloomed outside my screened window; the smell filled the room, scenting the curtains and the fluffy flowered quilt. Music drifted into my room from the hall.

The servants attended my grandparents on every day but Sunday. I enjoyed their company. Cook always dressed in a starched white apron, her hair netted and pulled back in a tight bun. She rarely spoke a word to me if Ninyah was present, but she jabbered constantly when I was alone with her in the kitchen and taught me how to make rice and buttermilk biscuits.

Mrs. Adair had been a maid all of her life, though she insisted I call her "the housekeeper." She was short and stocky, though not plump—more like an acorn squash than a watermelon. Her laugh was hearty like a donkey's bray, though she was all "yes, ma'am" and "no, ma'am" in front of Ninyah. She taught me how to polish silver, which I thought was a disgusting job, and the value of oiling the banister, down which I subsequently slid with greater ease.

My grandmother, Ninyah -
Sereta Taylor Jones

Mom

My great-great-grandfather -
Charles Penrose

My grandfather, Baba -
Shirley Penrose Jones

The Dark House on 14th East

Ninyah and Baba at the 14th East house

Our family early on at the 14th East house - Sandy, Mom, me, and Daddy

Our family later on at the 14th East house - Lucy, Mom,
Sandy, Daddy, and me

The Laird Avenue house

Ninyah and Baba's Military Way house

The four children at the Laird Avenue house - Clark, Sandy, me, and Lucy

Newspaper photo: Me, about to fly home from a visit to
Daddy in Alabama, shortly after the divorce.

She flies alone——Kathleen

9-year-old girl flies alone to Salt Lake City

Nine-year-old Kathleen ██████, daughter of Assistant U. S. Atty. Henry ████████, landed today in Salt Lake City with a load of Alabama cotton.

The little traveler took off from Birmingham on an Eastern Air Line plane alone. She flew here alone from Salt Lake City last week to see her daddy. She made the trip on Delta and United Air Lines.

BUT HER DADDY says that everyone from the president of Delta to stewardesses took an interest in her trip. Kathleen said that one stewardess fixed the finger on her doll. The doll had fallen and broken its finger on the trip from Chicago to Atlanta.

Then in Atlanta, Kathleen was met by another stewardess, who came to work an hour and half earlier than necessary, to meet the little traveler.

The cotton she took home to Salt Lake City was from her Grandfather ██████'s compress in Selma.

Daddy arranged for the press to be at my sendoff.

Me, Lucy, Clark, and Sandy when we lived in Ninyah's basement

Mom and Mort, Eric's father, during their brief marriage

Our Military Way "mansion," kitty-corner from Ninyah and Baba's house

The five children at the Military Way house - Sandy, Eric,
Lucy, Clark, and me

The 1st Avenue house

The East 27th Ward chapel

Me, at age nine, visiting Daddy in Alabama

Daddy at his desk in Alabama as an assistant attorney general

Daddy's new family - Daddy, Brad, Margaret, and Stewart

Me, at age fourteen, living with Daddy and my secret in Alabama

The Imperial Street house and the garage, the site of yet another secret

Me, in high school, an aspiring actress

Singing "Wouldn't it Be Loverly" from *My Fair Lady*

As Gladys, in *The Skin of Our Teeth*

As the ingénue, in *Good News*

In the chorus, in *Iolanthe*

Me, as Anne, in *The Diary of Anne Frank:* "I still believe, in spite of everything, that people are really good at heart."

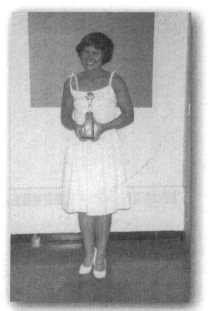

Winning Best Actress trophy at Northwestern University National High School Institute

Bear Lake - the Big House is in the lower left.

The Big House from the beach

Eric and I at Bear Lake

Me, a judge

The five adult siblings - Sandy, Lucy, Clark, me, and Eric

I recalled there was a butler, though this may not have been so. Baba himself might have been the one who pulled the velvet-corded tassel to summon cocktails. But if not the butler, who brought them? And who took my coat?

On Sundays, I ate breakfast with Baba and Ninyah in their bedroom or parlor. Baba cooked boiled eggs and toast, and brought them up on trays he carried from the kitchen. I sat in Baba's overstuffed chair and ate. "Manna from Heaven," I sighed, and Ninyah and Baba laughed. I thought Baba was as good as God.

On most Sundays, Baba took us for our Sunday drive. He drove into the canyons, up and down the Avenues, or out toward the salt flats. He bought us Popsicles, and we listened to *The Shadow* on the radio. Once he drove us up Emigration Canyon to show us where Grampa came over the mountains and into the valley. I looked up the mountain. "Where's baby Bertha buried?" I asked. "Doesn't she have a tombstone?"

"No stone." Baba puffed on his pipe. "We remember her much better this way, in our hearts." I decided I would be buried in the mountains, too.

Baba and I lined up dominoes and made them fall in a clattering line from one room to the next. He taught me to play Canasta, which he had learned from his mother, who had learned it from Grandfather Penrose. My mother had warned me to never lose easily, to fight to win no matter what, so I cheated at Canasta and Monopoly, but not with Baba. Even so, I seemed to always win.

———◆———

My first vivid memory of Baba is one of joy. He taught me about music when I was three years old.

A large mahogany table, extending the full width of the hall, stood in Baba's upstairs foyer. The table was so deep that when I climbed on my grandmother's cross-stitched stool and stretched my arms across it, I still could not reach the back. When I played underneath the table,

I ran my hands up and down the gigantic tree-trunk legs, which were wrapped with dark, wood-carved snakes. From the top of this table came the music that wafted into my lilac-scented room.

I was under the table one day when I saw Baba's legs approaching. I covered my eyes so he wouldn't find me.

"Where are you?" Baba sang. "Where is my little Kathy?" He walked back and forth. I could see his legs between my fingers. "No, not here," he said. "And not here. Where can she be?"

I put my hand over my doll's mouth and whispered, "Shhh."

"I have something to show my little Kathy, but I can't find her."

Should I open my eyes so he could see me? Should I tell him? Yes! I clapped my hands and cried out, "I'm here!"

Baba leaned down and poked his face in. He smiled upside down. "Ahhh, here she is. Come here, sweetheart, and I will show you something wonderful."

I scrambled out. Baba took my doll from me and sat her against the wall, bidding her to wait patiently. He lifted me up and settled me on one arm. "Look here."

A large wooden box sat on the table, a square and bulky thing polished so bright that Baba's suspenders were reflected back. "This is a phonograph," he told me. "This is where the music comes from."

I had heard the box singing, but I had never seen it.

"Here, I will show you how the music plays." Baba stood me on Ninyah's stool, and I was eye level to the box. He pointed to what looked like a sharp-toothed snake. "This is the tone arm. And that's a turntable," Baba said, pointing to a large round circle that looked like the lid of Ninyah's hatbox. In the middle of the circle a thin tube stuck out, straight into the air. Baba ran his thumb and finger up and down. "This is the spindle."

"But Baba, where's the music?" I asked, disappointed.

"Well, let's just see here." He turned to a floor-to-ceiling bookcase full of records. "Which one shall we play?" From a cardboard sleeve, he pulled a black disc as big as a plate, with a hole in the center of it. He lowered it onto the turntable, slipping the hole over the spindle.

"Let me! Let me!"

Thin lines were cut into the disk, circle after circle, like the age rings of trees. Baba twisted a fat button, and the disk began to spin around.

"Where's the music?"

"It's right here. In these grooves."

Could I believe what I couldn't see? Of course. I already had my fantasies and stories.

He picked up the snake's neck and placed its tooth in the grooves. I feared a howl of pain from the disc. What I got instead was a loud burst of melodic violins and a trilling piano. I was stunned and delighted. "It's magic!"

Baba laughed and said, "This is where the music comes from, Kathy. You may have music anytime you like. Now, why don't you pick us a record to play? I'll help you put it on." I picked a record with a picture of a cowgirl in a fringed skirt. Her hand was on her hip, and the other on a rifle standing at her side. I liked how she looked strong. She sang, "There's no business like show business," and I would come to believe that.

Music filled my grandparents' hall. It filled Ninyah's sewing rooms at the university, where she designed and made costumes, the theatres and halls where performers wore them, and the darkened auditorium of Kingsbury Hall, where I sat and listened to orchestras, operas, concerts, and musicals.

At home, a small radio sat by the side of my bed, soothing me to sleep at night. Sandy and I each had a small record player, too. Music filled my mother's room as well. She had a phonograph and then a stereo console. My family collected 78 and 45 RPM records, each housed in a sleeve—our treasures. We only touched the rims.

Over the years, I was denied food, affection, and approval, but I was never denied music. I dreamed of becoming a famous musical-comedy star.

Friends often marvel that I have memories of when I was that young. I wonder, too. Was it because everything took on such importance? Was it because of the ear-splitting volume of my world, the pain on my flesh when I was switched, the fear of the dark and abandonment, and then the juxtaposing and gratifying moments of fun and affection? Whatever the reasons, university archives and *Tribune* newspaper accounts confirm one event I recall vividly from a very early year of my life.

———◆———

I was three when I first appeared on the stage in 1947, the year of Utah's Pioneer Centennial. My grandmother enlisted me as an extra—a pioneer child—in a musical extravaganza depicting the story of several treks of the Mormon pioneers, beginning with Brigham Young leading his Latter Day Saints to the Great Salt Lake Valley and, looking over the valley, proclaiming, "This is the place."

Promised Valley was the first of the University of Utah's official Summer Festival productions, which were presented at the north end of the football field. In the fall, thousands of people sat in the bleachers to cheer the Utes, but in the summer, thousands of theatregoers came to see a sprawling spectacle on a massive stage. Between the ages of three and twenty, I was a part of nearly every production.

Each year, the stage was assembled from the ground up; for 1947's glorious historical pageant, it had to be big enough to hold horses, covered wagons, and hundreds of pioneers. I watched this enormous edifice rise up into the sky, a great mountain of wood and steel.

Underneath the stage, built among the support beams and piping, a labyrinthine catacomb of rooms was connected by tunnels and lit by bare bulbs hanging from lengths of cable. In one large room, Ninyah set up her costume tables and sewing machines, and hung racks and racks of costumes. The sewing ladies sat at the tables, chatting and stitching repairs.

Huge canvas tents were erected outside this underground city, lined up in rows, like houses on streets. The stars each had a special tent; the ballet corps and the chorus made their mysterious ways in and out of several others. This year, there was a tent for the pioneer children, too.

The pit in the front of the stage was large enough to hold the Utah Symphony, conducted by the famous maestro Maurice Abravanel. The sound system was the biggest and best available. Lights hung up and down tall poles along the sides of the stage and went on at dusk. The crowd arrived in a swarming buzz and milled about, chattering in anticipation.

On opening night, the sound grew like a summer storm rumbling into the valley. The stadium quivered with excitement. Backstage tension built. The actors, actresses, ballerinas, prop men, and scene changers murmured and hummed, and listened nervously to the orchestra tuning up. A hush quivered as the lights went down; the moonlight showered the stadium with chalky glow. The stage would soon be star studded, and I was a little girl bedazzled.

I was to play a pioneer child. Dressed in a red-and-blue gingham dress and a yellow plaid tie-on bonnet with blue ribbons, I would trek across the stage with my dear pioneer parents, several pioneer siblings, and the huge company of Latter Day Saints. The scene depicts one of the famous handcart brigades, in which a group of hearty Mormons rolled across the prairie in wagons loaded high with all of their belongings. But they were forced to abandon the wagons in a deadly early winter and trudge, cold and hungry, pushing and pulling handcarts through snow in the mountain passes, determined to reach the Promised Land. Some were rescued, but some froze or starved to death. It was all very grand and spectacular. Just my style.

This was a new world of color and joy, dancing and singing. I loved dressing up as someone different, having a different family—not just my Mormon pioneer family, but also the people who sang and danced and patted my head, who played Go Fish and Slap the Card with me, kissed and cuddled me, and toddled me down the field to the flagpole, where we lay on the lawn far from the lights, looking at the stars, listening to the crickets.

On opening night, amid all the excitement of scene changes, last-minute costume fittings, and missing props, I was instructed to "Stay put!" in Ninyah's costume quarters under the stage "until someone comes to fetch you to go on, dear." I knew that I had an entrance, that I was to go on with the Saints when the time came to cross the mountains.

Oh, it was hard to stay put. I could hear the shouts and talking; the songs and music piped thrillingly loud through the speakers that were set up in the tents and under the stage. The extravaganza was in full swing! I stayed still as long as I could. But the prairie called me, and mountains had to be crossed. Where was my pioneer family? I wanted to be with them, safe and sound.

In this anxiety, I left my grandmother's costume room and went searching. I wove through the pipes, waved at the other pioneers, and looked in the tents. I couldn't find them.

I decided to go out front, where the maestro was conducting the symphony. Abravanel was Ninyah's good friend, a gracious man whom we called Mo, who visited us at Bear Lake, where he lifted me to his shoulders, took me deep into the warm water, and galloped, pretending to be my seahorse as I shrieked with delight. I adored him, and he adored me. I would ask him where my family was. He would know.

I crunched along the gravel track that circled the football field. As I crossed the grass toward the maestro, I looked up at the stage, and I saw a miracle! The dancers were not pioneer ladies doing the do-si-do around the fire. What I saw was a fabulous world of swirling white angels!

Elegant ballerinas in white tutus whirled around. They pointed to the sky, they stood on their toes, and they flew across the stage in a glide, leaping, lifting their legs so high they could tap the stars. "Angels!" I gasped. "They are angels come from Heavenly Father."

(Years later, when the relatives chuckled and repeated this story, Ninyah explained that I had ventured out front during a dream sequence called the Cricket-Gull Choral Ballet, which depicted a Mormon miracle. When the pioneers settled in Salt Lake Valley, a swarm of crickets began to savage the starving Saints' crops. In answer to the pioneers' prayers, God sent seagulls to devour the crickets. The ballerinas in the ballet were depicting the seagulls.)

It took me only a moment to realize that Heavenly Father would want to see *me* dancing with the angels. I scurried up to Mo and tugged on the coat of his tux. Startled, he looked down. I yelled so he could hear me above the orchestra. "Mo, Mo, can I go on now?" He shooed me away, but I was not deterred.

The lights blazed on these beautiful, dancing angels, and I tugged again at the maestro's coat. He looked down at me, surprised I was still there. His face softened. "Kathy, dear," he said hurriedly. "Go on backstage to Ninyah." He leaned his head toward me and spoke in a rush, conducting all the time, never losing a sweep of his baton. "Go on now. Hurry."

I raced excitedly backstage. "Go on now," he had said.

I ran up the entrance ramp, and without a pause, I flew onto the stage. In my blue-and-red gingham dress, my yellow-flowered bonnet with the bright-blue ties, my sturdy brown shoes, and my gray muslin leggings, I joined the lovely white angels in their pale tights and leotards and snowy tulle tutus twirling. I became a short, squat riot of color in their midst.

I spun! I leaped! I held my hands way above my head and jumped from one foot to the other. I fell, but I picked myself up again. I rejoiced in my Heavenly Father's skies!

I don't recall how I got off of the stage. Someone gently led me. After that, I was a star. A ballerina tousled my hair. A lady with a bonnet like mine laughed and called me "precious little angel." A prop man who had been a stranger brought me lemonade. Ninyah hugged me over and over. "Such a dear girl," she cooed.

I thought then that it meant I had performed very well and that I had a superior talent. I am sure that this event nourished my dream of becoming an actress.

After all, I was a natural.

CHAPTER 17

NINYAH'S BASEMENT

———◆———

DADDY DIVORCED MOM. FOLLOWING THE divorce, which Mom always re-
ferred to as "your father's desertion," we moved to Ninyah and Baba's
house, where we lived in the basement for six months.

"Why didn't they give her the money from the sale of the Laird
Avenue house? To buy her own house? Or to support *us?*" Eric asked as
we read Mom's pleas of poverty in the court transcripts.

"I think it was a control thing," I said.

"Do you think that's where we get *our* control thing?"

It was true that I wanted to be in control. If I felt out of control, I
panicked. I wanted others to do what I said, to think what I thought. I
had to consciously settle myself down. This need was part of the reason
why being a judge was such a good job for me: I was in control.

But control had its dark side. I could abuse my power, making others
suffer. As did Ninyah and Baba.

"No," I answered. "We just didn't want to be like Mom. She had no
control over her own life; she had to control *us.*"

"Yeah," Eric fumed. "So she made ours miserable."

Unwilling to give Mom money, Ninyah and Baba nevertheless let
us live in their basement, although they spurned my mother, who only
begrudgingly accepted their charity. I was ten years old and numbed by
the changes. First, my father leaving. Then, the house being sold. Then,
moving to Ninyah's basement. I no longer felt special.

"We won't let the children live in a dumpy rental," Baba told Mom when we moved in. "But you must find yourself a better-paying job as soon as possible." Then he mumbled, "Or a better husband."

Mom had a secretarial job she liked at a plant called Seal-Tight, which made canning wax. She liked her boss, Mort Walton. "But he's married," she complained, though I didn't see how that mattered. "With four kids." She worked at other jobs, too, bringing home books to balance or working on the weekends, so I was left pretty much on my own to feed my younger siblings, get us all to church, and walk clear down to Wasatch Elementary in the lower Avenues, dropping Clark off at the babysitter's on the way.

She cried a lot and got bleary drunk.

That fall, Ninyah and Baba decided to send my older sister Sandy, then twelve years old, to Rowland Hall–St. Marks, an expensive boarding school in town, where she could receive "the quality education your mother should be providing." She came home only on weekends. They gave her piano lessons, too. I was resentful, left at home in their basement with my angry, depressed mother and the younger children to care for.

———•———

A chilly silence wedged itself between us all. We entered the house quietly, slipping through the long back hall and down the stairs. We didn't go upstairs unless invited to eat.

The basement was a dreary, gloomy place, lit only from narrow, rectangular casement windows high in the walls. The main room had a small fireplace, but the two rooms we used as bedrooms were damp and musty smelling. Mom slept in the largest of these, the girls slept in one bed in the other, and Clark slept on the living-room floor.

In the furnace room, we fashioned a kitchen. Baba installed a stove and a small fridge next to the basement washtub, which we used for water and sponge baths. Baba installed a toilet in a corner of our kitchen.

Next to the sink he ran a water pipe up the wall and attached a spigot. Around the spigot he jury-rigged a circle rod; we hung a shower curtain on it and wrapped it around us when we showered, the smell of cooked cauliflower mixing in with the shower steam.

In the darkest corner, behind the furnace, a half door was cut into the wall. The coal man dumped coal down a chute through this opening. We fed the furnace through its mouth, shovels of the black, craggy chunks. The flames licked at the coal, the furnace belched, and we got shiny and filthy with coal dust.

The furnace had five fat octopus arms stretching out over the kitchen. During the night, when I got up to pee, they reached out to grab me. I began to wet the bed again. Mom made me wash my own sheets.

I hated living there.

But we had a radio and a phonograph in Ninyah's basement, and my world was full of music. It consoled me and transported me to a different time, a different place, and a different me.

Occasionally, Baba invited me upstairs for music. I danced to the big bands: Benny Goodman, Harry James, and Glenn Miller. Baba clapped and hooted as I hopped up and down the hall to the "Chattanooga Choo Choo." My favorite of his records was Guy Lombardo and the Royal Canadians. I was sure that Lombardo's arm was reaching out to just me from the stiff cardboard album cover.

Ninyah bought classical-music albums and the score of each Broadway musical as soon as it was recorded. She allowed me to come upstairs and listen. I lay beside the phonograph table and sang along to *The King and I* and *Paint Your Wagon*. Years later, I lay beside that table and played *West Side Story* over and over until my usually tolerant grandmother begged me to stop.

Mom had talking records: men who told jokes, like Garry Moore and Danny Kaye, and poets who read their own poems, like T. S. Eliot.

"Here's a true one," she said of Eliot's "The Waste Land," and I heard him scratch out, "This is the way the world ends, not with a bang but a whimper."

Her favorite musical genres were blues and jazz. "Life is the blues," she lamented. In our basement living room, we listened in the dark to Sarah Vaughan and Billie Holiday, who sang like Mom talked: "I can't take it no more" and "You're a no-good man, but I love ya anyhow."

Mom played Judy Garland until I couldn't stand it, including "The Man That Got Away" and "Have Yourself a Merry Little Christmas," even in July. She sang along slurrily. She put her arm around me and complained, "Nothing good has ever happened for me, Kathy." She hugged me and rocked back and forth, crying until I wrested free.

"What about 'Over the Rainbow'?" I said, comforting her. But she warned me, "There is no 'over the rainbow,' Kathy. The wizard is a fake." She took another drink. "You have to be careful of everyone. There's nobody you can trust." She paused, and I was alert. I knew what was coming. "Like that asshole Sanders. He pays me shit."

Sanders was just one on her repeated list of injustices. There had been dimwitted Gerald at the bank, who got a bigger raise than she did, and flat-faced Mr. Rice at her Saturday job at the Red Cross, who didn't ever have to make the coffee. And now there was Mr. Walton at Seal-Tight, who "deserved a better wife than that tart he's married to." While I made dinner or did the dishes, she sat and recited her woes. "Pour me another drink," she ordered while relating the day's bad news. "Poor me," she punned, chuckling to herself.

Right after Daddy left, she lost out on a Wasatch School District job to a man who had a family to support: "What am I?" she yelled. "Chopped liver?" She slammed a pan on the stove. "I've got a family. Wanna see? Here they are, my goddamned family. Take a bow, girls." Lucy sucked her thumb, but I took a bow.

Her list fatigued me. How she wanted to be a lawyer, or a pianist. How she deserved to marry a rich man. How she shouldn't have had kids. How humiliating it was to be a secretary. How she couldn't afford nice things, though Lucy showed us her lacy underpants and filmy silk slips. Only seven, Lucy was in charge of Mom's finery, which she washed by hand and hung up by the furnace on a line.

Sandy just said, "No one to blame but yourself," and huffed out of the room. She stopped coming home from boarding school. I ached for the unfairness of it all.

And, of course, there was always my father. Mom called him names and was glad he was gone, but I missed him. He used to lighten her up a bit. "Get a grip," he would tell her when she got all soggy and bitter. Then he'd move the needle to another song and chug "wooo wooo" through the house, singing, "On the Atchison, Topeka, and the Santa Fe," stringing me behind him like a caboose.

"Come on, sourpuss," he'd say, chucking Mom under the chin. "Gimme a toooot tooooot."

In a good mood, my mother sang, "The hills are alive with the sound of music." I remembered my father singing, too. Lucy couldn't carry a tune, but Sandy sang high-class songs like "Beloved" from *The Student Prince* and "Un Bel Di" from *Madame Butterfly*.

I sang hymns.

"Music is one of God's languages," Sister Mallow explained when I asked her why we sang so many hymns in church. "When we sing, we are standing at God's gate, and our troubles disappear."

I could live with that.

———————

Eric and I gathered up the deeds and documents, and made ourselves some lunch. "I never could sing," he chuckled. "Though I tried."

I remembered his tone-deaf efforts. "You were a terrific audience, though," I said.

I had an idea for a token. At ZCMI, I happily browsed in the sheet-music department, selecting "Chattanooga Choo Choo" for Mom, "I Believe" for Daddy, songs from *On the Town* for Ninyah, and "Oh, My Papa," which I always sang as "Oh, My Baba," for my grandfather.

As I left the store, I realized I had picked out treasures rather than symbols of sorrow; the songs I picked were mementoes of joyful times.

Something was changing in me. That old furnace was scary, but it gave off heat for us. That dark basement was lonely, but it gave out music for us. Mom was tormented, but she gave up freedom for us. Was it all mixed together?

The music went into my bag.

At the top of Ninyah's steep hill, the gray house looked like a man's face peering down. The windows were eyes, large and shaded. The mouth was a bulky oak door. From the sidewalk, a manicured green lawn sloped up to the front door. Thirty steps led up a hill to the front entryway.

In the back, thirty more steps led further up to the garage, behind which was a field. Those back steps were the steps that seemed miles long when I fled up them to the field on that dreadful and wonderful day forty years ago, when Mrs. Adair showed me her magic mirror.

For a child with a vivid imagination, the basement was a scary but electrifying place. I sometimes invited friends to adventure with me to its dark interior. We snuck through the front bedroom, where the small rectangular window at the top of the wall let in a coffin of light, looking for a beast. We crept into Mom's bedroom, which had a window just large enough for a swarthy bogeyman to crawl through to hide in the room's dark corner, waiting to attack a small child. The deepest terror, however, lay in the kitchen, the dank forest of crevices and crannies in which the evil furnace lurked, its arms reaching out across the room, searching for children.

"Shhh," I cautioned my itchy friends. "The monster's there, and he has long poisoned fingernails." I slunk silently and slowly into the shadows, and then let out a piercing scream and cried, "Run for it!" We tripped over one another, shrieking up the stairs, out the back door, and up into the field, where we threw ourselves down and waited to be murdered.

I was not unhappy when friends refused to play along any longer. The creatures were far more terrifying, the agonies more excruciating, and the victories more glorious when I was pursuing terror alone. Some days I crept alone into the basement's secret and forbidding lair, and lost myself in my own adventures. Until one day, when I never played those games again.

At the bottom of the basement stairs was a closet. Ninyah had instructed me never to go into the closet, and it had remained locked since we'd moved in some months ago. I spied to see where Cook placed the key when she emerged from the closet, turned the lock, and retreated up the stairs with a jar of jam or string beans. She hung it on a hook by the back door.

I realized there was food in the closet, and by then I had come to realize that food was going to be a big issue in my family. Mom had cut way back on our food since Daddy had left. She argued with Ninyah about how much food Ninyah allowed us to eat when we were invited upstairs.

"I can't pay you for it," Mom grumbled.

"Sereta," Ninyah said, "if you can't feed your children, I will."

Cook hung the closet key above the milk cubby. It hung right there in the open, next to the back-door key. This would be easy. All I had to do was stay home sick from school on Cook's day off, and the closet was mine!

The day came. I feigned illness. Everyone was gone but Ninyah, who finally left at one o'clock. Mrs. Adair didn't come until one thirty, so I had only a small window of time. I jostled the key from its hook, and then I slowly inched down the stairs and stealthily approached the closet door. I inserted the key.

I did not admit to myself that I was afraid. But, in truth, I was so frightened that my hand shook as I turned the key. My skin prickled, and my throat was as tight as a sling, ready to snap and throw me back. As I turned the key, I thought I heard a mumble behind the door.

I couldn't stop my hand from pulling open the door, which widened its dark orifice. A hidden creature breathed on me! His breath was warm and fusty. Something smelled repellent and scabby. A gelatinous mass of a man with eyes so red I thought they were bleeding bent his black neck toward me. I yowled. Every ounce of courage fell out of me, and it was only by God's wind that I escaped his monstrous hand and fled.

Up the stairs I raced, through the back door. When I reached the field, I flung myself down in the clumped brush. I felt no thrill of escape, no safety, no joy. Sobs bludgeoned my chest until I hurt. "Save me!" I cried to no one. "Please save me!" I sobbed. But I knew I would not be saved.

Mrs. Adair found me there.

A note from Ninyah asked her to look in on me, as I was sick in bed. She quickly discovered my empty bed and searched the house. She found the basement closet door flung back against the wall. She shut it, ran up the stairs, and hurried up to the field.

"Oh, my dear child," she exclaimed. She fell to the ground and dragged me into her arms. "Are you breathing?" When she assured herself I was, she stroked my head with her old, worn hands and asked, "Whatever happened?"

"There's a vicious man in the basement closet, and he wants to kill me," I sobbed as she wiped dirt from my face and picked grass from my hair. "He has bleeding eyes and a great knobby hand."

She rocked me back and forth. We sat there for a while as she soothed, "There, there." I was afraid she would deny the man and I would be all alone again, left with a hideous and cruel enemy to tackle on my own.

"Kathy, my dear," she said. "All these monsters you make up and all the evil you strike out against, they are real in your mind." I was relieved that she understood my difficulties.

"Yes, it's a terrible thing," I emphasized.

"But they aren't real in true life."

Before I could argue, she continued. "They simply represent the challenges you must overcome." She hummed a bit, and I was somewhat comforted. "What you must do is remember what your father taught you." I paused. Which of his lessons? I didn't recall him seeing my monsters.

"He told you, 'Take only what is good.'"

"I don't remember that." I didn't even know what it meant.

"That's what he said. And if you do that, it will turn any monster in on itself." She lifted me up and brushed the dirt from my knees. "Come, I'll show you what I mean."

We entered the house. She held my hand and went into Cook's bathroom, where she took something from the medicine cabinet and put it in her apron pocket. "Now come with me."

We went down the stairs, I reluctantly following behind her, grabbing her hand with both of my own and bending over, not daring to look up.

I watched from behind her skirt. She opened the door.

She pulled a thin chain. A lamp flared.

The lamp was the most glorious thing I had ever seen.

In the center of the closet sat a narrow high-backed chair with heavy arms and a velvet cushion. At its side stood an enormous curved-arm floor lamp on two great iron legs. Wrought-iron curlicues wound around the lamppost like vines. Flower blossoms and leaves branched out from the bottom to top of the vines. Three light bulbs cupped in gold-fingered prongs rested on a brass bracket at the top of the pole. They were graced with a frilled lampshade of pale-red satin and dotted with fat red-and-black brocaded buds of crumpled silk that looked like roses.

"Here is your monster," Mrs. Adair smiled. "Actually, a rather lovely creature when you look at its good points and in a good light."

I was mesmerized.

"Which is what your Daddy was telling you."

Mrs. Adair reached in her pocket and brought out a small hand mirror. She placed my fingers around the teardrop handle and held my hand up so the mirror faced the lamp.

"Now, here's what you do with your monsters and all your evils." She switched off the light. She bent to her knees and pulled me in close.

I felt dread rise again, sure I could see the monster's bloody eyes. But I stood steady. Mrs. Adair held my hand tight with the mirror facing the monster.

"Shine the mirror on the monster, like this. Now you are turning its darkness back onto itself. Do you see?"

"Yes," I said, though I wasn't sure.

She pushed herself up from her knees with a slight groan and a loud exhale of breath. "Now watch in the mirror." She pulled a switch.

There was the beautiful creature lamp.

"Now you see it in the light. You see the monster's goodness shine out because the bad has been swallowed up."

———◆———

Shelves of glass jars containing fruits and vegetables, jams and jellies, pickles and tomatoes covered two walls. The other walls were piled high with stacks of books and magazines.

I asked Mrs. Adair why Ninyah kept the closet locked and why she wouldn't let me enter. She explained that this was Ninyah's sacred space, where, before we moved into the basement, Ninyah liked to come and sit alone to read her beloved magazines and favorite books, lit only by the lamp. I wasn't allowed to enter because the magazines were *National Geographic, Horizon,* and *Theatre Arts,* with pictures of naked people and coarse words improper for little girls to read.

I told Mrs. Adair that I knew all about sexy things, and I cursed every word I knew for her. She laughed and said she would see what she could do to wring permission from Ninyah.

From then on, Ninyah allowed me into the closet, where I sat for hours looking at sinuous Castilian women and muscled African men, Greek and Roman statues, and insects "doing it." I visited Norwegian fjords and Niagara Falls, and swam with dolphins off the Kona coast. I read plays and theatre reviews, and learned about Broadway, the Pasadena Playhouse, and method acting.

My dreams of evil creatures ceased. Instead I expanded my story writing and playacting. I became a wild-animal hunter. I traveled to exotic countries and fell in love with Asian men and Inuit women. I decorated my room in yellow and black, because those were the colors of the *National Geographic*. I stared at the stained-glass windows in church because they reminded me of the covers of *Horizon* magazine. Sometimes I sat in Ninyah's chair for hours, transported away from the dreary basement.

I admit that even today I can't define what exactly became clear that day. All I know for certain is that *something* became clear. I felt grown up and capable; I would meet my monsters and evils in a new way.

I did remember many of my father's lessons:

"Find the silver lining."

"Whistle in the dark."

"Look for skies of blue."

"Smile, though your heart is aching."

He was optimistic and hopeful, almost always willing to give the benefit of the doubt.

"You make life seem like a fairy tale to that girl," my mother criticized.

"Ah, my dear," he said, and smiled. "But it is."

"Oh, yeah?" she'd countered. "Have you ever read the original *Grimms*?"

Though I lost the actual mirror Mrs. Adair gave me, I used its message in my teaching, legal, and judicial careers. I tried to turn the mirror toward my students when they misbehaved, my divorce clients when they were vindictive, my adversaries when they hurt me, and the people in my courtroom—the abusive and neglectful parents, the recalcitrant children. I tried to give their evil enough time to wear out and absorb itself. Then I turned the light on their hopes and needs.

I imagined the mirror shining until the good shone out.

But then the recent past had descended on me. I had lost the mirror.

———◆———

Eric and I drove to what had been Grand Central, our childhood grocery store, to buy dinner. In the vegetable section, I found my token—a large gingerroot. Fresh gingerroot is generally squat and gnarled, with stumpy limbs coming off a stocky trunk. But this piece was long and fat, scabbed with burls like blisters, with two trunks. Several long arms stretched and twisted out from the trunks.

It was the furnace; it was the lamp. It was Daddy gone and Mom going crazy. The perfect token for Ninyah's basement.

It weighed over a pound—twice the weight of my heart.

CHAPTER 18

RICH GIRL, POOR GIRL

———————

MOM FOOLED EVERYONE. SHE MARRIED Mort, her boss at Seal-Tight, who left his wife and four children for her. Ninyah and Baba were friendly to her again. They approved of Mort because he was rich, successful, Mormon, and from the north—Wyoming. Furthermore, he was elegant—tall, with a bounteous head full of thick, wavy salt-and-pepper hair; broad shoulders, like Paul Bunyan's; a dazzling smile; and a cherubic face that reminded me of Michelangelo's seraphs. He charmed us all, buying the girls white gloves, chucking Clark under the chin, complimenting Ninyah and Baba, and kissing my mother in public, which caused her to blush and giggle. Not only that, he was an exotic inventor—he held the patent on a new sealing wax for canning.

So when I was eleven, after all those dreadful months in Ninyah's basement, we moved to a mansion kitty-corner from my grandparents' house, on an even higher hill, so close that from a small second-floor balcony I could see Ninyah's purple lilac bush climbing the side of her house like a feather boa. We would live there only a year.

Our Military Way house held, to our relief, my mother's joy. My aunts and uncles told me that Mort was the only man she had ever truly loved, the love of her life, and I believed it. For the first seven months we lived there, she smiled a lot, laughed uproariously, sang and danced around the house, and even hugged and kissed us. She didn't drink—Mort prohibited it. She didn't smoke in front of us either, though I know she did in secret (I could smell it on her). I wondered whether Mort knew she did, too, and whether that's why he left several months later. I thought Mom must have done *something* to scare him away.

It was grand to be so rich after being so poor! Sandy was ecstatic. She came home often from Rowland Hall–St. Marks those first months. She took singing and piano lessons, bought new clothes, made new rich friends, and took on sophisticated airs.

I was ecstatic because there was so much food! I remember the kitchen more vividly than the rest of the house and took to studying at the kitchen table, with an alert eye on the fridge.

At the Seal-Tight factory on the industrial north end of town, large barrel-shaped tanks seduced us into climbing their ladders to the top, a dangerous prank I shudder at today. Tall smokestacks belched out fire and streams of steam. I jokingly told my friends that my stepfather made the wax the Mormons used to seal their families for eternity.

Mom traveled a lot with Mort, so they hired a caretaker for us: a tall, broad woman, with a face square as a chessboard and bushy eyebrows. My mother called her our governess and addressed her as "Miss." She liked that but told us, "Just call me Jerri." She brought her nineteen-year-old daughter with her as our cleaning lady. Sherri was a bouncy girl, as narrow as her mother was broad, her elbows poking out like doorknobs. When she wasn't cleaning, she played cards, jumped on the beds, made mud cakes, and romped with us. The two of them lived in our bright basement, in what Mom called "the servant's quarters": a large bedroom, a small living room, and a bathroom.

Other rooms wove through the light and spacious basement: a library; a recreation room, in which we had pool and Ping-Pong tables; a sixth bathroom; and a large family room, where, in front of the largest television I had ever seen, Jerri and Sherri and all us children gathered to watch *I Love Lucy, Kraft Theater,* and, right before everything fell apart, a Disneyland show about Davy Crockett.

I had a spacious bedroom all to myself, with a brand-new phonograph and a radio by the side of my enormous bed. Lucy was afraid to sleep alone, so I let her sleep with me. At night, we were allowed to listen to the radio until we fell asleep; our favorite show was the *Tennessee Ernie Ford* show. "Today is National Peanut Day," he quipped. "And if you don't think that's important, ask any elephant." I wrote all of his jokes in my journal and incorporated them into the plays I was still producing.

I co-opted for myself the second-story balcony that was cupped by a wrought-iron rail. Here, I wrote in my journal, read books, and placed my dolls on little chairs and read to them from *The Children's Friend*, a Church magazine. The play pieces from my favorite games, Monopoly and Go to the Head of the Class, became characters and props for little plays I produced for imaginary audiences.

In our living room, Mom played on the biggest, most beautiful piano I had ever seen. She called it "my grand." Sometimes she sat on the closed lid and sang sultry songs like "I Got Lost in His Arms" while Sandy accompanied her.

Best of all, we ate all the food we wanted.

Jerri and Sherri were our constant companions, Jerri was our surrogate mother, teacher, and cook: instructing, tut-tutting, and snuggling us. Sherri was our playful friend. We had what would be the last of my childhood fun! That winter we built snowmen and forts, and roasted marshmallows in the fireplace. The following summer we played in our vast yard and in the untrammeled fields behind the house, building forts and digging holes, playing hide-and-seek, and climbing trees. At Halloween, Jerri and Sherri built a spook house for us in the basement. I manned the door, answering knocks, refusing to allow entrance to adults. The children had to descend to the basement. They wound their way through the dark and eerie labyrinth, plunged their hands into bowls of plucked-out eyes (grapes) and gooey intestines (cooked spaghetti), and stroked the hair of a beheaded hag's head as it moved back and forth on top of the table, tongue lolling out, eyes crossed (that was Sherri). Eerie music played. Spider webs (Jerri's gauze) grazed their faces. Only after negotiating this trail of terror could the children receive their treats. Once in a while, the disembodied head gave out a bubbling scream, and a child went crashing back up the stairs, refusing the gumdrops I offered as consolation.

On the only Christmas morning we spent in this house, we bounded down the wide, winding staircase to a huge tree glittered with color and light. A new bicycle stood beside my other presents, which were piled higher than I'd ever seen, even in the movies. My stocking was filled with goodies and small gifts. Mom was already at the piano playing "O Holy Night." Nothing ever surpassed that sight, not even Ninyah's massive, copiously lighted trees, decorated with bubbling candles, porcelain ornaments, candy canes, and tinsel.

One day in early spring, Mom announced, "You're going to have a baby." I was startled, because Daddy had told me babies come from a girl's stomach. I had no clue about conception. "I don't want to have a baby," I whimpered, clutching at my stomach.

Mom laughed happily and took me in her arms. "*I'm* having the baby," she said, beaming. Still, I thought I might be the one pregnant, that a baby had entered my stomach when Daddy had taught me about the cave. I watched for signs.

Mort did not seem happy about the coming baby. Mom stayed home, and Mort was gone more and more. The house soon held sorrow. Lying in my bed, I'd hear their muffled quarrels: Mort thought we children were out of control, Mom wanted Mort to make more money, and so on. Sandy came home less and less, and when she did, she spent time with her friends or at Ninyah's house. Lucy contracted rheumatic fever and spent several months in the hospital. Clark disappeared into loneliness and inattention. More and more, I played on my balcony, or went climbing in the foothills, or wrote stories on a small desk set up in the library next to the servants' quarters.

In August, Mom gave birth to my baby brother, Eric. I loved him with the mighty love only a child can have for a baby. He slept in a crib in the alcove dressing room off the master bedroom. I stood watch over him, standing on a stool to turn him over every once in a while, playing with his fingers, telling him stories, singing to him. I was the only one who could quiet his crying.

In September, Sandy went back to public school. Ninyah told me she was now sending *me* to boarding school at Rowland Hall–St. Marks for my own "educational head start." I didn't want to go. Even though the mounting tension at home was disturbing, I loved my new family, and I had made friends in the neighborhood. But Ninyah insisted. She gave me a record of the musical *Kismet* and a quilt, which was silver on one side, dark green on the other. She checked me into Rowland Hall–St. Marks and took me to my assigned room. I had a bed, a bureau, and my phonograph. I sat on the quilt and cried.

"Kathy, dear, your mother and Mort need some time to resolve their differences," she said to comfort me. But I knew what *that* meant—it would all come crashing down.

I quickly grew to love Rowland Hall–St. Marks. Aunt Henry, the housemother in charge of the boarding girls, was a thin, wiry woman, with graying hair pulled back in a bun. She gathered us each night in her bedroom parlor, where we sat at her feet while she instructed us in moral values. The girl who had been best that week got to wear a lovely necklace Aunt Henry's mother had given her. I was a troublesome child, and it took me many weeks to win the necklace. When I did, I lost it.

I had strict and knowledgeable teachers. Every day I had mandatory study hall until dinner. My intellectual acumen blossomed. I was encouraged in my studies, particularly in music and writing. Although I fretted and complained, as I had learned to do from my mother, I actually enjoyed school and thrived. I learned academic discipline and gained a deep love of learning.

———◆———

As a judge, I encouraged the delinquent kids in their schooling. Every Friday, my probationers returned to court for what I called Automatic

Report. If they had perfect attendance at school and their grades were improving, I let them go. If not, I put them in detention for part or all of the weekend. I assigned themes, art projects, whatever they seemed to excel at.

One of my probationers, Tyrone Manning, was an extraordinary artist. As a condition of probation, I required him to draft a graphic comic book about child abuse for me to reproduce and hand out to abused children and their families. His book was breathtaking. One of the illustrations in his book shows me as a judge celebrating a child's escape from abuse. I encouraged Tyrone to seek employment. He was the youngest person ever hired at a tech firm in Portland. Sadly, shortly thereafter, he drowned in the Columbia River Slough, where he was swimming with friends.

Though most probation officers appreciated these efforts, many were irritated at the time they had to waste appearing at Automatic Report with their charges. This was yet another way I disturbed the juvenile-court status quo. Eventually, I excused those officers and simply conducted the hearings without them.

———◆———

At Rowland Hall–St. Marks, I conspired with two other troublesome girls to sneak down the fire escape, which was outside my bedroom window. We'd walk to Snelgrove's to buy ice cream, or downtown to play in the Temple grounds. We were never caught. Some nights we sneaked into the lavatories and played Monopoly or jacks until midnight. Sometimes I sneaked out alone to wander and walk. I often walked the twenty-seven blocks to Military Way, hid across the street, and watched my house.

I was rarely invited home.

Two months after Eric was born, Mort left, and we were suddenly poor again. Years later, I learned that he had gone off with a large share of my grandfather's money. He had coerced Baba into liquidating most of his assets and investing in Sure-Tight. Then he stole the company money and fled. The company plunged into bankruptcy. Baba and Ninyah never recovered their wealth. I wonder now whether Mort planned it all along, marrying my mother to cheat my wealthy grandfather. My uncles thought so. "A wily crook," they called him. "A charlatan."

Mort may have gone away with the money, I thought, *but we got Eric, so the joke's on him.* That's how I saw it, though Mom didn't. She cried, pouted, got sloppy drunk. Ninyah yelled at her, and she yelled back. She pounded on the piano as she drank, turning love songs into tempests. She shouted out her rewritten Rodgers and Hammerstein lyrics: "Oh, what a shitiful morning." She seethed while she hammered the keys. As her binges wore on, she became maudlin, singing ballads and blues, her voice plaintive and wracked as she moaned off-key: "They're playing songs of love, but not for me."

Baba died two months later of a stroke, leaving Ninyah in desperate financial straits and dumbfounded that Mormon Mort had turned traitor. "He killed your grandfather," she told me in a rare moment of visible despair. Ninyah sent the *Tribune* a lovely picture of Baba for his obituary. In the photograph he was sitting in his overstuffed armchair, smoking his pipe. When the obituary was printed, however, the Mormon-owned newspaper showed Baba with uncharacteristic puffed-out cheeks and a little hole in his mouth—the staff had excised his pipe.

Ninyah never went to Church again. When I asked her why, she took a deep breath, pursed her lips, and said, "I don't care to discuss that, dear."

I was heartbroken.

All this betrayal in less than a year.

Now Mom brought me home from Rowland Hall on holidays and every weekend. I see now that it was for companionship; I became her confidante.

I didn't fully understand the heavy crush of sadness that descended upon me, but I felt it in my bones. My feet developed an odd coldness; they remain cold to this day, long after the rest of my body has warmed. When I heard we would have to move, I began to eat furiously and quickly gained too much weight. I've had a weight problem ever since. Mom dismissed Jerri and Sherri. A dark silence came over our house, interrupted only by my mother's weeping in the night.

In my room, I played my records as loud as I dared to drown her out—songs about strangers in paradise and never walking alone. I missed my father and sang: "Oh, my Papa, to me you were so wonderful." I held Eric, fed him his bottle, changed him, rocked him, and put him in bed with me. Mom didn't even notice.

Mom's list of injustices now included Mort. "That sonofabitch Mort!" was the only name she ever called him anymore.

When I could, I continued to disappear into dreaming, walking, singing, and making up stories, skits, and sermons. To these strategies, I added prayer. I prayed Mort would come back. I prayed we wouldn't have to sell the house. I prayed Mom wouldn't start drinking again. When my prayers weren't answered, I decided to report God's neglect to my new Sunday-school teacher and ask her advice.

I don't remember anything about this woman except her voice, which was pinched, as if she had a clothespin on her nose.

"First of all, Kathy, our Prophet says you must pray both morning and evening," she said, her hands folded neatly in her lap, "and in a quiet place. Do you do that?"

"I do." I knew a thing or two.

"You must always be on your knees."

"I am."

"You must use proper language, using Thee and Thou and Thy and Thine. And you must pray in the name of Jesus." She lifted a hand and pointed a finger at me. "The power of your prayers depends on you."

I tried again. I rewrote my prayers using good words. I prayed with energy, love, and a good heart, as instructed. I prayed for Mom and Daddy, Ninyah, my siblings. But God still didn't help us with food or money or making Mom happy, so I went back.

The Sunday-school teacher seemed irritated to see me again so soon. "Well," she said, "did you give thanks for your blessings?"

"I did."

"You have to help and do all you can yourself to make your prayers come true."

"I do." I defended myself, thinking of my allowance money going to Mom, of how I took care of Eric, and of how I'd taken up the chores when Mom let Jerri go. I felt defensive. I didn't want to cry.

"Well"—she shifted to her other foot—"God answers prayers in different ways than you expect sometimes. You must always ask for guidance from the Holy Ghost."

Suddenly I felt demolished. "But I don't have the Holy Ghost," I admitted, panicked. "I'm not baptized yet."

"How old are you?" she asked, shock in her eyes.

"Eleven," I said shamefully.

"Well, there you have it. You should have been baptized at eight. You've disobeyed the Gospel." She was done with me.

I told my mother I wanted to go back to Sister Mallow. "Honey, she's gone, gone, gone," Mom said, pausing, lighting a cigarette. "She got pregnant." I was flabbergasted. She smiled at me. "How do you like *that?*"

I have since looked for Sister Mallow, done a genealogy search on the LDS ancestry site, called the stake president to find her full name and whether she had been excommunicated. He refused to give me any information. I have found no record of her. At least, none that is open to me. So I imagine. I imagine she is happy. I imagine she is married to the man who is the father of her child. I imagine they live in Idaho.

———————————

Decades later, Eric and I stared at the Military Way house. I looked up at my balcony. "The house isn't a mansion, after all," I said, and laughed. And the balcony, which had seemed so large and on which I had spent so many happy hours, was tiny. Everything now seemed small, shrunken.

"I know I was just a baby," Eric said, "but I'm sure I remember being in a crib, and you were leaning over me."

I smiled, ironically thinking, *Can we have memories so young?*

"You kept me safe, didn't you?"

So many events were compressed into such a short, happy period that they seemed a dream to me now as I looked up at the large red-brick house. But there was the sloping lawn we had sledded down in winter; there were the shrubs and trees in which I had built my impenetrable fort. And behind the house, I could see the field in which we found a large hole in the earth, dug it out further, boarded it over, and turned it into a large neighborhood clubhouse. We lighted it with candles and made up elaborate rituals, passwords, and incantations. The hole was our hideaway until we accidentally set the roof and field on fire and escaped with our lives—and mandatory lessons at the firehouse.

Eric and I had left the motel that morning and spent the entire day in the Military Way neighborhood, walking the streets, watching the house, sharing thoughts or thinking them in silence. The sun was now lounging in the western sky. Time to go back.

My mother loved bearded iris. She told me it was a female flower, independent and paradoxical, willing to flaunt its colors yet maddening romantics with its lack of smell. In the long yard behind the Military Way house, she had attempted to grow a garden, which Jerri had tended when Mom was traveling with Mort. Only the irises thrived. One day Jerri brought Mom a large vase of deep-purple irises she had cut from the yard.

"Well, Jerri, thank you," Mom instructed her gently, "but you mustn't cut the irises while they are living."

Jerri's eyebrows lifted. "Why?"

"These flowers look strong and bold, but they are really quite fragile and don't last long if cut." Mom paused, smiling, rubbing the silky petals across her face. "However, if you leave irises to die in their natural place and then cut them down to the base, you can dig the rhizomes up, divide them, and replant them. Then flocks of iris will multiply and cover the field. Some are inferior; some are more beautiful."

I was amazed. What else did my mother know that I didn't?

"I see," Jerri acceded. She didn't cut them again.

I think of my mother as the paradoxical iris; we are her divided rhizomes.

———•———

I felt reckless, my old rebellious self. I marched right up the steps and around to the backyard, heedless of being caught. To my astonishment, there was a large spread of iris stalks in a wide path along the back of the property. Though they were no longer blooming, they were standing quite tall and rigid in place, waiting to be pruned down and separated. There must have been hundreds of them.

I walked brazenly to the flowerbed and, with my penknife, dug a stalk out of the ground, rhizome and all. I carried it happily to my car and put it, still clumped with dirt, in my token bag.

CHAPTER 19

ALL THE WORLD'S A STAGE

———◆———

WHEN BABA DIED, HE LEFT Ninyah with little money; to prevent her humiliation, my three uncles took over Ninyah's support. Although she continued to earn a modest wage as the university's costume mistress, they had to sell her mansion and move her to a more modest house on 11th Avenue. It was a long slide down for Ninyah. Even so, the location was far enough above our house on 1st Avenue, where we had moved next, for her to escape our working-class squalor.

She gave Mom the silent treatment again. But she lavished love on me.

By now, Ninyah's name was well known in theatre and music circles in Salt Lake City. To me, she was just Ninyah. But to the wide world beyond me, Ninyah was the great and talented costume mistress, the elder Sereta Taylor Jones, whose "costuming was rapidly becoming legendary," as one review effused.

She was as regal as her name: tall and lovely, with a Grecian face and a thick hill of hair combed and piled meticulously on the top of her head. She had perfect posture and exuded an aristocratic air. She wore her "good breeding," as she called it, like a fur coat.

She continued to design for the university and community theatre groups for pleasure and out of necessity. From her imaginative mind came ideas, which she put to paper. From the handmade patterns, bolts of cloth, and spools of thread emerged the sweeping satin gowns of duchesses, the double-breasted suits of gangsters, fanciful and frilly frocks, and stiff, wavy petticoats that fanned out like crinoline chande-liers, along with penguin suits and the head of a donkey.

The ballerinas, actors, singers, and dancers came to her for fittings. She bent and pinned, and tucked and pulled, until a woman rolled her eyes, or a man snorted, and then Ninyah would demand imperiously, "Do you want me to make a costume that fits, or would you like to look like a lumpkin? Now stand still, turn, bend over, and be quiet!" The female lead, the chorus girl, the boy dancer, the opera star—all would be silenced by her magisterial tone, and would turn, bend, kneel, whatever she wished.

From the time I could walk, she took me with her to Kingsbury Hall, where, in the catacomb basement underneath the stage and auditorium, she commanded closets of costumes, rooms stacked with bolts of mate-rial, dressing rooms, fitting rooms, and a long, wide room full of sewing machines, cutting tables, and a staff of sewing ladies.

For years I trailed along after her. I was taken under her ample wing and allowed to follow silently at her feet. I sat in a chair or on a stool, or slept on a soft couch in her office. I watched the ladies sew, especially a kind, quiet lady named Ruth, who had very thin glasses that kept falling down on her face. Ruth lifted her finger over and over again to push the glasses up, but her knee never stopped pressing the pedal that ran the machine. A feeder tube reached down from the body to the base. The feeder had thin silver arms, like fangs, that pressed the cloth down. I watched Ruth guide the lengths of material through the feeder. I feared the feeder would grab her fingers and eat them, and watched with fas-cination, a part of me hoping they would. But Ruth was too quick, es-caping every push at the last moment. She lifted her hand to push her glasses up. Her eyes never left the garment as she sewed.

"What're you staring at, little one?" she said, startling me, because how did she know I was looking?

"That's pretty material," I said, grasping for an answer.

She laughed. "This old brown tweed? You're a little kooky." That's what she and Blanche called me: Kooky Kathy. She gave me bumpy black licorice candies to suck on.

All the sewing ladies became my friends. To Myrtle and Marie, I was "Kathy, sweetie," and to Ethel and Pearl, "Hey, kid." Heads bent over their work, they sat pinning, cutting, and sewing. I thought of them then as lucky. They didn't work as secretaries or adding figures in columns like Mom did. They got to hold chiffon, silk, brocade, and chenille. Under their fingers material sprang to life, took shape, became flowing and winding, decorated and adorned. Wigs and masks and wings arose from their hands.

They laughed and told stories at lunchtime, and shared baloney sandwiches with me. They moved effortlessly through closets jammed with long rows of costumes of frogs and fairies, kings and queens, a bear, a scarecrow, a nutcracker, and tutus for the ballerinas. They talked about their children, sewing, or "things."

"We're talking about things, dear, so you shoo." But they wouldn't make me go. Instead, they lowered their voices and continued to chat.

I was already a good chain stitcher.

"This chain stitch is a useful stitch," Ninyah instructed. "See how you can grab the thread at the end of the whole long row of stitches you've made, yank it, and the whole chain of stitches unravels?" She tugged at the thread, and with one thrust of her arm, the two pieces of cloth she'd stitched together fell to the floor, floating away, not looking back. "We use this stitch because it has stretch, and flexibility. We can undo it to fit the costume to a different person."

I imagined using this wonderful stitch. I would chain stitch my dolls to each other, my sheets to my bed, my mother to me. And then, *voila!* If the sheets were dirty, if my dolls were mean, or if Mom yelled, I could just pull the string and I'd be free.

Years later I was delighted to recognize this ingenious stitch. It holds together bags of sugar, pet food, and bird food, and if you pick the right thread, you can pull the opening apart in one sweep of the arm.

"But," Ninyah warned, "the stitch isn't dependable or permanent. Don't use it for something you want to stay put. For that, you would use the lockstitch."

It was this magical chain stitch I loved, practicing it for the thrill of ripping it out with one yank. It bent; it yielded. I was the master. I could create it and then make it disappear. I practiced it for hours, unbinding the fabrics like a magician.

My audience loved me. "Look here, ladies," I announced to the sewing room at large. "I am the Colossal Kathy, and *this* is Stella the Stitch. Now you see her; now you don't." How they cheered. I used it at home and in my fantasies.

I wonder now whether Ninyah had some ulterior motive in teaching me the chain stitch, which she used in this world of make-believe. Maybe she just wanted to keep my little hands busy during the many hours I was in her care. Sometimes I waited for her in her large office, where she kept high, wide bookcases full of art books and magazines, pictures of paintings and costumes from all ages, and her voluminous sketchbooks full of her designs, in which I imagined myself on every page. When I was tired of leafing through them, or of ironing the costumes, or of separating the buttons by color and size into boxes, I practiced my chain stitches.

Probably Ninyah simply wanted me to learn how insubstantial the chain stitch was compared to the lockstitch, which is double strong and stays fast. It binds pieces of fabric together so tight that they are very difficult to separate—you must use a seam ripper to pry them apart.

Maybe she was teaching me something else. The lockstitch holds. But it requires trusting in the future, in the permanent nature of your creation.

———◆———

Mom's long descent accelerated when Mort left. She now had five children to raise by herself. She was angry and impatient. She started up again on her orange juice and vodkas, which I made for her regularly. Once, when I was younger, a man had come to our house to repair a bathroom leak. He rummaged in his tool chest, murmured a curse, and then said, "Can you get me a screwdriver, girl?"

"Yes, sir," I obliged. I went to the kitchen and made him a vodka and orange juice.

Now on 1st Avenue, home was once again a chaotic, unpredictable place. I never knew when Mom would be drunk or sober, electric angry or fresh-air sweet, in a furious rage or playing happily and singing at her now much-smaller piano. Ninyah seemed somehow to know when storms were gathering. All of a sudden, when Mom was raving or was sloppily depressed, Ninyah swept in, scooped me up, and carried me away. I was also old enough now that I could call her to come, which I did, and which she did.

She appeared like an avenging angel coming to save me. She swept through the front door without knocking. "Well, well, well, here you are, darling," she announced, as though I would be anywhere else. "Come along with me. I'm off to Kingsbury! Dress rehearsal, you know."

She addressed my mother thunderously. "Sereta!" Mother stilled her tirade or looked up from her weeping. "I'm taking Kathy." There was nothing to do but obey.

"Suit yourself," Mother said, snapping, or sullen and simmering.

Off I'd flee with Ninyah. I imagined I was escaping the brute in the dungeon or the snake crawling out from under the rock or the crouching panther. Gone was Mom slamming pots or threatening suicide—the scariness of it all. Off I'd fly with Ninyah to the magical world of music, song, theatre, and dance.

Before I was ten, Ninyah gave me small jobs to do at the costume department and paid me ten cents an hour. I hid the money from my mother, walked to the Tower Theatre, and watched *Creature from the Black Lagoon* for fourteen cents. I didn't pay tithing on my wages.

As best she could, Ninyah taught me to sew. I was a mediocre seamstress, however, lost in dreams of becoming an actress, or a writer, or both. I worked in her costume department for years on and off: after school, in the summers, whenever I had free time. Under her tutelage I learned the difference between silk and satin, the quality of different threads, and how to use attachments for the sewing machines. I learned what costumes were appropriate for what time periods, how to put stays in bustles and petticoats, and how to coordinate colors. Eventually I became a dresser to the stars, fetching their drinks, zipping them into their costumes during rushed costume changes, and enduring the verbal abuse of the prima donnas.

Ninyah companionably gave me lessons about sewing, or acting, or the politics of theatre. Before Baba died, I'd often spent overnights at Ninyah's house. When we lived in her basement, she would invite me up for tea-time, when she would tell me a story or teach me a morality lesson. One Saturday morning she sat in her parlor across the hall from the bedroom, writing letters at her large mahogany desk. Baba lit an early-morning fire for her there. I had stayed the night before, and this morning I sat on a tall-backed Victorian settee in front of the fireplace. Baba brought us tea and small sugar cookies.

That morning, she put down her pen and told me that the sewing machine had been one of the most important inventions ever. "A hundred years ago," she said, "a little tailor in France had been sewing all day by hand. That's how clothes were made back then." She let this sink in. "In the factory where he worked, he watched as the ladies looped their threads with hooked needles. *How fast they are!* he thought. *Hundreds of stitches a minute, almost as though they were machines!*" I thought about how long it took me to make a few stitches. My eyes widened.

"That little French tailor was a Mr. Thimonnier," she went on, pronouncing it in French. It sounded like "Mr. Tim Onay." "This Mr. Thimonnier had the idea of making a machine to do the stitching. 'Here it is!' he exclaimed when he was done. 'Let's show Napoleon, and he can use it to sew all the army uniforms.'" I could see hundreds of soldiers with their machines, stitching away at their uniforms. "That's how he invented the sewing machine."

She poured some tea into a delicate china cup, one with primroses and leaves and little scalloped edges. She squeezed lemon into it and dropped a cube of sugar in. With a silver filigreed spoon, she stirred. Then she handed it to me. "Have a biscuit, dear," she said when I had taken the cup. "Hold your cup properly. That's right." She laid one little cookie on a plate and set it on the table next to the couch.

"Well, Mr. Thimonnier liked to name his machines, like you name your dolls." Ninyah pulled up a straight-backed Victorian chair next to the fire and sat close to me. "He named his first machine Couseuse."

Over and over I said the name: "Coo-soos, Coo-soos."

She showed me a picture of a machine shaped like an owl. "The sewing machine was just one of the machines that have freed women from work," Ninyah concluded. "Now your mother doesn't have to work as hard as I had to."

I had never seen my mother sew a thing, fast or slow.

I watched as the ladies made the machines purr. There were several different kinds of machines. One had a hand wheel at the right of the needle, and Myrtle would turn the wheel to run the needle through the needle plate. Blanche operated her machine by pressing her knee against a pedal that hung down under. The sewing machines hummed and buzzed soothingly. Costumes grew from under their fingers and flowed onto the bodies of real people to make them into someone else: King Richard's humpback coat; Stella's satiny nightgown; the fat lady's skirt, which, in *The Nutcracker*, hid twenty children beneath its stays; and the best Mother Goose ever created!

———◆———

It was Sunday, and the costume room was abuzz. The entire sewing staff was working in preparation for opening night of a Shakespeare play. Ninyah no longer went to church, but she had picked me up after Sunday school and brought me with her to work. I was a junior seamstress. I was twelve.

Ninyah stood at her cutting table in the costume department at Kingsbury Hall, pinning a filmy paper pattern onto the long length of red brocade. I sat practicing a stitch on a tall stool Ninyah reserved for me at the end of her long table.

Her words came out muffled through a cluster of straight pins she held in her mouth. "Oo yoo ahnt oo be ih uh hlay, 'arling?"

I paused, interpreting. Ninyah often talked to me through pins, or while threading a needle, or when her teeth were engaged in snipping a thread, so it took me only a moment to decipher.

Did I want to be in a play? Was there any doubt? I had been in many plays, ever since I could walk. But always mute. This time I might be allowed to speak or sing. I might become famous.

"A play? Oh, Ninyah, yes!"

I sat breathless, waiting for Ninyah's answer.

Following the pinned pattern, Ninyah began to cut out the bodice of the Elizabethan gown she had designed. The garment took magical shape under her long high-knuckled fingers. Behind me, sewing machines hummed on the tables, which were lined up to the end of the room. The sewing ladies murmured together as they pushed cloth under the presser feet, guiding the pieces forward, not trusting that the feed dog would follow an exact line without their assistance.

Gray-haired Blanche had been humming, a habit that irritated flat-faced Myrtle, though I liked it. She often hummed tunes, and I tried to guess what they were.

"*Romeo and Juliet* by Tchaikovsky," I chirped.

"Um hmm," Blanche purred, her lips locked as she concentrated on maneuvering a thread through the eye of the needle. "What a talented girl you are." She started another tune and then lowered the note, seeming to search for just the right pitch. "How 'bout this one?" She thought she'd stump me this time.

But it was "Some Enchanted Evening" from the latest record Ninyah had bought me, and I knew it. Oh, I had her now! I was *that* clever. But before I had a chance to show off this talent, Ninyah had asked her question.

I heard and understood her invitation, even over the clickety-clack of the needles lockstitching the fabrics together, even over Blanche's humming, even over Marie and Myrtle's chattering back and forth. I stopped stitching. I didn't blink. My lips parted, and my legs tightened around the stool. "What play?"

Ninyah had used up her pins. "We're doing *South Pacific* this year for the Summer Festival," she said, carefully pressing the pattern to the cloth with her hand so as not to stick herself with the pins. "There's a part for a little girl in it."

She picked up her finely sharpened scissors, sliced through the slippery fabric with one swift clamp of fingers to palm, and moved quickly forward through the material. Shreds of unneeded fabric and pattern slipped to the floor as she pulled the bodice toward her in swift movements.

I lowered my sewing to my lap. "Would I get to talk and sing?" I asked, hardly daring to hope. When Ninyah didn't speak for a time, I realized it would just be another walk-on part. Disappointed, I felt a pressing down behind my nose, in back of my eyes, that awful, heavy cloud of hurt. Whenever this happened, I pretended there was a lost lake behind my eyes and that once the hurt emptied into it, the skies would turn blue again. I willed my disappointment into the deep, turbulent water, which spooled turquoise and silky warm like Bear Lake. Then it didn't hurt anymore, and the tears didn't come.

I breathed as quietly as I could. I stole a glance at Ninyah. She was quiet, concentrating on her cutting, so I picked up my stitching, afraid to ask again.

"Yes," she said, finally. "You'll sing a song with a little boy. And you'll have lines as well."

I was breathless with joy.

Ninyah took up the fabric she had cut, clipped the bodice on the skirt with a clothespin, and set them at the edge of the table. "Myrtle, here!" she commanded loudly.

Myrtle stopped what she was doing and came to get the pieces she would seam into a gown. "Got the sleeves yet, Mrs. Jones?"

"They'll be along," Ninyah said.

All the ladies got along pleasantly, so long as everything was on time and well made. The ladies adored my grandmother, and they told me so.

"But don't be handling that fabric with dirty hands, dear," Ruth would warn me. "Ooo-eee, no!" The ladies nodded knowingly at one another.

Ninyah took me to a tryout, where I read a script and sang a song. There was no one else at the audition except her friend, Dr. C. Lowell Lees, the director, known as Doc and beloved by the theatre department. "Well, let's see what you can do, honey," he said.

He gave me a couple of the lines to read. Simple lines, like "Papa, you're home!" and "Yes, Nellie," and "We will, Papa." I read the lines with great fervor. I paused meaningfully. I lowered my voice. I lifted it lyrically. I repeated the lines again to give different meaning and then again until Doc held up his hand.

"Excellent," he chuckled. "Well felt." He winked at Ninyah.

Then he asked me to sing something. I had practiced a song Baba taught me—"I'll Take You Home Again, Kathleen." I sang my heart out.

I sang out my happy heart that was with me all those days at Kingsbury Hall, when I sat at my perfect grandmother's side; my curious heart that followed her expectantly in and out of the sewing room and the auditoriums; and my writer's heart that rummaged down the long racks in the costume closets, fingering the material, breathing in the deep odor of wool and the light scent of silk, inventing stories. I sang out my frightened heart that escaped to the fabric storeroom, where I organized the bolts alphabetically by fiber and color, creating order and safety, and my astonished heart that carried me backstage, where I gazed transfixed at the looming light board, a long slanted board with handles that went up and down with hundreds of buttons to push in or pull out to change the way light played from darkness to glory. I sang out my yearning heart I held in the darkened auditorium, where I sat with Ninyah while she watched the costumes at work and made notes for the sewing ladies of what had to be altered or redone, and my envious heart with which I watched the actors on the stage as they altered life and relived it.

I sang as though my life depended on it. "I'll taaaaake you hoooooome agaaaaain, Kathleeeeen. To wherrrre your heart will feel no paaaain." I put all my passion into it. I lifted my arms, clasped my chest, and put the back of my hand to my forehead.

I sang for Ninyah and Baba; for my mean, crazy mother; for my father, who had abandoned me. I sang for a way out of my house, to be free from the noise and hurt, for my brothers' and sisters' escapes. And I sang for my Heavenly Father, to whom I promised eternal obedience if I could just win this part.

"Well, my goodness, honey," Doc said, chuckling and giving me a hug. "It's not *that* big a part."

It was. And I got it.

———————

I could never sew properly; I stopped working in the costume shop when I went to Alabama for ninth grade. But I never lost my love of the theatre. In high school, my beloved drama teacher replaced Sister Mallow as my mentor, and drama became my primary passion, though running away came in second.

I was in school plays, community plays, speech tournaments, and drama competitions. Of all the roles I played before and after high school, my most beloved was Anne in *The Diary of Anne Frank*, from which I took my mantra to believe in the basic goodness of all people.

For the next decade, I took on different roles in the ongoing U of U Summer Festival musicals and operas. When I wasn't a performer, or dressing the stars, or on stage crew, I sneaked out front, milled with the crowd, and strolled around among the audience, listening for praise. It was exhilarating for me both as a child and as a young adult.

I received tuition scholarships from theatre schools—Northwestern University, Pasadena Playhouse, and BYU—but I couldn't raise the money for living expenses. So I went to the University of Utah, living at home. Because I was Ninyah's granddaughter, other students believed I was favored. I wasn't. In fact, I landed few parts and became quite discouraged.

I received no encouragement from my mother. "Acting?" she scoffed. "Get a *real* job."

Desperate to get away from home, I married in 1965 at twenty-one and left Utah for Oregon. Portland State College had no drama department at the time. Although I continued to perform in community theatre, my dreams of becoming a professional actress faded. I had two sons; I became an English teacher.

I married with a chain stitch; it unraveled.

But I was lockstitched to Ninyah. I now own her mahogany desk. In a secret cubby I found a letter from Orson Welles inviting her to come to Hollywood to costume him in *Macbeth*.

What would I have done if she had gone?

———

Eric did not have the same love of theatre, so when he was using the car to visit his childhood haunts, I walked to Kingsbury Hall, where I found my tokens: a Playbill for the current show, a script someone had left on the light board backstage, and a thin strip of red silk I found on the floor in the basement.

In the lobby of this great building, and in the lobbies of the new Pioneer Memorial and Babcock Theatres, hung ornate, gold-framed, bigger-than-life oil portraits of all the greats of the University of Utah theatre department during the 1950s: Maurice Abravanel, conductor; C. Lowell Lees, director; William Christensen, ballet choreographer. Similar portraits and photographs on the wall memorialized other fine teachers and directors.

There was no portrait or photograph of my grandmother.

I imagined I heard my mother's voice. "Of course not." She lingered over the end of her cigarette and then stubbed it out. "She was a woman."

CHAPTER 20

IRONING

———◆———

WHEN I WAS THIRTEEN, I started Kathy's Klassy Ironing Service, which became a thriving business. I advertised in the newspaper, placed flyers in mailboxes, and posted notices on apartment doors. I charged thirty-five cents an hour, giving 10 percent of my earnings for tithing and most of the rest to Mom for food.

Even though the neighborhood was poor, I garnered plenty of local customers. Folks who seemed to have nothing else to be proud of sent out their ironing. I collected bags of clothes, worked my magic on them, and then piled the neatly pressed and folded garments into a plastic clothesbasket or the customer's pillowcase, and delivered them back. Not just clothes, though—sometimes even sheets, socks, and rags.

If I thought there'd be a problem with getting paid, Mom drove me to deliver the finished ironing, and the customer paid up when they saw her. Mostly, however, I pulled the clothes back and forth in Clark's red wagon. I rigged a pole to the wagon and hung the shirts and dresses on it. When the wagon was loaded, the wheels wobbled lazily, trying to follow in a straight line as I walked from house to house, first up toward Federal Heights, where the richer folks lived, and then farther down the Avenues.

Mom bragged about me to all her friends, and I basked in her praise. "Kathy's the world's best ironer," she said. And I was. I still am. For years, not realizing how neurotic it was, I ironed everything, even my underpants and jeans.

My father had been gone three years by this time. I could still see him standing in the hallway the night he left, when he said good-bye. The brown leather belt he'd used to strap me with was wrapped around his old suitcase to hold it shut. I wished he would stay. I sat on the floor and wouldn't look at him, just ran my fingers over that rough, frayed belt. I felt lost—dead, really. He knelt down and wrapped his arms around me. His face came close to mine, and his aftershave lotion smelled sweet and spicy.

"Don't you touch her." Mom came up from behind. "Get out."

One of my regular customers was Mabel Jensen, five houses up across 1st Avenue. She had six children, all under ten, and no husband, so she gave me lots to do. The clothes were thin threaded and bare, requiring careful ironing. Some people in Salt Lake City were disapproving about single mothers, but I never held that against her. My mom was divorced, too.

Sometimes Mabel's basket was filled with dirty clothes, so I had to wash them before I could iron them. I didn't mind, because I got sick on the smell of ironing dirty clothes—an acrid smell, or sweet like rotting fruit. I enjoyed turning a basket of disheveled clothes into a basket of clean, neatly pressed, fresh-smelling little girls' dresses, little boys' summer shirts, and pillowcases. Sheets, too—but only hers, the doubles.

One week I found a man's long-sleeve white shirt in Mabel's basket. Surprised, I pulled it out and held it up to the light. Sunlight shone through the cloth. I pressed the fabric to my cheek. It was linen! The embossed tag set out the washing and ironing instructions in fine script. The shirt was tightly woven; strong silk thread secured the whalebone buttons, and the seams were double stitched. A stiff strip of heavier material between the collar and the yoke straightened the collar. Such a shirt!

Daddy had several such shirts that he wore only to the office and to fancy parties. He was the most handsome of all the lawyers and clerks. Once, when Mom was in a pout, Daddy took me instead to a fancy dinner and introduced me as his "darlin' Kathy." Men bent over and shook my hand; wives murmured, "Aren't you sweet?" Given how Mom didn't like Daddy, I was surprised that everyone at the party did.

"Excellent job today, Hank." A large man slapped him on the back. "When're you going to open your own practice and put this clerk stuff behind you?"

He didn't succeed at private practice, not in Salt Lake City, where Baba, Ninyah and Mom berated his incompetence. But when he returned to Alabama, he became an assistant attorney general and then a well-respected labor lawyer with his own law firm.

I turned the man's shirt over in my hands and lifted the sleeves to peer at the underarms. Not a single stain on any inch of the shirt, even under the arms. A man's shirt usually smells sweet when the hot iron presses nearly invisible markings of old embedded perspiration, yet this shirt smelled fresh as a lily.

Daddy hardly sweated at all, even at Saltair, where we wrestled or played ball on the beach of the Great Salt Lake in the hot sun. And when he mowed the lawn, no sweat then, either; I walked behind him, raking up the grass. In fact, Daddy had very little hair under his arms or on his chest. He would say, "Beware of men who have too much hair on their chests; they are half-wolf!" When I noticed hair coming in under Sandy's arms and on the special hill by her cave, I asked her whether she was half-wolf. She slammed the bathroom door in my face, yelling, "Don't you know anything, creep? Now scram."

"I know more than you think," I yelled back, thinking about Daddy and Laird Avenue. But it was true; I didn't know girls got hair, too. In fact, I was not precisely certain of how women got pregnant. There was no comprehensive sex education in the schools in the fifties, and there was certainly none through the Church. Or at home—not in a responsible way.

Given what happened later that year, it was fortunate I didn't get pregnant.

I held, and then stroked, Mabel's man's luxurious shirt. I wrapped the arms of the shirt around my neck. I pressed the broad front of it tight to my chest, held one sleeve out in my hand, and danced with the shirt.

It took me a whole wondrous hour to iron the shirt. A shirt like that must be ironed in a quite particular way. I spread a clean towel on the kitchen table. I placed the shirt on the towel, smoothing the arms straight down to each side. I sprinkled clean water over the shirt, on the neck, the chest, and down the arms, and then I sprayed the shirt with a starch that smelled like overripe cherries, more heavily at the collar because a stiff collar adorns the neck and calls attention to the face.

I folded both sleeves in over the chest. Then I folded the shirt in half, lengthwise, arms inside. I caressed this rectangle down with my hands, stroking it until it was free of wrinkles. Then I rolled it up from the bottom to the top in a tight little tube, damp between my hands. Next, I squeezed the tube lightly in my hands—squeeze and release, squeeze and release—to press the damp into itself, to wet the shirt all over. For a while, I stood with the tube in my hands, my mind drifting, staring out the kitchen window at the weedy backyard.

Daddy had loved linen. I had to be very careful when I ironed his shirts. "Linen is a dangerous cloth," Mom said, and it is. Easy to scorch, it must be ironed at just the right temperature.

Daddy used to watch me iron. He chuckled, "Little miss, you should be a judge—you have a fine judicial *temperature*, not too hot, not too cold." He laughed. I blushed with pride. "And you should be a writer. You're so good at *irony*." He liked his own jokes, though I didn't always understand them.

Linen shirts must be stretched out so that the iron glides over the threads, slipping back and forth with just the right amount of heat to leave the texture smooth and alive, almost glossy with the pleasure of the press. Too hot will blister.

Daddy said, "Love's like that, too."

Mom just waved her hands in the air. "You fill that girl's head."

I preened. "See here, Daddy, when you iron the sleeve, you must make a pure, crisp crease from shoulder to cuff."

"A straight line to God," he agreed.

Mom pooh-poohed Daddy's idea of God and Heaven. When I came home from church on Sundays, he would lift me up into his lap and say, "You are on the right hand of God."

He taught me Baptist hymns we sang before bedtime. "God of Earth and Outer Space" was my favorite, though Mom hated it. To further irritate her, he broke into "Jesus Showed His Nail-Scarred Hands."

She hissed at him, "Hank, sing something pleasant!"

Dad whispered to me, "Well, He did, didn't He?"

I wasn't sure about Mabel's man, but Daddy liked to get out of his suit coat as soon as possible. When he got home from work, he would be so eager to play catch, he didn't even hang up his jacket. He just tossed it over the back of the chair.

"Henry!" Mom yelled. "Who do you think I am, your servant?"

But we were long gone to the backyard. At dusk, he carried me in on his back, my nose buried in the earthy smell of his starched shirt collar. The shirt was mussed and sometimes dirty from play, but he didn't mind.

I imagined Mabel's man playing with her boys in just such a way. Maybe he would let me play, too, once he realized what a splendid ironer I was. He would notice the back of the shirt and exclaim, "Why, this pleat is exactly one inch wide the entire length, my girl." I wouldn't reveal the secret: I cut a cardboard strip one inch wide and folded it in the pleat before I pressed it beneath the hissing iron.

Ironing a shirt is usually easy enough. But ironing *this* shirt was a sorrowful thing. My father took all his white shirts with him when he left. I searched the house in vain, looking for one to wear or to keep under my pillow.

The hardest part of ironing Mabel's man's shirt was moving the iron back and forth over the front panels, deftly slipping the tip between the whalebone buttons. I remembered how I lay beside Daddy sometimes; how I rested my cheek on his chest; how I heard his heart beat so strong and steady, so fast sometimes; how his arm had curled around me, holding me peacefully, so I could sleep; how he had taught me about my own little buttons; how he had told me I was special and that he would never leave me.

I was careful not to cry on the shirt. Tears are not pure. They stain.

I slept with the ironed shirt hanging on my bedpost. It rained that night, so the next morning, after breakfast, I scotch-taped four long sheets of waxed paper together, front and back, and laid the shirt down inside them. The shirt was fully protected. Only the curved handle of the hanger poked out. As I loaded the basket of clothes into my red wagon, I felt stuffed up and gloomy. I fixed the shirt on the bar, pulled the waxed paper taut, and centered the shirt on the pole, making sure it wouldn't fall. I set off for Mabel Jensen's house with my umbrella. Despite the drizzling rain, I dawdled, tapping my boot in shallow puddles, looking for cross plugs and cracks in the sidewalks. Too soon, I was approaching her front yard.

Then suddenly I had an idea. Maybe Mabel's fella was living there, a new father to the children. Maybe she would introduce me. Maybe I could iron his shirt again.

I unhooked the shirt and raced up the steps. Ralph opened the door and retrieved the basket, lugging it in for me. "Ma" he called out, "Kathy's here." He turned to me, eyes disgusted. "Drunk," he muttered, and slammed out the front door.

"Don't bang the fucking door," Mabel yelled, stumbling in from the kitchen. She ran her hand through her hair. "Hi, Kathy." She fumbled through her purse. Things fell out. "Well, I don't know where I put the damn wallet," she said. "I'll have to pay you later, OK?"

"I guess so," I said. I was suddenly afraid. "Shall I just keep the shirt until then?" I couldn't leave it with her.

"What shirt?"

"This one. This man's shirt." I held it out, sorry to give it away.

She came at me, grabbed the hanger, and tore at the waxed paper. The shirt fell to the floor. I gasped, reached for it. She pushed me away, scooped it up.

"Where the hell did you get this?"

"It was in the ironing basket." The stuffing in my chest was on fire.

She tore at the paper until it came completely off. She grabbed the shirt off the hanger. Then she did the unthinkable! She twisted it like a rope, grunting, her voice a low scowl. "You told anyone about this?"

"No. Why would I tell anyone? What's the matter?"

"Well, don't you tell anyone, you hear? This was all a mistake."

"Yes, ma'am. I mean, no, ma'am."

As she slapped the shirt against the table, it caught on the metal trim and ripped. She sat down, and her head fell to her arms. I couldn't move.

She lifted her head. "Get out. I'll pay you tomorrow."

I ran from the house.

When I told Mom what happened, she told me not to worry about it. "It was just a shirt," she said.

I didn't go back for my money.

———◆———

Eric had wanted to use the car the next morning to visit his old school and to look for some documents at the University of Utah library. I had arranged to meet him at Makoff's tearoom, where Ninyah had taken me many times so long as I behaved appropriately, removing my white gloves daintily and sipping my tea with my little finger crooked. I picked a table in the corner, away from the crowd.

I planned to tell him about Laird Avenue and the beginning of my first terrible secret. But he bolted into the tearoom in a wave of excitement.

"What a morning, I've had, Sis!" he gushed. He was so ebullient, his joy was infectious.

I laughed. "Tell me."

He had been to the University of Utah campus, where he relived giddy memories of his days as a journalism major and as editor of the university newspaper. He had been wildly successful in college: academically superior, well liked, and exceptionally creative in the communications department.

He had not lived at home.

"I looked for a record of Dad's patent on Seal-Tight wax," he said. "I couldn't find it. But Professor Blanchard is still there, and he remembered when Mort set up the factory and what a big deal it was for Salt Lake City. And I saw Rob, my old KSL-TV mentor. He and I had coffee and talked about my early newspaper stories." He smiled and added, "And our exploits." His colleagues had not been surprised to learn that Eric had become a well-regarded investigative journalist and a TV technical creator.

Eric looked at me, smiling proudly. "I became an inventor, didn't I?" he said. "Like my father."

He babbled happily on. I kept quiet. The moment for my confession had passed.

It was easy to fall back into silence. We children had learned to keep secrets about our mother's alcoholism, about our tawdry home life, about our poverty. Silence had kept us safe from harm. The habit was deeply ingrained.

After lunch, Eric drove to the library building, and I walked to ZCMI to shop for the tokens I'd decided upon.

I bought a small travel iron.

Then I moved through the store to the men's department. In accessories, I fingered a man's leather belt. A saleslady approached me and asked whether she could help.

"For your father, is it?" she asked. I nodded.

"I'm really not sure of his size," I said.

She unhooked several belts and held them up to me. "Is he slim or stocky?" she asked.

"Well, he's very handsome," I said, catching the irrelevance. "Let's see, a bit stocky, muscular." I felt an ache in my throat and hurried on. "Rather short, for a man. Like me." I laughed, nervously. "He gave me his short stature."

She laughed and said gently, "I'm sure he gave you much more than that, dear."

She put her hand on my arm and smiled. "Let's see. This one has more holes than the others. It will likely fit. What do you think?"

It was brown. I bought it.

CHAPTER 21

BIRMINGHAM

———

ERIC DROVE ME TO THE 1st Avenue house and dropped me off across the street, in front of the old apartment building in which several of my ironing-service clients had lived.

The house was for sale, empty. I walked up the front-porch steps and peered in. I looked through the living-room window and the open hallway to the kitchen, where I had set up my ironing board and labored into the night. I felt faint. I turned my back to the window and slid to sit. There was so much more to remember.

Alabama.

Shortly after my father left and returned to Alabama, I flew to Birmingham for a week-long visit. Mom insisted that I stay with an aunt while I was there. I like to think she was protecting me.

It was a happy, uneventful visit. I have a photograph of my father and me sitting by the side of a swimming pool, his arm around me. He also arranged for the newspaper to take a photo of me getting on the plane to go home, a smiling, waving, brave little nine-year-old girl flying for the first time—clear across the country, alone.

During the next three years, Daddy called us children sporadically. He didn't pay child support, as Mom complained, but he sent gifts. After Mort left, he and my mother talked on the phone every time he called; sometimes they talked into the night.

When I was thirteen, Daddy came to visit us. He had remarried and had a stepson, Stewart, almost my age, and a new son, Brad, now three. Even so, during the visit, my parents fell in love again.

At that age, I didn't question how this had happened, or appreciate how inappropriate it was. Now I realize it was a sign of how self-absorbed, even selfish, both my parents were, willing to disrupt my father's new family, as my mother had been willing to disrupt Mort's before that. I marveled that I had no fears, no doubts. Only hope.

"I'll be divorcing Margaret and remarrying your mother," he told me. I was giddy with happiness and expectation. Our family would be together again. No more single mother. No more stepfathers.

But it didn't happen. The days went by, and winter stumbled into spring. Mom watched the mail, listened for the phone, drank more, and sat at night by the piano playing furious tunes—tarantellas and marches. One night, wakened by faint sobs, I crept to the door of Mom's bedroom.

I heard her on the phone. "But you promised." She was crying. "That's what you say now…Since when?" I couldn't make sense of the conversation, hearing only one side of it. "Never mind, Hank, just forget it," she said, slamming down the receiver. Then, silence. I crept back to my room.

The next morning, Mom went on a tirade, breaking everything breakable in the living room, throwing vases and ashtrays, figurines and glasses. We knew to get out of her way and scattered. I hid in my room, anxious for Sandy, Lucy, and the boys. Where were they? Were they safe? Would Mom come after us too, break us like dolls?

I was furious, too—at Mom. She must have done something wrong, something to scare Daddy away again. It was her fault, and I made her pay. I was rude and sassy one day, sullen and sulky the next. I made mistakes in the cooking, was late with her morning coffee, scorched her blouses. As the awful weeks went on, my grades fell.

I was in the eighth grade at Bryant Junior High School. One day I decided that I didn't want to take the prealgebra test, so I coerced my friend Dwayne into helping me call in a bomb scare. I stood in the phone booth outside the principal's office, put in my coin, and called. Dwayne stood watch at the office door to see who picked up the phone.

"Bryant Junior High School," the receptionist, Abby, chirped.

Dwayne nodded at me and raised his hand in an OK. She was listening, all right.

"Yes, well, I'm calling to warn you that someone has planted a bomb in the school." I lowered my voice to create the impression I was a man.

Dwayne gave me a thumbs-up. She was taking this seriously. I could imagine her face, twisted by fear. "Is that right?" Abby said. I heard alarm in her voice.

"Yes," I grunted. "So you'd better make all the kids go outside, or they'll get blown up."

Dwayne was looking at Abby and then looking at me, giving me the go-ahead signs. I could tell from his face that this was going well.

"This is quite serious," said Abby. "Will you just hold on while I get the principal?"

"Sure. Thanks," I said. "You won't be sorry."

I gave a thumbs-up back at Dwayne, and he smiled. Then, abruptly, he turned and ran down the hall. This was puzzling, but I decided it was good news. It must mean Abby was shooing all the kids out of the office.

Suddenly, Abby appeared at the phone-booth door. She pushed it open. "Well, what have we here?" She took the receiver from my hand, hung it back on the hook, and said, "Come with me, little lady."

I was expelled, which was not good news, because this was not my first expulsion. I had been expelled from first grade at Uintah Elementary for kicking. I was then expelled from Wasatch Elementary for throwing Al Binney over a railing and breaking his nose. I was ultimately expelled from Rowland Hall–St. Marks for many infractions, lastly for insulting the principal, Mrs. Core, by calling her a "dirty rotten old apple core" at an assembly, in front of everyone.

There was nowhere else for me to go to school.

Mom showed her usual contempt, which, by now, I was steeled against. "You're nothing but a troublemaker." And "You never do anything but cause me pain." And "I'm at the end of my rope with you." She added a new one: "You are completely unlovable."

I was stung.

"Yeah, is that so?" I retorted. "Well, let's ask Daddy how lovable *you* are."

———•———

I am ashamed when I recall that crack. As a judge, I feel great sympathy for the children of quarreling parents. What I've only learned slowly, however, is that children do damage to their parents as well, with their cruel jibes, insults, and nasty accusations, flung out from unresolved pain and hidden truths.

"How sharper than a serpent's tooth," Shakespeare wrote of a thankless child. How true of a child's defensive, but poisonous, bite.

———•———

My mother's shoulders fell, her stunned eyes went blank from shock, and her lips parted. I saw that I had hit my mark. And I was glad.

"Fine," she said, not with vitriol but with sorrow and bitterness. Her voice barely audible, she said, "Fine. Go live with your father, if you think he's so great."

———•———

That summer of 1958, when I turned fourteen, I took the train by myself to Birmingham to live with Daddy and his wife, Margaret, her thirteen-year-old son, Stewart, and their four-year-old son, Brad. I believed I would find a new and more wonderful family.

Coming into Chicago, the train passed rows and rows of falling-down wooden shacks in which colored people lived. Black men sat on tilted porches, puffing on cigars. In dirt yards, black women hung tattered clothes on lines strung from dead trees to sagging roof arches.

Scruffy black children, clothes torn and dirty, lined the railroad tracks, waving at the train, looking up with smiling faces.

These were not the African American people my mother extolled. She never spoke of the finishing school she attended in New York. Rather, she enthused about Ethel Waters singing "Suppertime" on Broadway; she sang songs from *Porgy and Bess*, which she had seen when it opened in New York in 1935; and she enthused about Lena Horne, who had performed with Cab Calloway's band at the Cotton Club in Harlem. She told me that a dignified black man had written a song called "I'm Just Wild about Henry," which she sang to my father in a Southern accent to irritate him.

"It's 'Harry,'" Daddy would grumble.

My Church had taught me well: black people were marked by the color of their skin so that we could identify these premortal cowards who had sided with Lucifer in the Prelife. And Daddy taught me his Baptist belief that dark sin was the mark of murderous Cain and that coloreds were being punished for the sins of their fathers.

Mom felt differently. "What do you suppose Jesus thinks about all this prejudice?" she challenged.

When Ninyah arrived to pick me up one evening, Mom was playing swing music.

"Why are you bringing that jungle music into this house?" Ninyah asked irritably.

"Look here, Mother," Mom snapped. "See these keys?" She pointed at the piano. "Black and white."

I was scornful of my mother, so I accepted the racism of my father and grandparents instead. It made sense to me as a religious construct. But I thought we shouldn't be so mean to people we didn't have to live with, people who were already suffering and paying for what I believed had been their premortal choices.

"That's just another form of prejudice," Mom said.

The African Americans I saw in those Chicago slums seemed to confirm my grandparents' racist views. In my train seat I sat riveted, afraid the train might stop and I might be required to disembark and stand among the people called "niggers" and "coons." I was afraid for my safety. Yet another part of me felt daring, tempted to meet these forbidden people. They were exotic to me, and the possibility of a new adventure gave me a small thrill of excitement.

I would make no black friends in Alabama, however.

I realize now that I had moved from my racist Church and my racist city to live in the racist South with my father's racist family. Schools were segregated. Drinking fountains were for "Whites Only" and "Coloreds Only." White children rode to school in the front of the bus, blacks in the back. I didn't question it then. My transition in this regard was smooth as butter.

———◆———

My new family was not what I had hoped for. My stepmother, Margaret, was a dark-haired Southern beauty who had all of the arrogance and hauteur of a Southern belle. Her anger was as violent as Mom's, and her disappointment in my father as virulent and vocal. My half brother Brad had coal-black hair and thick lashes to match; he was as handsome as Daddy and as even tempered. I took to Brad immediately, but not to my stepbrother, Stewart, who didn't take to me, either.

Margaret doted on Stewart, who was aloof and odd. He was skinny, soft skinned, and full hipped, a beautiful boy. Lovely long eyelashes, thick and dark, shaded his cedar-brown eyes, which were flecked with gold. I saw him pinch his cheeks until his pale face took on a pink hue. Margaret manicured his fingernails for him and was teaching him how to pluck his eyebrows. Circling like silent ships in a night sea, he and I rarely spoke to or acknowledged each other. He stuck close to Margaret.

Daddy fixed up the back porch as my bedroom. He installed a wall heater, built me a solid bed with a drawer in the bottom, and hung black-and-yellow plaid curtains over the row of windows looking out to the yard. Beulah, the cleaning girl, had to walk through my room and out the porch door to hang the wash in the backyard. The porch itself was an add-on, so the bathroom window looked out into my bedroom.

Daddy placed a hollow door on sawhorses to serve as my desk. When I stood beside my desk, I could see into the bathroom, so Daddy hung a shade in there. But Stewart never pulled the shade down. He knew that I watched him as he stood at the sink and plucked his eyebrows. Once I watched him apply lipstick. He turned toward me, rubbed his lips together, and then came to the window and kissed it. For weeks, no one removed the red press of his lips from the glass.

My arrival seemed to cause no stir in the ongoing life of my father's new family. Margaret nagged Daddy, just as Mom had. Daddy answered her braying with the same silence or muffled replies. Sometimes she yelled and went on tirades, just like Mom. Stewart ignored me. Daddy was happy to have me there, I could tell, but I was disappointed in his new family.

Still, I was impervious. By now I had learned how to disappear. I went for long walks. I listened to music in my room: "All I have to do is dream, catch a falling star." I wrote adolescent love poems in my journal: "Oh, darling, the wind whispers your name / For you I forego fortune and fame," and the like. And I read. Brad climbed in my lap and I read to him—his books, and stories I wrote just for him, in which he was the hero.

I entered Homewood Junior High School, where no one knew me, no one knew I was a troublemaker and a sinner, and no one even knew I was a Mormon. I felt like I had a new start, an opportunity to make friends, be a scholar, and be loved.

"This is your chance, little darlin'," Daddy agreed. "You will create a whole new you."

———

One night, Daddy and Margaret had a vicious row. Margaret was screaming and throwing things. I heard Daddy yelling, which alarmed me.

Then I heard him crying, which unnerved me. I could feel Margaret sizzle. The noise was worse than any exploding I'd heard at Mom's houses. I imagined I saw Hell. The Devil was shrieking at the Lord in a death fight for the right to the earth's souls. I was riveted at my desk, listening. Where were the boys? Were they safe?

Brad came first into my bedroom, carrying his blanket. He pulled my cracked door open and padded softly to my side.

I hopped up on the bed, took him onto my lap, and began to tell him the story of the Mormon Saints, a story he loved to hear. He asked no questions. Somehow he knew that what was happening outside my room was big, bigger than anything that had happened before.

So big that Stewart, too, came into my room. He walked in, didn't say a word, and acted like nothing was wrong. "Whatcha doin'?" he asked nonchalantly. "Well, I might as well hop up there with you guys."

We three sat there together, stuffed animals pulled into our chests, my yellow quilt tucked around us. Listening. Stewart leaned over and pulled the quilt up over Brad's shoulders. I gave Brad my favorite rabbit; he sucked his thumb. Stewart scooted closer, and I put my hand on his and squeezed it.

Stewart's and my first and only camaraderie began and ended in that night's war, that turbulent, cacophonous battle between Daddy and Margaret that went on and on, relentless. We didn't have the maturity to recognize yet that we were border states about to separate into sides: one for secession and one for union.

As the fighting escalated, Stewart said, "Let's sing camp songs." We sang to Brad: "Shadows fall o'er the earth, darkness falls anew," to the tune from Dvořák's *New World Symphony,* a camp song both Stewart and I knew from his Baptist and my Mormon camps. Brad stared ahead and said nothing. The noise did not abate, so we moved on to "Ninety-Nine Bottles of Beer" and "The Worms Crawl In, the Worms Crawl Out"— more frivolous and louder.

The door flew open. Margaret hurled her fury into the room. "What the hell are you boys doing in Kathy's bedroom? Get out of here." She grabbed Brad by the arm, yanked him free of the blanket, and jerked the rabbit from his hand, tossing it to the floor. Still holding Brad, she went for Stewart. His leg buckled as she pulled him from the bed. "What the fuck are you all doing back here like a bunch of cowering shits," she accused, dragging him harshly to the floor. "Haven't you ever heard fighting before? Get up." She pushed him toward the door.

She turned back to me. "And you, you little bitch, I've had it with you, do you understand?" Her spit sprayed. "'Kathy this' and 'Kathy that.' Do you understand?"

"What did *I* do?" I yelled defiantly, my fright taking voice. "Where's Daddy?"

"You want your daddy?" she sneered, her lips lifting over her teeth. "That fucking limp-dicked asshole of a bastard who can't make a living or screw his wife? Him?"

Daddy came thundering in through the door and smacked Margaret on the back of the head. I was shocked. When Margaret stumbled, she dropped Brad; his head cracked on the floor. Stewart scrabbled forward to cover him with his own body.

"Don't you talk like that in front of these children!" Daddy commanded.

"Ha!" Margaret whipped herself up and slapped Daddy's face. "You're useless."

Daddy grabbed her hands, clamped them together, and spoke right into her face in a low, trembling voice: "You're not exactly a woman to make a man useful, Margaret."

There was a momentous silence. Margaret pulled her hands free, stood erect and rigid, and glared at Daddy. Stewart shot up and grabbed her around the waist. "Momma, stop!" She put her arms around him. Brad grabbed her ankles and held on. He wasn't making a sound.

"Well, sir, we'll see about that, won't we?" Margaret snorted. She took Stewart's arms from around her waist, leaned down, and picked up Brad. "Let's go to bed, boys," she said. "Good night, Henry." The door slammed.

Daddy stood for a moment and then walked toward the bed and sat down by me. He put his hand on my head, letting it rest there for a while. Then he climbed up on the bed with me and curled his legs up under him. He pulled me in close and covered us with the quilt. My ears felt the nub of his pajamas—flannel, white like snow, covered with little blue stars, my Christmas present to him last year. When Daddy laid his cheek on my head, his slow tears felt like warm puddles in my hair. We sat there for a long time. His heart beat out; I finally buried my head in his lap.

From Stewart's room, through the wall, I heard Margaret's high-ringing laughter, then conversation, and then low murmurings. I heard low moans and soft whimpering. I heard a drawn-out cry. I heard quiet, soothing words. Then I heard silence. The noises, and then the lack of them, felt strange and ominous. I thought it all beyond understanding.

I didn't sleep, and neither did Daddy. We sat on the bed all night. Morning light shone through my yellow and black plaid curtains. I counted the threads as they wove back and forth through the cloth. As the room drew light, I looked into the shadows on the ceiling and fol-lowed them down the walls. I looked up to see Daddy's eyes, staring ahead, unseeing, deep as a bog, musty and dark.

From then on, Margaret and Daddy rarely spoke. Stewart didn't speak to me again. He mostly walked around with his head down; at other times he held himself up, arrogantly, as though daring me to say something. I ignored him. I had no stepbrother. He was a cipher, meaningless.

Margaret moved into the boys' room, moving Brad out. She con-verted the hall closet into a bed nook for him, which he and I decorated. We pinned up his Disney poster, put his teddy-bear sheets on his foam pad, and hung his toothpick mobile from the iron rod. Everyone talked to Brad. He was the demilitarized zone.

Margaret slept in Stewart's room, in Stewart's bed, with Stewart. The door was always locked. I know now that the sounds I heard were the sounds of sex. She continued to sleep with her son for the rest of the year that I remained in Alabama. Brad slept in his hall cubby, never in the room with his mother and half brother.

When I look back now, I am stunned that the family just seemed to accept this arrangement. Margaret and my father must have discussed it, must have argued about it. But I heard nothing. No one asked questions. No one tried to save Stewart. I never spoke of it to anyone, though I knew it was unusual and against my Church principles. I didn't like either Margaret or Stewart, so I ignored it, pretended it wasn't there. We went about our lives as though this incest was acceptable. Our maid, Beulah, once asked Margaret whether she should put Margaret's ironed dresses in Stewart's closet. Margaret told her, "Mind your own beeswax, girl!"

I didn't want to sleep in my back-porch room anymore, so Daddy let me sleep on the couch in the dining room, just a few steps from his bedroom door. Each night he stayed up until Margaret had gone to bed, and then he came to sit by me on the couch. He stroked my head and sang to me: "I believe for every drop of rain that falls, a flower grows." He kissed me on the head, then the cheek, and then one night, on my lips. "Good night, sweetheart," he said, and then he was gone.

I must have known what was going to happen. I had learned, though I don't recall how, that these things do happen, but I had not imagined they would happen to me. Not to me, because I loved my father and my father loved me. And so whatever happened, it couldn't be like what happened to other girls, who didn't understand their fathers, whose fathers were drunks and screamers who never spent time with them, teaching them about the stars, singing them songs about hope and faith, and helping them with their homework.

I am sure now that Margaret's rejection of my father, her incestuous relationship with her son, and the silence and inaction in which we all conspired made my father's actions more possible and, in an odd, deconstructed way, more palatable to me. He was protecting me. Somehow.

CHAPTER 22

FOR EVERYONE WHO GOES ASTRAY

———◆———

IN OUR MORMON CHURCH CLASSES for teenagers, I had been taught what the Gospel required of me: chastity and clean thoughts. Purity of mind and body. I could not date a boy steadily until I was sixteen. Even at sixteen, I could not hold his hand, because handholding led to kissing, and I could not kiss until I married. I could not let anyone touch my private parts, even through my clothes. That was evil.

If I let it happen, I was to repent.

But I thought then that Daddy was different. As I lay on the couch that night in Alabama, his lips on mine, I was confused. As he whispered good night, I bit my lip. But I didn't push him away. After all, he was the person who loved me best and always had. He had already taught me about my buttons and my cave, and I had accepted his lesson.

I began to fade out, drifting into a dreamlike state. If ever he kissed me on the lips again, if he touched me in my cave, if anything happened like that, then I was sure he would make it be OK that something like that was happening to me, his little girl, his favorite daughter.

When I think of those moments, I realize I had retreated into an imagined place, where I calmed my fear and trepidation, allayed my suspicions of betrayal, and reconciled myself to my father's behavior. Counselors assume that he had been preparing me all along for this night, a process called grooming.

For years, I didn't believe it. I believed he'd loved me, had parented me well, legitimately gained my trust, and that what happened developed logically and organically in that fraught household. I think that was why I allowed it to continue for the rest of the year.

I trusted my father unequivocally. In all of the court cases of familial sexual abuse over which I presided, the child's trust was the common denominator. A betrayal of that trust was the lit fuse, the detonator that sets off the explosion in the child's life.

But what confuses me still is how to assess the damage. Is it a bomb, wiping out landscapes and lives? Or is it a firecracker, confined to a damaged space that can be restructured and repaired? Or is it a sparkler, a splashing flash of light?

———

One night, in Birmingham, I was lying on the couch reading Norah Lofts's *The Town House*. I remember the book now as a book not just about a house, though I loved houses, but about a family, a close and loving family, because that's what all the books I read that year became. The Nancy Drew books, *Gone with the Wind, Great Expectations,* and research books on great men of the South—I turned them all into books about houses and families who lived together in harmony in those houses. I disappeared into the stories, the characters, and read hour after hour, during all of my spare time.

"Do something around this goddamned house," Margaret growled at me. "All you ever do is read!"

"Make me," I challenged, not willing to endure the same abuse Mom had meted out. I had Daddy again. "I'll tell Daddy," I taunted.

She threw things at me, sometimes not to hit me but to scare me and to try unsuccessfully to upset Daddy, who would just say, "Now, Margaret." He gave me a key to his closet, and I closed myself in to protect myself. She threw a stick of butter at me, which missed and hit the wall. She left it, and then ordered Daddy to clean it off, but he let it stay. Beulah, who had begun to roll her eyes at the goings-on in our house, was ordered to leave it as well. Leery of Margaret's rage, she did. It dripped down the wall in the heat, dried in a crust, and stained the wall for good.

Her abuse worsened. She threw a pot of boiling potatoes that hit the couch where I sat. Daddy and I cleaned it all up, and set the cushions outside to dry, so I could continue to sleep there. She clipped buttons off of my skirts; Daddy sewed on new buttons. She sang, or chattered, to interrupt my reading, sometimes cutting pages out of my books before I got to them. Life became a nightmare from which I found comfort in my father's arms.

Daddy never complained about my reading. He brought law books home for me to read. "Read this case and tell me what you think," he suggested. So I read the Alabama Supreme Court cases and gave him my opinions. "Hmmm," he always said, "I'll have to think about that." He brought home a copy of the *Plessy v. Ferguson* case that made "separate but equal" the law of the land to emphasize his support of segregation. But I knew from my friend's lawyer father about the *Brown v. Board of Education* opinion, which overturned *Plessy*, and I made him bring it home for us to debate.

"If we're all equal, why do we have to be separate?" I asked, when I told him I agreed with the decision.

He just laughed and said, "Well, you're a little young still, my small solicitor. Someday you'll understand."

He didn't have to think about that one. His racism was well ingrained.

———————

Now in Salt Lake City, I sat across the street from the 1st Avenue house, on the steps of the apartment building, noticing that it was getting late in the day. On the hills above me to the east, the huge white U was emblazoned. If I left the 1st Avenue house now, I could hike there; or I could visit East High School, where I succeeded academically and theatrically on my return from Alabama; or I could drive to the last house I had lived in before I married—the Imperial Street house.

But I knew that I must stay where I was seated and that I must remember the night in question—the night in the Birmingham, Alabama, house that wrapped itself around me and never let me go. And then I must choose a token for the memory, which I would throw into Bear Lake, where I imagined it would be sucked up—all that damp and watery waste of wanting.

If I didn't do that now, I never would.

So I stayed.

———

That night in Birmingham, I was lying on the couch, reading Norah Lofts. The time had slipped by, and it was very late. Margaret had long since disappeared into Stewart's room. Daddy had said his good nights. Then I heard him stirring, and then he was sitting on the couch at my side.

"What are you reading, honey?" He slipped his arm around my thighs.

"Just a book, Daddy."

He didn't say anything, but he took the book and laid it on the floor. He took both of my hands in his, and we sat there, looking at each other.

"Are you OK, Daddy?"

"I'm fine," he said softly. "I'd just like to sit here awhile, OK?"

"Sure."

He reached over me to turn off the floor lamp. I could smell his Old Spice cologne and the soap he washed with. As he reached past me, the skin of his neck was close, a warm, clean-shaven skin. "Let's just sit here awhile, OK?" he repeated into the dark, and I was silent.

My body knew nothing, but it suspected everything.

I was a fourteen-year-old girl, raised to be virginal and holy. I was to save myself for my husband, who would be God's emissary to salvation, who would pull me through a curtain in the Temple ceremony, say a magic word, and call me by my secret name.

Already I feared that I might not be allowed in the Temple because I wasn't totally pure. Actually, I considered myself a sort-of-bad girl: Olive and I had stolen apples and books; we put dog poop in sacks on door-steps and lit them with a match, and then we rang the doorbells and ran away to hide and watch people try to stomp out the fires; we jammed car horns and watched people throw open the hoods, looking for crossed wires.

As for kissing, I had only ever kissed one boy, the previous summer at Bear Lake, behind a haystack, and not really even then, since his cow-boy hat got in the way. But that didn't mean I hadn't thought a lot about kissing. I had stretched out on Olive's bed, and we had practiced kissing. We explored our bodies. We drew sketches of breasts, which Olive called pop-ups and I called buttons. Her breasts were big, and mine were small, so we drew breasts the size of watermelons and golf balls. We drew the nipples to look like raisins and walnuts. We took fruit from Olive's fridge and made breasts out of peeled grapefruits and dried prunes, and then ate them.

Olive called men's things "whangies"; I called them "thingy-fishies." She called women's things "do-dangs"; I called them "caves." We drew pictures of whangies rubbing against buttons. We sucked each other's nipples, pretending to be baby cows. We lit our drawings on fire in Olive's garbage-burner bin, dancing and chanting. We had sleepovers, wrestled on the bed, drew pictures on each other's backs, and slept cud-dled together like spoons. I cupped my hand over Olive's blossoming breast, and she let me rest it there. She covered my tiny hillocks with her own hands and promised me mine would get as big as hers, though they never did.

This was before her mother caught us. Then Olive moved away. I missed her.

All the activity with Olive had filled me with a hot pleasure. I didn't confess any of this pleasure to my bishop, though I knew I should re-pent. I felt hardly any guilt—after all, Olive was my friend. We loved each other. I was sure Jesus would let me into Heaven in spite of the Church's damnation.

Love, after all, was everything.

That night in Alabama was entirely different. I'd been only nine when Daddy first found my cave. Now I was almost fourteen. I had seen much of the world, I thought, and was experienced. And even though it wasn't perfect here in Alabama, I was away from the mother I hated so much.

I was scared, but in an odd way. After all, I was with my beloved father, who was scared, too, I could tell—his face was warm, his body trembled a little. I had to trust him, trust that I would be all right. Maybe he was going to teach me something, and maybe it would be something I would enjoy knowing.

Daddy bent down on the couch and brought his body close to mine. His feet, in his shiny black shoes, upon which I had so often stood while he whirled me around in a dance, remained on the floor, but his body, from the waist up, bent over me, his chest to mine, his lips kissing my hair, my forehead, and my nose. His hands brushed my hair and then held my cheeks. He kissed me on the lips: a long, held kiss.

"I love you, Kathy," he said softly in my ear, "so much," and I wrapped my arms around him. I held him, not out of fear, though I was scared, but out of knowing I was loved. I felt this meant he was mine, that he may have gone from my house, but he would never go from me. I hugged him as tight as I could, and though the kiss burned on my lips, though his sweat was wet and sticky on my face, though his hair took on an acrid smell and his grasp of me was too tight, I was thrilled above the terror, secure above the falling, joyous above the dark wonder.

He lifted me from the couch and carried me into his bedroom, pushing the door shut behind him with his shoe. He laid me on the bed. He sat to untie his shoes, unbuckle his belt. He slowly stood to take off his shirt, his slacks, his underpants. The bedroom was flushed with the light from a full Alabama moon outside, which blazed into the room. The scent of the daphne bush sifted through the window screen; somewhere down the block, a car radio was simmering with soft music.

Daddy climbed on the bed, sat on his knees by my side, and took off my pajamas. As he lifted them off, I saw the little red hearts on the pajama legs. My white pajamas with little red hearts, his white pajamas with little blue stars. This soothed me, made me feel somehow that what was happening was right and just.

"Margaret sleeps with Stewart, you know." Daddy's voice cracked beside me.

"I know that, Daddy," I said, not knowing what it meant. I knew only that Daddy needed me to say I knew. He pulled me toward him, turned me over, and cuddled my smaller body into his. It was like an ocean curving over a shell, waves and waves and waves, and me, ebbing and flowing in the current, being shaped. "It's an ocean, Daddy," I said.

———————

I am lying in his curve. He crosses his arms over my chest and feels my nipples gently, rubbing them between his finger and his thumb. A wave crosses from his fingers through my chest and down my arms; a wave washes up from my legs to my head; a wave turns over itself. I am in Bear Lake, swimming, somersaulting, diving.

I feel his thingy grow like a fish, a puffer fish, a long, puffing eel. It swims on my back up and down, and then he puts it between my legs, and I can feel it swimming in and out of my legs.

He turns me over. "I'm going exploring," he whispers. "There's a cave down here. Can you feel me exploring?" And I can. Like a school of fish, his fingers swim one by one into my cave, now all together in a school. I feel strands of seaweed waving; I feel lacy fins sweep the walls of my cave. This is new; this is terrifying. The cave is dark, the moonlight doesn't reach inside, and yet the fish know where they are, swimming all around, playing in the dark. My terror is more than fear. It is light breaking through...and sound, muffled and tinkling. It is jellyfish pulsing in streams of silk, fluorescent tetras beaming color. I scoot into my father; I am sure he will find a treasure.

"Does that feel all right? Are we exploring together?" he asks softly. What else to say but yes to my father, to this strange sensation.

"Now," he says, gruff and with a choke, "there is a very kind sea creature who wants to come in. But he is big. Shall we help him?"

"No, yes." I am afraid.

"No, yes," my father echoes. "All God's creatures. All God's creatures."

I feel the creature, and it is big. But my father helps him in with the fishes. He pushes in, pushes in, and suddenly I am no longer in the swaying, watery ocean. I am in its storm, pierced by stalactites, stalagmites, the teeth of the sea monster. I feel a shock so great, so piercing, I am certain the cave has exploded. The sea creature writhes and shifts. He can't get out, though he tries; he pushes in and pulls out, and goes up and down, looking for escape, and I scream. But my father's hand loves my mouth, his arms love my body, his mouth loves my neck. I can feel my father struggling to catch the monster. I can hear him hissing. I can hear his moans as he squeezes the monster to death. The monster is crushed. I feel his blood.

"I have him!" Daddy finally shouts, breathless. "I've pulled him out." He has saved me. We both cry with relief.

———•———

This is how I remember it, my father saving me, even though I know that "My father raped me" is the proper description. The accurate narrative is: "My father had sexual intercourse with me when I was fourteen." The prosecution would angrily sum it up: "The father betrayed the child's trust." Still, through all my years, through the confessions to counselors and the counselors' kind assurances, I never lost the sense that my father and I went exploring together. He was the guide; he took me near death, and then he saved me from it.

———•———

Daddy soothed me to sleep. He cleaned the seawater out of my cave, bathed all the hills beside it, dressed me in my hearts and himself in his stars, and sang me a song while I lay in his arms and fell away into sleep. I don't remember the song he sang, but, knowing my father as I did, it was a hymn, or a sacred song—something like "Smile" or "There's Never a Prayer Unanswered," because those were the songs I loved him to sing. Those were the songs that made me sleep.

As an adult, I looked for the lyrics to these favorite songs. I found the song I loved best—"I Believe." One of the lines reads: "I believe for everyone who goes astray, someone will come to show the way."

Who?

I slept with my father many times after that night and throughout the year. Some part of me, however, refused to sleep with him every night. I often told him I didn't want to do so, that I wanted to be alone to read or study or simply sleep bundled in my own body. He did not pressure me. But just as often, I wanted to. I felt a need to have him physically close to me. I enjoyed the sex.

And as with Stewart and Margaret, nothing was questioned or spoken about. As the months wore on, however, Margaret and Daddy, who did not sleep together again, continued to argue, snap, or growl in low voices. I closed my ears. I went for walks. I didn't want to enter into their struggles. Stewart and I never spoke. Brad grew quiet and played alone. The adults grew self-absorbed. The children were not saved.

———◆———

I loved my father in spite of his abuse—and even, in part, because of it. I didn't want him to stop, or to leave me. I depended on him, on the physical relationship and the closeness. I wanted his love forever.

I lived in a no-man's-land, buried in a foggy miasma, a place where this secret hid and then haunted me. I carried it everywhere. It exposed me when it darted out in juxtaposed forms: a strong respect for sex, yet fear for my children's sexual discoveries; excessive repulsion at one sex scene in a movie, yet rising excitement in another; cold indifference to sex at times, yet wild desire at others.

It strung me up like a marionette: moving my arms to close around my chest when a lover reached for my breasts, or moving my legs without commitment when I made love, and alternatively, opening my legs in invitation, or opening my arms in acceptance of a lover. My brain formed odd calculations whenever I was called upon to think about or analyze sex or affection. I was in a fog of confusion.

Even as a more mature adult, I had no words for it. I sought counseling but sidestepped the truth and found no peace. I thrust my secret away and pronounced a permanent estrangement. But the exile returned.

This is the space sexual-abuse victims inhabit with their secrets. "What happened? What didn't happen? What do I feel? And who is to blame?"

———————

When I visited the Laird and 1st Avenue houses, I began to find my words. And my own truth:

What shamed me was not that my father had sex with me. What shamed me was that he left me. That I could not hold him.

CHAPTER 23

JUDGING

———◆———

IT IS DIFFICULT TO WRITE about the pleasure.

In my twenty-one years of presiding over child-abuse and child-neglect cases, few experts testified successfully that different children might experience sexual abuse in different ways. Pleasure, love, safety, and devotion—these emotions were unacceptable, unbelievable, and presumably coerced.

If a child told a counselor, or testified in a closed hearing, "I want to have Daddy move back in," a psychologist's usual explanation, the prosecutor's argument, and the judge's opinion were, "The child may think she wants to be back with her father, but she doesn't understand." Or "It isn't in her best interest." Or "She's too young to know what she wants."

And "Give her time; she'll learn what he's really done."

But to the children, and often to the parents, their own dysfunctional family is a special unit, and its complete dismemberment can cause more harm than good.

Did I, as a judge, always probe these issues? Can I say that I always had the courage to ask a witness, "Can this man be rehabilitated? Will we harm the child by cutting off all contact with her father? Is there any benefit that might come from reuniting this child with her father?" I can't say that I examined the possibilities from every angle in every case. I remember many silences.

I was afraid to be labeled "soft on sexual abuse."

As a judge, I was very alert to the harm sexual predators cause victims, to the terrible pain youngsters suffer when violently offended by strangers. Common sympathies, and mine, are very much with the victims.

I was acutely aware, as well, of betrayal children feel when offended by someone they know, love, and trust, especially in family abuse. Acknowledging that the father wrongly uses the power imbalance to victimize the daughter, shouldn't the sympathies for the child also include a consideration of her bond with the abuser, her love for him, and the damage total separation might cause? Shouldn't we treat them both? Heal them both?

Shouldn't a state, with the power to separate a family, first use that power to save it?

Even though the ultimate goal of the state was not only to rescue children but also to rehabilitate the family, treatment and services were rarely designed so that a sexually offending father might someday reconnect with his child, even return to the family.

It was a system bogged down in bureaucratic status quo. Thoughtful suggestions and imaginative solutions weren't encouraged or accepted; they were stifled under the burdens of red tape and conservative traditions.

Even if the question of guilt was up in the air, professionals erred on the side of the child by presuming the father was guilty. The plan to remove him from any contact with his daughter was considered to be in the best interests of the child. These presumptions reflected society's views of sexual offenders as the worst kind of criminals—disgusting, irredeemable, and evil. Some of them are.

But some of them aren't.

———◆———

In the mid-1990s, Oregon's Multnomah County child-services agency offered and paid for multiple excellent services for the daughter and her mother—psychological evaluations, individual counseling, support groups, and financial aid. Yet for the father, little was offered and much was usually required.

He was moved from the home and denied any contact with his daughter and often with his other children, even those not offended. While still supporting his family, he was required to seek other housing at his own expense, which he could not afford. He was required to take a test using a plethysmograph, an instrument that measured his arousal to children. Electrodes were attached to his penis. He was shown pictures of children in various postures and forms of undress. This test was periodically repeated until he registered "normal." The cost of the test was usually beyond his reach. He was required to attend and pay for sex-offender counseling. The waiting lists were long, and the cost prohibitive.

Before he could see his daughter again, or return to the family, he had to comply with all requirements. The process took months, sometimes years.

Compliance rarely occurred.

He was overwhelmed and gave up.

In my years on the state-court bench, in the cases over which I presided, and in other cases of which I was aware, no sex-offending father was reunited with his daughter or family. After many years on the bench, reading medical studies and listening to expert testimony, and as a periodic teacher with the National Council of Juvenile and Family Court Judges, I came to believe that it is possible for a father to experience remorse and rehabilitation, for his children to accept his apologies and understand his behavior was harmful. He can learn to take all the necessary steps to create safety for his children, and the children's mother can learn to better protect her family.

A repentant father's return might be his own and the family's rescue, and the salvation of his grieving daughter, who loves him, needs him, and forgives him.

———◆———

"All sex offenders are evil," my friend asserted, unconvinced by my arguments.

I never thought so. True, many might be damaged beyond repair—predators and pedophiles, serial offenders. Evidence indicates that these men rarely change. They should be kept away from possible victims. And some families probably cannot be rehabilitated, too deep in their dysfunction—my father's second family, for example, smothering in double incest.

But the question remains: Isn't there such a thing as a "situational" offense, in which the circumstances must be examined? Isn't this a proper distinction that ought to be explored when planning for family treatment?

There is the one-time offender, for whom recidivism is unlikely. What should we do with him?

There is the predator who waits in the bushes by a school, kidnaps a child, and rapes her. He never repeats his crime. How long should he be incarcerated?

There is the serial predator, who stalks and rapes several victims. Should he be locked away forever? Executed?

What about the eighteen-year-old who has sex with his fifteen-year-old girlfriend with her consent, which is statutory rape? Should he serve time? Be registered for life as a sex offender, the registration following him to employers and residences forever?

What about the drunk father who on one occasion touches his daughter's vagina, or places his penis between her thighs? How about on two occasions? Ten?

What of the brother having sex with his brother?

What of the twenty-five-year-old, five-foot-tall, female high-school teacher having sex with her sixteen-year-old, six-foot-two, 190-pound, sexually active student?

Even more puzzling—what about a father-daughter incest that is begun with a power imbalance but proceeds on the basis of love?

Are there no permutations? No complexities? No necessary considerations?

What of my father, who, if caught, might have spent the rest of his life behind bars? Would anyone have cared how I felt about that? I would be sent home, to my mother's house and her carelessness. Would anyone investigate *those* harms?

I wish now that someone had acknowledged my mother's dysfunction. Surely someone must have or could have known. Intervened. I wish my mother and her children had been offered family counseling, my mother enrolled in alcohol treatment and parent training, and services brought into the home. Perhaps we could have salvaged our family.

I wish my father had been caught at the beginning, when family counseling may have saved our family. I would have wanted him to remain in the home, with me, as our family healed.

As for my father's second family, could social-service agencies have interrupted the double incest and rehabilitated us? Probably not. But certainly my father and stepmother could have been required to engage in free sex-offender counseling. My father could have been helped to identify the sources of his anger, to end the incest, and to stop immediately—what I only understood decades later—his inappropriate use of his child for his own comfort and his revenge against his wives.

I would have wanted the system to insist that my father take full responsibility for both his passivity and his actions.

I would have wanted an apology and an assurance that I was not at fault.

I would have wanted to continue an appropriate relationship with the father who had loved me so well, been so good for me in so many ways, and saved me from all other harm.

Even now I can barely write these words, afraid of the scornful reaction, afraid of the disbelief by those who read them, afraid that my words will be degraded and disregarded, challenged by those experts able to tell me how I should feel and what is best for me and other abused children.

Detractors will accuse me of inventing my memories and patching together my armchair recommendations for treatment. More well-meaning critics, even compassionate friends, will say I have remembered and interpreted events erroneously, that my hopeful plan for such families as mine is fanciful, impossible. I will be told that I am not yet in touch with the appropriate anger I must feel to heal, suggesting that I suffer from repressed, unreleased, and unresolved anger and shame.

No wonder I have kept silent.

I admit to being ashamed, but not to shame. I did not blame myself or feel worthless.

Nor was I ashamed of having been abused.

Rather, until I made my journey back home, until I relived and rethought my father's abuse, I was ashamed of not feeling what society prescribed. Instead, I felt benign about the abuse—horrified but accepting, betrayed but also loved.

I ponder the effects of incest on me. Complicated, of course. Enduring, yes.

For many years, I claimed that the year I spent in Birmingham with my father had been the happiest year of my childhood. I made many positive changes then. In school, I earned excellent grades. I became an avid reader. I discussed all of Daddy's cases with him. He took me to court with him, asked me to analyze the lawyers' performances and the witnesses' demeanors. I continued to keep my daily journal, adding to it almost every day of my life thereafter. I wrote poetry, stories, and songs, and performed them for my father, who called me brilliant, beautiful, and good at heart.

Friends seemed to gather around me that year, seek me out, in part because I had such an interesting "Northern accent" and in part because I was kind and friendly. Daddy encouraged me to stand up for kids who were teased at school, and although he disagreed with me about discrimination against African Americans, he encouraged me to stand strong in my changing beliefs.

I became self-assured and proud of myself. When I stood before a large audience of Rotary Club members to give my speech on great men of the South, I was confident. Daddy's secretary had typed my speech on long, legal tissue paper and bound it in a WILLS AND TRUSTS blue cover, on which Daddy had amended: "*She* WILLS *succeed* AND *I* TRUSTS *she is the best!*" He sat in the audience beaming and took me for ice cream when I won first place.

I even had a "boyfriend," Bucky Cochran, who was forced to be my partner because we were both short. I never let him press close when we danced at the ninth-grade parties or hold my hand. Because, really, I belonged to my father.

As the year went on, however, Daddy grew more distant and aloof. He was not as attentive to me as I was to him. I slept with him less often. He didn't come for me; instead, I went to him. He seemed lost in thought when I struck up conversations with him. I tried harder to retain his favor, cooked for him and gave him stolen gifts, but he was less and less responsive.

I recall being confused at the time, but I was too young and inexperienced to understand. For years I tried to justify his withdrawal: perhaps he had been lonely and wasn't anymore; perhaps he had hoped to make Margaret jealous, to hurt her, and when that didn't seem to work, he lost interest in me; perhaps he began to recognize that what he was doing was wrong.

As hard as it is for me to admit it now, I think he simply tired of me.

At the end of the school year, I begged Daddy to let me stay in Alabama to finish high school. He said no and told me that my mother loved me and wanted me home.

"No, she doesn't, Daddy," I countered. "She tells me all the time she would have been so happy if it weren't for me."

"I'm sure you misunderstood her, Kathy." He took my chin in his hand. "What she said was she would have been *un*happy if it weren't for you." I told him he was wrong. I didn't understand why Daddy continued to make plans for me to return to Salt Lake City.

"Daddy, I want to stay here. All my friends are here. I'm a good student. I want to go to high school here. What about you and me, Daddy? Who will sing to me and read my stories? Who will take me for dinner and ice cream? Who will talk to me about why segregation is the true path, and why stars fall out of the sky, and why Robert E. Lee was a great general? Who will I sleep with, Daddy? Who will take me into warm waters and curl around his little shell?"

"You're going home, honey. Your momma wants you home."

"I don't want to go home. I won't. Not to Mom or anyone. I'm staying here!" I called him names. "You shithead. Bastard. Asshole!"

"Now, you don't mean those things," he said, and smiled. And he tried to take me in his arms, but I pushed him away. "There's no need to get so upset," he soothed.

I was enraged. And hurt. I had seen a girlfriend at school get dumped by her boyfriend. I was being dumped! And he wasn't even telling me that it was over. I sulked and pouted and begged. Margaret walked around the house with a smug look on her face—Stewart, too. They were against me. I thought Daddy was against me, too. He had turned.

In Salt Lake City, so many years later, as I sat on the steps across from the 1st Avenue house, I felt these losses again. I absorbed his betrayal and his rejection. That year had been a well of replenishment and wonder, and I drank deeply from it. But I no longer thought of it as my happiest year. In fact, I realized now it was, perhaps, my saddest.

I sat there, fifty years old, staring at the house I'd lived in thirty-five years earlier, and finally refused to push away the memory of our final moment.

At the train station, on the platform, as the porter called, "All aboard," my father hugged me good-bye. I smelled his sweet scent, felt the soft texture of his jacket, and tasted the cool of his cheek. His touch came to me in a wave of pleasure, curling in, melding with the tears building. I stepped back to look at him, to beg him one last time.

On the train platform, lonely already, I asked him, for the final time, "Daddy, I just don't understand. Why must I go?"

And he said, "Because, sweetheart, it's your little sister's turn."

———

I loved my father, and was in love with him, although I came to understand, sadly, I must admit, that he did not love me as I loved him. I think of him as a lost love, a failed relationship.

Nothing has ever changed the good he did for me. But I have come to realize the harm as well.

I had very little contact with my father after that. He never called or wrote. He had tossed me over like a summer fling. I hated him for his betrayal, but I longed for him and was inconsolably sad. I wrote him long love letters and then tore them up. I called him but hung up before the phone was answered. I moped for the first year of high school, was sullen and surly. Mom noticed that I didn't seem to like boys, or go to parties anymore, so she sent me to a psychiatrist, ironically named Dr. Darke, who tried unsuccessfully to make me more feminine and alluring and more attracted to boys. Mom never asked what we talked about, which was never the truth.

I'm not sure I ever learned to trust an intimate relationship again, though I would marry and divorce, take a lover for a while, and then have a long-term partner. I am still alert, wary, and cautious that I might be betrayed. This attentiveness, this suspiciousness, made me a tenacious trial lawyer and a thoughtful judge, but it interfered mightily with my relationships. The flint that flicks and lights the fire of true intimacy was permanently dulled.

"I only believe in the mountains," I explained dreamily, years later, to a questioning friend. "They're steady."

"Well, I hate to disillusion you, Katharine," she said offhandedly. "But earthquakes happen every day on the Wasatch Front. The earth is never stable."

———◆———

Decades passed with no paternal contact. In 1986, when I was forty-two years old, I received my last, strange message from my father.

Incoming mail at the juvenile court traveled under many eyes: first through the downtown main courthouse mailroom; then by carrier to the juvenile courthouse, where the clerks sorted the mail and sent it upstairs, where it was again separated by staff; finally, it was placed in a judge's box.

One day, a postcard appeared in my box. By then, the word had spread, and the staff watched to see my reaction as I pulled the card out.

On the back my father had written: "Kathy, darlin', I knew you would get a kick out of this. Missing you. Love, Daddy."

On the front of the card, a sexy, comically overdrawn Vargas-styled woman stood on a pier with her back to the viewer. She was holding a fishing rod. Her voluptuous butt cheeks were flowing over a thin swim thong that hugged her crack. She turned at the waist to face the viewer. Her right breast ballooned out of a skimpy swim top that barely covered her nipple. Her plump red mouth was formed in a surprised O, as though she had been caught doing something naughty. At the end of the fishing line she had hooked a large fish. Posted on the pier was a sign: NO FISHING.

"Why would your father send you something like that?" asked my clerk.

I had disappeared. I was perfectly calm. I tore the card up and tossed it in the shredding bin.

"Don't be silly," I replied. "This is some crackpot joke." I turned to the gaping staff. "My father's been dead for years."

CHAPTER 24

SHOULDERING THE WHEEL

———◆———

SIX WEEKS AFTER I RETURNED from Alabama, I received a tearful call
from Lucy in Birmingham. "Please come and get me," she begged, sobbing. I didn't ask her why. She didn't tell me the truth for thirty years.

She gave me a reason. "It's my birthday," she snuffled, "and Daddy's,
too." When she had been born on his birthday, she had become his
birthday present from Mom. So she had looked forward to them sharing the birthday together. "He's going out with Margaret instead," she
sobbed. "How can he do that?"

My mother was unresponsive to Lucy's plea to come home. "She
wanted to go," Mom said. "She can just stick it out like you did."

But I fretted. Lucy was the gentle child. She had uncommonly silky,
feathery white hair. People stopped us on the street and exclaimed,
"Why, that's the most beautiful hair I've ever seen." As she grew older,
her hair remained white, cottonwood fluff in a spring breeze, flying
about on unseen waves of air. At an early age, she wore heavy, black-
rimmed eyeglasses with thick lenses that stood out against her white
hair and gave her a mad-scientist look.

"You'd better be smart," Mom told her, "because you'll never get by
on your looks." She called Lucy "the ugly child," and Lucy thought it was
true. Her little face was a shadow of sorrow, eyes deep and watery, her
mouth rarely upturned, her voice seldom heard. But she figured out
how to live in that house, and she did it silently, shrewdly.

She was a good girl, hushed, thoughtful, and vulnerable. She was smart; her little brain was an orchestra tuning up, listening, and holding different notes. Then out she came with a symphony of finely tuned ideas, organized and harmonic, usually in the form of a poem.

I had just turned fifteen when Lucy called from Alabama. She was twelve. Against Mom's wishes, and without her knowledge or permission, I bought train tickets with my ironing and babysitting money and went to rescue Lucy. I left Mom a note on the table: "I have not run away. I've gone to get Lucy. We'll be home in few days." As far as I know, Mom never called Daddy to see whether I'd made it.

I was savvy then, hurt and hardened. I looked at the Chicago tenements with a sharper eye. I avoided strange men. I felt mature, independent, and capable. As soon as I arrived in Alabama, I took the bus to Daddy's house and walked right in.

"Well, look who's here," Margaret snarled.

I helped Lucy pack her bags.

Daddy stood there as we left the house. "How're y'all gonna get home?" he asked. As we waited at the bus stop, he drove up. "You sure?" he asked, but when we ignored him, he said, "Well, have a good trip," and drove off.

Lucy and I didn't talk much on the bus, or on the train. She was reserved and solemn. I was alert and watchful. We had a layover in Chicago and spent a long night sleeping on a bench in the train terminal. I considered myself quite brave. I had saved my sister. From what, I didn't know yet, but I suspected.

When we got home, Mom might have said, "Well, welcome home. Not so great at your dad's house, is it?" But I don't recall her saying anything. Lucy unpacked her bags, and we all went on as though she'd never left.

I remember very little of the trip. I think now that I had to have been terrified, both of the train trip and of seeing my father. I had to have been stunned by his indifference. If so, I have repressed the memory.

I do remember the sound of the train wheels and the smell of cigars in the Birmingham train station. I can see the cracks in the sidewalk as we walked away from his house and the sour look on Daddy's face when he rolled down his car window. I recall buying apples for Lucy and me to eat, stealing a Big Hunk candy bar in the Chicago terminal, and the cold of the bench we slept on. Otherwise, I recall nothing. Today, decades later, I am uncomfortable in train stations and anxious on trains.

Repressing bad memories became a pattern in our family, as did silence. We five children really didn't need to talk about our lives; we simply understood one another, because we lived in the same experience. I am sure that Lucy and I knew something terrible had happened for us both—we held hands on the train ride home and slept on the wide station bench snuggled close together. But we didn't talk about the abuse for another thirty years, when I learned that Lucy—reticent, analytical, perceptive Lucy—had, unlike me, sized up our father immediately when on her birthday morning she had awakened to find him rubbing his penis on her thigh.

Horrified, she had called me. Suspecting, I had gone to save her.

——◆——

Eric and I cooked up a fine meal at the Stansbury Suites. We had been eating mostly takeout food, supplemented by the occasional healthy dinner—fish, a salad, a vegetable, and fresh fruit for dessert. That night we broiled steaks, baked potatoes, dobbed them with sour cream and real butter, and double-scooped the double-chocolate-fudge-brownie ice cream for dessert, followed by coffee with Bailey's. Sated on chocolate and high on Bailey's, I mustered up the courage to tell him about Dad's abuse and my conflicted feelings.

"Oh, Katharine," he said. "I'm so sorry."

We were each on one end of the sitting-room couch, feet touching. He let me talk until I was done and then moved over to sit beside me. He put his arm around me and gave me a long hug. We sat in silence until a sudden thought occurred to him.

"Lucy! What happened to Lucy then?"

"She only stayed a month or so," I answered, deflecting the question. "She called me to bring her home," I said. "So I did."

"Of course you did," Eric smiled. "That's so like you." He leaned back on the couch and put his hands behind his head. "Lucy. Little Lucy. Our master chef. Queen of the Chore Wheel."

I laughed.

"That damn Chore Wheel was your fault, Kittens," he teased.

———◆———

I was ten, and Daddy was gone, so I performed only for Mom. I sang her a song, a new hymn I had learned in Sunday school: "Put your shoulder to the wheel, push along. Do your duty with a heart full of song."

"What a good idea," Mom said. "A wheel to push on." She invented the Chore Wheel—we were bound by it the rest of our childhoods, from Laird Avenue to Ninyah's basement, to Military Way and 1st Avenue. When I finally left home from the Imperial Street house, I ripped it down and took it with me.

Although Clark, and later Eric as well, were regularly assigned boy chores—empty the wastebaskets, take out the garbage, in the summertime mow the lawn, in the wintertime plow the snow from the driveway—for the girls, Mom made a big wheel out of cardboard, with another slightly smaller wheel pinned on top of it with a gold two-pronged clip. The smaller wheel spun around on the larger one.

On the outside rim of the large wheel, Mom printed our names—Sandy, Kathy, Lucy. On the smaller wheel, she drew three pie sections. In each she recorded, in pencil, all the regular chores of the day. She rotated the wheel around until a list fell under one of our names.

One pie might read: "Do the dishes, sweep and mop the kitchen floor, put in a load of laundry, bring my coffee." Another might say: "Clean the bathroom, dust living room, fix dinner." Sometimes she erased a chore, or added another. Sometimes she listed chores whether they needed doing or not. We were never certain what the chores might be. When I complained, she retorted, "I'm training you for the real world."

She pinned the Chore Wheel to the wall. Every evening she would turn the wheel around. That way each girl knew before she went to bed what her chores were the next day. If Mom was mad, she'd pencil in an extra chore. Sometimes she did this after we went to bed.

On Friday night, she added extra chores to do on Saturday and Sunday, things that were done once a week: "Clean the furnace room, shampoo the carpets, clean out the fireplace, scrub the kitchen shelves."

You never knew which pie section you were going to get, or what the chores would be, because she didn't spread them out fairly, using them to punish us with gross chores like cleaning grout with a toothbrush or wiping the dirt and grime off the furnace pipes.

We had until midnight to finish our chores. We heard her walk around the house after we went to bed, inspecting the finished work. When something wasn't done to her satisfaction, she came stomping into our bedroom. We stayed still, each of us hoping it wasn't our chore she'd settled on.

One night, she slammed the door back. "I'm sick and tired of your laziness."

This time it was Sandy she pulled from the bed. "Get up there and mop the floor better." She smacked her.

"Mom, it isn't my turn!" Sandy shouted, yanking away.

Lucy cried out, "It's me, it's me! I'm sorry."

Mom turned on Lucy. Another slap. I pulled my pillow over my head. A loud shout. Somebody running. Somebody following.

Mom yelling at Lucy's back, "I'm at the end of my rope! Don't you girls understand? Can't you ever think of anyone but yourselves?"

"Mom, I'm—"

"You're hateful. You're all ungrateful wretches!"

The door slammed shut. Sandy and I were quiet in the dark, making sure Mom wasn't coming back.

"Thank God it wasn't me," I said. I was cramped up with fear.

"It will be," Sandy said. "Hold your horses."

This was true. Mom spread her disapproval around. It was unpredictable, terrible as a volcano. She could erupt.

But when all was said and done, we girls knew how to do chores. That meant we knew, sooner than the boys did, how to escape—how to move out and live on our own.

Mom added cooking to the Chore Wheel, and by age six Lucy had to learn. Though I had been cooking for years, Lucy had no idea what to do. I taught her. "Here's the can opener. Here's the oven, the stovetop. Here're the sharp knives, the cutting board. Here's a list of what to make for dinner." She stumbled along, learning the rules. Get out two pots with lids. Open a can of spaghetti and a can of peas. Turn the stove to medium and dump the cans into the pots. Turn on the heat. Wash the lettuce leaves, one per person. Spoon out the cottage cheese. And so forth.

I taught her that if you made the salad last, the main dish would burn on the stove while you were still opening the peaches. I taught her to heat things longer in the oven than on the top of the stove. Don't heat the chili on high. The lime Jell-O with shredded carrots must set before you could serve it up. Once, when she realized the Jell-O wasn't hard yet, she served it anyway, in a glass, as a joke. Unamused, Mom ordered us to "Drink up. Can't waste food." It went down slimy.

Lucy became our best cook. With money earned from our jobs babysitting and ironing, Sandy and I paid her to do our cooking and many of our chores, thinking we had the best of the deal. Canny little Lucy—she got rich on us.

Eric and I washed and dried the dishes. "Great meal," he said of the steak. Stansbury Suites provided wood-burning fireplaces; he struck a match to a Presto log.

"And a nice quiet dinner," I said, joining him on the hearth.

"Yes," he said. "That was nice."

He paused. "I have such awful memories of our dinners."

———◆———

One suppertime Mom scolded three-year-old Eric when he refused to eat his beef potpie. It had been my turn to cook the meal, and I had cooked the pies on too low a heat.

"I don't want it," he whimpered. "The bottom is gooey."

I sympathized but said nothing. I didn't want to get into trouble.

If anyone could soften Mom, it was three-year-old Eric: his little cowlick sticking up from the middle of his head, his legs swinging back and forth against the booster chair, his pretty eyes blinking cobalt blue like his departed father's. "Don't wanna." His shoulders pushed back, his back stiffened.

"Eat it," Mom rasped. "Eat every bite." He clamped his mouth shut. Mom turned to look at each of us. "And you will all sit here until he does."

"Come on, Eric," said Lucy. "Just take it a bite at a time, honey."

Lucy scooped up a good piece of beef. "OK, I'm an airplane." He watched her move the spoon around in an ascending and then descending arc. He tentatively opened his mouth a little. Then, as Lucy whirred the spoon around, he opened wide. She flew it into his mouth.

"Now, this one." Lucy scooped the slimy dough onto the spoon and buzzed it in a circle. This time, he gagged, but swallowed it. Again and again. "Almost done."

Suddenly, in a great arc forward, Eric threw up. Globs of beef and carrots, vaguely identifiable, chunks of potatoes and ribbons of dough, spewed across the table in a splashy projectile. Nothing moved but a slow dribble coming down Eric's chin.

Mom rose slowly. I expected her to shout and curse. She just stood there. Eric's mouth stayed open, his tongue pushing food out.

She pinned her eyes on Eric and then on us.

Lucy sat back, pressing herself into her chair, looking at her lap; her white-topped head was all I could see of her. Sandy crossed her arms.

"Mom!" I said, rising. "It's OK."

"Sit down," she said to me. "You eat it!" she ordered Eric. "You hear me?" Her chair squealed on the linoleum as she pushed back from the table. "You girls pick it back up, and you eat it, young man."

She stood for a moment by the table, surveying the mess of vomit, her five children subdued before her. Then she left the table and walked to the hallway door. "I'm going to bed."

She closed her bedroom door. We all sat there, not moving.

Then we moved in concert. We didn't have to discuss it. We simply knew we were not about to make him eat his vomit.

I picked Eric up and took him to the bathroom, stripped him down, and bathed him. Sandy, Lucy, and Clark cleaned up.

It is as though, as one, we recognized the common enemy and moved against her. We just carried on as though not much had happened, communicating without words, maneuvering toward peace.

There is a book by Leo Lionni—*Swimmy*—in which little fish are afraid to come out of hiding because of the danger. They discover that if they all join together, they become what looks like a big fish, and thus they avoid peril.

This is how we all got out. Each of us was forced to struggle individually, like shipwreck survivors in a tossing sea, yet nothing the others did prevented each child's escape. We secretly aided one another through our support, by our mutual hopes for each sibling's success, and by complicit conspiracies toward freedom. We talked among ourselves when we could, shared our fears and hopes when we dared, and helped as best as we were able. Sandy married and fled into social work. I did, too, into law. Lucy followed into music. Clark disappeared into himself. Eric escaped into television.

We were each injured, but we made it to shore.

One Tuesday, it was Lucy's turn to make the evening meal. After school, we waited for her to get home and start to cook. Dinner was always at 5:30 p.m. on the dot. At half past four, still no Lucy.

From the couch, I watched for her arrival. I looked out each minute into the yard, past the tall brick apartment house, and down the street. At the table, Clark sawed his legs back and forth in his chair. We were anxious, watching and waiting. What would Mom do if she came home before Lucy? She'd yell, "What the hell's going on? Where's Lucy? Where's the goddamned dinner?"

She'd turn on me. "Where is she?"

"I don't know!" I'd defend myself. "She had violin today, I guess." We protected one another that way.

"Violin?" she'd say, incredulous. "Violin? You think that's more important than dinner?"

We waited. By fifteen minutes after five I knew we would all suffer what was about to come, and I was angry with Lucy for doing this to me.

"Little shit," I mumbled. I kicked at the table.

"Stop," Clark said.

"Where the hell is she?" My voice was ragged.

Clark began to rock in his seat. "I don't know. I don't know."

I can't think now why I didn't make Lucy's dinner for her when she was so late. Maybe it was the thrill of not being the one in trouble. Saved.

I began to pace.

"Goddamn it, she's such a brat." I turned on Clark. "She doesn't care anything about us and what might happen to us." My fists clenched, unclenched. Panic grew all hairy and dense in me. I was spinning out of control.

I banged the table again with my foot. Then Clark's chair. Harder.

"Stop it!" Clark yelled.

I deliberately walked to the coffee table.

Another me, sitting on my shoulder, said, "What are you doing, Kathy? This isn't right." I didn't listen.

I picked up an ashtray and threw it straight at Clark's face. He saw it coming, a glass cannonball whirling, a betrayal of the largest sort, something that could not be understood except to dodge, to avoid it. He bent sideways and tried to cover his head with his arms under the table.

"Why are you mad at *me*?" he gasped. I felt crazy. What was happening to me?

Suddenly, Lucy came bursting into the house, and everything was frantic. She flung her books on her bed and ran to the kitchen.

"Where the hell have you been?" I yelled.

Without answering, she slammed a pot on the stove, opened the chili cans, dumped the chili into the pot, slung the tablecloth on the table, and raced to set the table. She threw the salad together—pulled the lettuce leaves off the head and plopped them on plates, scooped the cottage cheese onto the leaves, forked a canned pear onto each scoop, dabbed the pear with mayonnaise, sprinkled paprika on top.

She flew to the cupboards for the crackers, salt, pepper. She poured our milk, made Mom's screwdriver. I was mesmerized by her speed. I was breathless with hot anticipation. Sandy came upstairs, looked at the clock, and said snidely, "Happy eating, everyone."

We heard the car coming up the driveway, stopping. Quickly, Lucy grabbed the pot from the stove, spooned the chili into the bowls, ran to put the pot in the sink, hurried back. We scurried to our seats, ready to receive Mom.

"Please, God, let it be OK," I prayed. "Let nothing be wrong."

The back door opened, the screen flapped shut. Door closed. In came Mom. She was there in the doorway to the dining room!

We sat in paralyzed silence. She looked at us sitting there. She looked at the table.

"Where's my hello?" she said, but none of us could talk, strung up by fear and hope. Mom came slowly into the dining room and set her things down on the desk. She took off her coat and hung it on the hook. She moved toward the table and stared down at each of us in turn. She looked carefully at the table.

She walked over to her place, and then, as though she'd figured something out, she put her finger in the bowl of chili. She drew it out. "It's not hot," she said.

She grabbed at her cheeks, flattened her face with her palms, and uttered a low, pained howl. Then she breathed in, bent down, and grabbed the ends of the tablecloth, bunching the edges in each hand. With a mighty exhale of breath, she brought the cloth toward her as she rose up to her full height. She looked like a demonic minister rising from the pulpit, arms swinging to the left and then up, inciting the congregation to new heights of shame.

In one mighty heave of the tablecloth, she pulled everything off the table. A fury exploded.

The bowls spiraled. The white tablecloth was covered with red chili, the dishes clattering toward us off the sides of the table. She yowled and whined like a terrible wind. The food landed on the table, on the floor, on us—everywhere. Dishes broke, silverware scattered. Eric was wide eyed. Clark scooted down in his chair, and I leaned over him, my full weight pressing. A knife cut my hand. Lucy let out a short wheeze and put her hand to her cheek where the cocktail glass hit her.

Sandy clambered up. She grabbed the table, lifted it up, and slammed it back down with a crash. "Stop it! Stop it! I can't stand it anymore!" She raised her fist at Mom.

I didn't care about the chili on my back, the mayonnaise sliding down my arm, or the blood on my hand. I jumped up, grabbed Sandy's arm, and cried out, "Don't!"

Then it was quiet. Chili seeped down the wall. Sandy pushed me off her. I landed on the floor.

Mom stood there, stiff and on fire. I thought to look for cover but did nothing, went nowhere. She dropped the tablecloth. Her shoulders fell down. She looked straight at each of us in a blaze.

"I hate you all," she said softly. She turned and walked into her bedroom without saying anything else. We heard the lock turn on her door.

Lucy sat in her chair with her hands clasped between her knees. Clark and Eric were wide eyed and stunned, their sobs muffled. I felt exhausted from the humidity of the house. There was no air; we were breathless in the wet heat of fear and longing. We just sat there, five children in a smothering silence.

I looked at the chili on the wall. It had stopped running.

Sandy stood like a sentry at her post, her face red and mottled, unreadable. Then she turned to us. "This is just bullshit!" she roared. "I can't stand it in this house."

She picked up a bowl from the floor and hurled it at Mom's figurine on the coffee table, shattering both. She left, slamming the front door.

I knew then that my mother was crazy. I felt both sorrow and panic. I felt like I weighed three hundred pounds and was stuck in quicksand. I felt like flying away. I couldn't breathe.

But I had to take care of Lucy and Clark and Eric, who was only seven. It was up to me.

I moved to Eric, put my arms around him, and gave him a hug. "Let's clean up. OK?" He moved slightly in my hands. His blond hair was bleeding with chili juice; beans stuck in it like little barrettes.

"We'll pretend we're on a mission to Africa, feeding all the starving children. See?" I bent down and picked up a pear, put it in a bowl. "We'll just collect every possible scrap of food to feed the children."

Eric slid off his chair, got down on his knees with me, and began to scoop up the food from the floor, put it in a bowl.

"Me, too," Clark said. He knelt down on the floor, but he just sat there, his leg touching mine.

"I'll help, too," Lucy said, slipping from her chair to my side.

"This is for Sambo," Eric said, the only black child he had ever seen. "Him and his three sisters."

I didn't know whether Sambo had three sisters, and most likely he wasn't hungry. But I replied, "And his brother, too."

I picked up some crackers. "Here, honey, these will be good." He began to finger them.

"There's plenty of food here for Sambo's whole family, Eric," Lucy said from under the table, "and they'll love us because we bring them food."

"That's right!" I said perkily. "Let's sing a hymn as we go, shall we?"

We sang "Come, Come Ye Saints": "All is well. All is well."

CHAPTER 25

THE GENEALOGY OF COOKING

ERIC AND I PLANNED TO go together to the house on Imperial Street, where Mom had unaccountably moved us when I was seventeen and Eric was seven. Sandy, nineteen, spent most of her time away from the house; Lucy, twelve, cooked and cleaned. I have few memories of Clark there— "Of course not," he told me years later, "no one does."

Imperial Street. Where my second secret resided and waited to pounce.

We started the day at Starbucks, watching the sunrise. This was the time of day my daily relationship with my mother began.

My sisters and I took turns bringing Mom her coffee in bed. She taught us how to do it. She was strict about compliance. First, get up precisely at 5:30 a.m. Put the water and coffee grounds in the percolator pot and turn on the stove. As soon as the water perks up into the glass bulb on the top, turn the stove down. The coffee will perk to perfection on its own without more watching. Now prepare the tray: a coffee cup and saucer; cream and sugar in separate small servers; orange juice from *her* juice jar, not the watered-down juice jar she prepared for us; and a cup of jam. Make toast. Do not burn it at all, not a bit. Butter the toast to the edge of the crust. Put it and the morning newspaper on the tray. Now go into Mom's bedroom and shake her gently awake. She may be in a bad mood, so stand back a bit. Open the shades. Hand her the frilly lavender bed jacket. Quickly go back to the kitchen and pour the coffee. Bring the tray to her—don't spill the coffee on the napkin.

If all went well, this was the time of day when Mom was most relaxed. She sat up, plumped her pillows behind her, steadied the tray, and took her first sip of coffee with her eyes closed. Then she smiled at me. Maybe took my hand, patted my arm.

"It's a new day," she sighed, and sometimes added, "You're a good girl, Kathy." I lasted all day on that.

Now when I watched the sunrise, I felt each new day in my whole body: in the way my flannel shirt brushed my arm, in the sharp smell of the air, in the hardness of the wood bench on which I sat, or in the grainy softness of the sand. I still believed in the promise of a new day—although I know now, of course, that like all promises, this one can be broken.

———◆———

At home, food became scarce. My mother continued more rigorously her decade-long budgeting, which included a set allocation for the purchase of food. On long sheets of accounting paper, she carefully wrote each source of income, the amount she netted, the amount she paid on bills, and the small balance left, out of which she bought food.

When she worked on these sheets, she left them where they lay on the dining-room table: the sheets spread out, the calculator with the hand-pulled lever, the pencils and small pencil sharpener, the overflowing ashtray, the empty drink glass. We would have to move them off when we set the table and back on, in precisely the same place, when the dishes were done.

I resented those budget sheets.

"Look at what I do for you!" she whined, pointing to the columns. "You think this is easy? I am trying to save money," she explained when we complained that there seemed to be so little food in the house. "You don't need to eat so much."

She began to measure the food, to hide it and to ration it out. She rewarded our good behavior with food—an apple, a glass of milk, a coveted half piece of Wonder Bread with a thin spread of peanut butter.

By the time I was sixteen, I had learned what love is: from my Church, salvation, *if* and only *if* I didn't sin; from my father, sex and physical affection; from my mother, food. Looking back, I realize that we always had enough food to stay healthy, but we never had enough to completely quell our hunger. My hungers combined, scrambled themselves together. I was always praying for more. Even now, enough is not enough.

She planned the cheapest menus she could devise, relying on daily sales for which she would send me to the store on my bicycle. To my mother, eating the food was very nearly a waste of resources, diminishing what food was left for the rest of the week. The best cooking required as few ingredients as possible.

I think now my mother saw cooking as an almost-spiritual event, and the kitchen was a chapel. Each meal was a crusade. Feeding five children was a holy struggle, a battle with the budget. We were her little army of cooks, armed with shrewd strategies. We were to perform miracles.

She had three rules.

Rule 1: Waste Not

As one strategy, Mom tempered the use of supplies, cutting us down to just what was needed and no more. She thinned out our juices and made servings just a bit too small. She used one less strip of meat, a smaller dollop of mayonnaise, or two nuts instead of five. She bought days-old bread, diluted the powdered milk, and stretched the hamburger with crushed crackers.

She didn't allow us to waste a thing. After the canned pears were spooned out from the can with a slotted spoon, she poured the remaining syrupy juice into the pitcher of orange juice made from concentrate with an extra can of water.

"Mom, that's icky," I complained, but she made me drink it.

"It's nutritious," she commanded.

"It's gross," I insisted. "It's too sweet."

"Then water it down!" she barked.

I didn't know the words then for obsessive-compulsive behavior. I only knew that I hated our meals: shopping for them, making them, and eating them. I resisted and pouted.

I didn't know when I had pushed her too far until one day she turned on us.

"Please don't do the peach juice," I begged. "There're stringy things in it."

"Then drink it fast," she ordered. "And don't talk back!"

"I can't talk back," Sandy said. "I'm gagging on the juice."

Mom threw the juice jug to the table. It spilled and ran over the edge.

"Well, you just wasted it," Sandy dared.

"How dare you, you little shit," Mom growled. "I work my fingers to the bone for your food." Her voice reached its apex. "And what do I get?"

No matter how many times she said this, I'd steal a glance at her fingers. They looked OK to me.

Rule 2: Be Grateful

She told us what eating was—it was partaking of the blood and flesh of the Lord. "You are very blessed to have this food," Mom said at each meal.

I began to connect the food with God, which gave me comfort. I saw that every crumb, even the littlest of these, mattered. At church, the crust of the white Wonder Bread was the flesh of Jesus. Grape juice was His blood. Surely this was true at home as well.

Every night we were required to make a "salad." I opened a can of pineapple reverently, placed a spear on a hillock of cottage cheese, dropped a dollop of mayonnaise on top, and anointed it all with a sprinkle of paprika. These spiritual fantasies gave me a way to look forward to the evening cooking.

I shaped the body of Christ into a round patty of corned-beef hash, pressed a small depression in the middle with my fist, dropped a raw egg in the crater, and baptized it in the oven. One evening I forgot the egg until late in the process; the hash was overcooked, and the egg was undercooked. It looked like a corpse. "Dear Lord," I said in prayer as the family sat, our heads bowed, "thank you for allowing us to eat the dead, rotting body of Christ."

"Again," Mom chided.

"Good drink, good meat, good God, let's eat," I prayed, irritated.

"One more time, if you know what's good for you."

I mumbled more-appropriate thanks. We began to eat. I looked over at Lucy. She was eating her pale peas with concentration, even contentment, as though this meal were edible, even delicious. In the middle of the hash sat the shiny, barely baked egg. There was a red thread running through the yellow.

"That's God's eye," I said, pointing at the quivering yolk. Lucy hesitated. "Look, it's all pussing and weeping because Jesus is all mashed up—that hash is His body. You can see the intestines. Oh my god!"

"Kathy, stop that," Mom snapped, but I was on a roll. Lucy began to whimper.

I poked her cottage cheese with my spoon. "Ooooh, this is His snot and mucus, and that pear is His dead butt, all white and pale," I pricked the pear with my fork. "Jesus is naked on your salad plate. Are you really going to eat Him?"

Lucy began to cry. Her little sobs gave me enormous pleasure.

"Ew! Your peas are poop!"

"Poop?" Horror filled her eyes.

"Everybody shits when they die. It just falls out. Little green poop plops."

"These are Jesus's poops?"

"Yep, and—"

Suddenly Mom's fist landed on the side of my face, and I heard the crack of her hand as she crushed my ear.

"Shut up! Stop it right now!" she roared.

I spun around and slid off my chair. I heard the high whine of wind.

"Now get up and eat." She yanked me up and slammed me into the chair. I pretended there was no sound in my head and wiped my snot. I glanced at Lucy. Her face was as white as her hair, and she was gulping softly.

She was the sweetest of the sisters. I knew that. I don't know what propelled me to treat her so badly. I made promises to be good and immediately broke them. I snuffed out a spider she was corralling to take outside. I put gum in her shoes. I called her "bottle eyes." Even while I was teasing or pinching or pummeling her, I knew that I was being bad. But I couldn't stop. Another me would say to myself, "Stop that. You are being mean, and God will punish you." But I would go right on. I especially hated myself in the middle of some heinous torture I was inflicting upon her.

Who was I really torturing?

Lucy had her hands in her lap, twisting the paper napkin. I felt miserable. I wanted to tell her I was sorry, I wanted to make it up to her, have her like me again.

"I lied," I told her. "It's not God and Jesus."

She looked hopefully at me. I could make this right for her. But the temptation was too great.

"It's Joseph and Mary," I said.

She burst into tears.

Rule 3: Eat Every Bite

Of all the meals Mom taught us to cook, her favorite was pork and beans. She opened up a big can that had a slippery glob of pork fat floating in it. "Come to dinner," she trumpeted. "Pork 'n' beans tonight."

No one knew which bowl hid the thick lump. Mom's rule was that whoever got it had to eat it. I poked a fork stealthily through the bowl. If I found something firm, I watched until Mom looked away. Then I plunged my fork down into the fat, pulled it up, sneaked it down to my lap, wrapped it quickly in my napkin, and pocketed it. Then I pretended to thrust it in my mouth. I gagged. "Ugh! Oh, this is so awful, blech! Why do you make me eat this?"

Mom fixed her eyes on me. "It's protein," she said. "You're lucky to have it."

Sometimes, however, there was no escape, and I had to swallow it. So I pretended I was a prisoner of war—it was this or starve. My loved ones were waiting for me; I had to survive. When I made it home, I'd fall into their arms and gasp, "I ate pork fat for you."

If I hesitated to eat it, Mom stopped eating, sat straight up, and said firmly, "There are starving children in Africa who would be very grateful for that food."

What amazes me now is that I always took that admonition seriously and began to fret about the foodless children in foreign lands, imagining them to be the very children I had seen while sitting in Ninyah's closet sifting hour after hour through *National Geographic*. I had fond feelings for the children in those secret pages. Not just in Africa and Peru, but in Appalachia and New Mexico. Were they really starving?

Mom's chastisement worked on me, and I ate every scrap, but Sandy snidely offered to "ship the damn stuff off" to the starving children, who, she insisted, would refuse to eat it, too.

"Is that so, smarty pants?" Mom took the pork fat from her own bowl and put it in Sandy's. "You may not leave the table until you eat *all* of it." These predictable transfers of Mom's pork to someone else's bowl occurred often enough for me to believe she detested the blubbery gob as much as we did.

———•———

Eric and I sat on the lawn, across the street from the Imperial Street house.

"You know, for all her bitching and moaning about how women were treated unfairly," he said, "she never made us boys cook."

"It used to bug me," I responded. "You and Clark got to shovel the walks and take out the garbage, but we had to do all the 'girl things.' She was a paradox, wasn't she?"

"Among other things," he said, and laughed, his lip curling.

When I look back now, I realize that pork, even a glob in the middle of beans, was a luxury. My mother probably bought it on sale and thought it was a treat that we didn't appreciate. She had many disappointments, and our response to pork and beans was likely one of them.

Though she locked up the best of the food in her closet, she had likely done it because she didn't have the money to feed us better and she didn't want the food to run out between paydays. But her food mania, and our disastrous meals together, had unintended consequences for us. Today, as adults, all five siblings have eating disorders. For years I hoarded food, ate in private, and avoided preparing sit-down family meals for my own children. Whenever we did manage a meal together, I was tongue tied, vaguely frightened for what I thought was no good reason. I had learned to hoard what I had and steal what I didn't have.

Eric and I shared many of our experiences of our mother. Although each of us had already selected tokens for our different fathers and for our different Church experiences, we talked together about what we should choose to embody our mother.

"Something edible," I said, and laughed.

"Of course!"

Food. Our curse.

We went shopping for our tokens. We went to a grocery store and walked up and down the aisles together, crazily buying childhood food that was still being produced. That evening, we carried three paper sacks into the Stansbury Suites and unloaded them, first with giggles and then uncontrollable laughter, the manic hysteria that built whenever the siblings reminisced about our mother and food.

We stared at the pile of food in disbelief. What should we do with the lime Jell-O, canned green beans, and processed cheese slices? The potpies, the Wonder Bread? We sorted out the most meaningful food and put it all aside as tokens. We took the rest of it to a shelter.

It took me years to realize that having food was a sickness for me, sometimes mild, like a cold or the flu, sometimes more insidious and permanent, like eczema or the neuralgic aftermath of shingles. Over the years, I realized how closely this obsession was connected to, and twisted up in, the Church's doctrine of food storage, my grandparents' cornucopia of plenty, and my mother's refusal to feed us in a normal and loving way.

All I knew was I was anxious without food nearby—because I was not prepared for God's coming to get me in the Millennium; because I was loved by a grandmother, but unloved by a mother who used food so unconventionally against me; and because I was simply, unaccountably hungry. Food was love. And safety.

I began to hoard food, buying in bulk and stacking cases of food in the garage. I began to cook large portions of food and freeze them in dinner-size containers, label them carefully and stack them in the refrigerator and the freezer, then in a second large stand-up freezer in the garage, and then in my partner's parents' freezer.

Food was everywhere—I grew it, planned it, bought it, cooked it, ate it, canned it, and froze it. I saved it, and it saved me.

When I was depressed, I rose at three or four in the morning and began to cook—not just one thing, but several. One early morning, during a particularly obsessive spell, shortly before Eric and I traveled back to Salt Lake City, I woke at three with an uncontrollable desire to cook. By five that morning, homemade marinara sauce simmered on the stovetop burners, tuna casserole baked in the oven, and banana-bread batter waited in baking pans to follow the tuna casserole. I sat on the floor, where in large pots I alternately mixed hamburger for meatloaf, picked basil leaves for pesto, and dipped chicken parts in crushed Rice Krispies for chicken tenders.

My partner, wakened by the racket, stumbled into the kitchen, stood above me for a moment taking it in, and then said, gently, "What's wrong with this picture?"

Completely missing the point, I said, "It looks like we need a second stove."

CHAPTER 26

LITTLE REVOLUTIONS

———◆———

THE DAY HAD BEEN SO hot that Eric and I stayed in our Salt Lake City air-conditioned suite all afternoon. We cooked a large pot of spaghetti for dinner—with real noodles. As he tasted one for doneness, I laughed. "Remember when Sandy threw a canned spaghetti noodle on the ceiling to see if it was cooked enough?" We both laughed. "She must have learned that from Cook."

"We all kept trying not to look at the ceiling. We were afraid Mom would see it. She would have killed Sandy."

Eric drained the noodles, spooned the sauce, and we sat to eat. "She was a terrible mother," he mused.

"She was," I said. "But we paid her back big-time, didn't we?"

"We sure did," Eric agreed. "But boy, we were a handful."

———◆———

As Sandy and I entered our late teens, we began our revolution, pulling Lucy and the boys along.

At almost eighteen, Sandy was a model of rebellious behavior for all of us, and we were mostly willing students. At sixteen, I was the most reluctant, still of a mind that I could save Mom. Lucy, thirteen, home from Alabama a year, was quiet but willing. Clark was eleven, and though not yet fully committed to our rebellions, he went along.

But Eric, nine, the youngest and feistiest, became the leading war-rior against Mother's abuses. His guerilla hits continued until he was banished from the home five years later.

Sandy sassed her, ignored her, and mumbled snide comments under her breath.

Lucy sneaked out of the house at night and sneaked her boyfriend in, left clues for Mom and then denied them.

Clark tore pages out of her magazines.

Eric crawled through the ceiling crawl space to a hatch in Mom's bedroom closet, lowered himself into the locked closet, and stole the food.

Sandy and I short-sheeted Mom's bed; Eric hid her false teeth. We "forgot" to give her phone messages, put sugar in the saltshaker and vice versa, called her at work over and over although we weren't supposed to, put glue in her wigs and sand in her gas tank.

In the middle of night, I jammed her car horn, watching from the window as she sped out of the house in her nightgown and curlers and frantically searched for the source of the blare.

One Thanksgiving, she had a tantrum and broke most of the dishes. The girls pitched in our job money, and for Christmas we bought her a set of unbreakable Melmac dishes—the cheap and decidedly low-class alternative to china. We wrapped it extravagantly and put a card on it that said: "For all you do." Mom got teary when she picked up the box and read the card, and gave us such a loving look that we looked guiltily at one an-other. She opened the box and pulled out the tissue hiding the surprise.

As the gift and its intentions registered, her smile faded. She simply looked at us, said, "Thanks," and took her coat from the chair. "I'll be back in a bit," she said. Out the back door she went, down the steps to her car. She backed out of the driveway and drove away. She was gone for an hour.

She was still in her lavender nightgown. She called it a peignoir. We laughed at her and called it her "pig-wah."

Mom had the occasional date, and she insisted that the five children hide downstairs in the basement so her date wouldn't know she was a single mother until he had fallen in love with her. One night, she was aflutter in anticipation of an upcoming date. She primped all day like a preening bird.

Unbeknownst to her, we had prepared. Mom was in her bedroom, putting on the final touches. We sneaked upstairs and watched for her date to arrive. We opened the door as he came up the walk, invited him in, and greeted him enthusiastically.

"Hi, we're Sereta's five children."

He stood there awkwardly as we lined up quickly in a row and smiled sweetly. All together, taking little mincing steps, we sang "If Mama Was Married" from *Gypsy*. We reached the chorus, which we sang out loud and longingly, our hands in prayer formation: "Oh, Mama, get married today!"

By that time, Mom had come out of the bedroom and was standing in the dining room, dumbfounded, her mouth slightly open, her eyes bright with shame.

"Really, Sereta," the man said coldly. "You didn't tell me."

We never saw him again. Mom stopped dating.

———◆———

Eric and I laughed as we recounted these exploits. But suddenly a heavy sorrow descended over me.

For days I had been feeling confused: intent on my anger and resentment yet pulled another way by pity. Now as we recalled our "mischief," as we called it, I realized that we had been much more than a handful. We had been cruel. Defensively, yes—little warriors, underdogs in a great war—but cruel nevertheless.

Even so, Mom had not left the field. I had to give her that.

Sandy escaped first. It happened when she was eighteen. I was sixteen. It was the Christmas season.

We girls had musical talent and were good performers, which Mom encouraged. She paid for Sandy's singing lessons. I took piano, Lucy the violin, the boys horns.

Sandy was the best of the bunch; she sang the lead in school musicals and solos in church. I could play the piano passably and sing fairly well, if others were around me, so I made a good choir girl. Lucy's violin was magic.

It was under Mom's fingers, however, that the piano came alive, chasing all chaos from the house in a sweep of beauty. The piano stood in the living room, taking up most of the room. We were not allowed to touch it, except to practice or to clean the white keys with a damp, soapy cloth and to oil the ebony-black surface. Mom lovingly lifted the lid and propped it up with a rod that folded out of the padded keys and strings. Everything sparkled from her attention. She sat to play, and out of that piano came the loveliest notes.

When she sang, her smoker's voice filled the room—that deep alto voice, rough like bark, vibrant and dense. Her notes played and her voice sang, and the music was as rich as a calm spring midnight, lit by moon.

Sometimes, in the late-night hours, we lay in our basement bedroom and heard Mom singing "Ol' Man River" or "Can't Help Lovin' That Man of Mine." We crept up the stairs and sat squished together at the top, listening. Sandy put her arm around me.

Some evenings, when Mom had had a few drinks, she'd say, "Come on now, girls, let's have a concert." We'd drop whatever we were doing, because this was special. We gathered around the piano. Clark and Eric sat on the couch—our audience. Mom played, Sandy's soprano was sweet and clear, and I harmonized. Lucy followed on her fiddle, her head bobbing up and down, her arm flowing back and forth. Clark and Eric clapped and hollered: "Hoorah! Bravo! Encore!"

Mom stood and bowed, spread her arms to a broader audience, and gave a speech. "I have the most talented children any mother can have!" She pointed at Sandy. "Of course, Sandy is no Maria Callas." Then she pointed at Lucy. "And take Lucy, she's no Jack Benny." She then swept her arm to point at me. "And take my Kathy—" She paused. "Pleeeeease, take my Kathy." She laughed uproariously. We didn't get the joke, but we laughed, too, just to laugh with her.

At Christmastime, during Sandy's senior year in high school, she was chosen to sing a solo of "O Holy Night" in the city's all-high-school concert. To accompany her, she chose Lucy, who practiced for hours in preparation. I was only a sophomore, but I had been chosen to sing backup with the senior choir. We three girls practiced together, singing/playing, "The stars are brightly shining," and we were the stars.

On the evening of the performance, all five of us were dressed, excited, and ready to go, but Mom was in a funk. All morning she'd been lying on the living-room couch, in her lavender peignoir and a matching robe, asking for juice, or crackers, or a head rub.

"Come on, Mom, get dressed. We're all ready to go. We have to be there an hour early," Sandy said.

She groaned. "We can't go. I don't feel well." She held her stomach.

Sandy stood looking at Mom for a minute and then walked to the table, took the car keys from Mom's purse, and put them in her pocket. "Fine. We'll go without you. I'll drive."

"But Mom," Lucy pleaded, "this is so big! The whole city will be there. Please come! You've got to hear Sandy's solo. She's so good."

"And Lucy's violin, too," I coaxed.

Something changed. Mom looked puzzled, irritated. Her mouth twitched. We were all quiet, just standing there, watching a shift. It was as though Mom had decided on something.

"No, you won't," she said, sitting up slowly. She looked at Lucy and me. "Girls, I need to ask you a favor."

I was only sixteen, so I didn't know everything, but I believe I knew what was about to happen. Years later, I understood that on this night, my heart began to freeze. For decades, it would not thaw.

"What, Mom?" I said. My body felt crushed with disappointment.

"I need you all to stay home. I am very, very sick."

We stood in silence. Something foggy was seeping in, sucking out all the air, leaving everything damp.

Mom had a temper, but she never took it out on the boys. Eric was her baby; she called him her favorite child. Clark she ignored; he reminded her of our father. Years later, Clark would describe himself as "the nobody in the family, an afterthought, which required no more thought."

Instead, Mom took her temper out on us girls. She yelled and screamed, shot invectives and insults that wounded us, and guilt-tripped us. "I may not be around much longer" was her favorite. She tried to commit suicide several times, but we always saved her and doted on her for a while after each rescue.

If she couldn't get what she wanted by yelling for it, she staged a fit. She fell on the floor and quivered as though from an electrical shock or an epileptic seizure. Or she grabbed her stomach, curled up in bed, and moaned as if in pain. We called it her Mad Fit. We knew she was crazy, but when it happened, it was a powerful storm.

It always worked with me. I was an excellent savior, rapt through fear. I would fall in line.

"Mom," said Sandy, chilly as a winter post. "We won't stay home. We have to go."

I couldn't feel myself breathe. A tempest was roiling. There was a dark, threatening pause.

"You don't understand," said Mom, standing shakily and then rising to her full height. "I am your mother, and I am ill. What if I die while you're gone? I will be here all alone, dying, with no one to summon help." She let this sink in. "As your mother, I am asking you to stay."

Sandy laughed, but Lucy began to cry. "Mom," she said softly, still not giving up. "I'm playing the violin."

"Is a violin more important than your mother?" Her voice deepened. "Are all those strangers who come to hear you play more important than your mother?" Her voice was strident now and angry. "Will that make you happy, to come home and find me dead?"

"No, Mom," I said, "of course not. No one is more important than you. But why don't you come and sit right in the front row. You'll have the best seat, right in the front. We'll watch you and make sure you're OK."

"Stay!" she said flatly. "I am ordering you. You *will!* And that's that." No one spoke, but there was thunder in my ears.

"No."

No? Where did that come from? Clark and Lucy were looking at Sandy, so I looked, too. She stood rigid, her face hardened. Then again, from her mouth, came "No."

"What did you say?" Mom's voice was low, ominous. Her eyes were lightning cracks.

"I said no, Mom. We are going."

My eyes couldn't leave Mom's face. It was gray and washed out. I saw her then at what I know now is a young age—late thirties. Yet I recall her as old and haggard. For a shocking moment, I could see the toil of raising five children as it played out in the shadowy lines on her face and in the deep V-shaped wrinkles above her nose. Her fine golden hair looked thin and insubstantial. Her stooping body was a wreck of hardship. My heart broke for her and began to harden.

To underline this extraordinary act of rebellion, Sandy took my hand, and then Lucy's hand, and backed us toward the door. "Come on, girls. Mom will be fine. Clark, you take Eric and go get in the car." They ran out. Lucy buried her head in Sandy's arm; I looked over my shoulder as we turned.

Mom dropped her arms and clenched her fists at her side. "How dare you?" she commanded. "How dare you talk to me like that? How dare you defy me?" She walked straight over to Sandy, grabbed her by the shoulder and slapped her face.

Sandy slapped her back. Mom stumbled.

"You ungrateful bitch! I've given everything I have to raise you girls. And all alone, working two jobs. No help. Not from anybody. You think I get any help from your father? That bastard? Your grandparents?" She made a spitting sound. "I do not! Nobody helps me. I take care of you all by myself."

She began a gulping sob. I thought these were real tears. But this didn't stop her raging on. "And is this what I get?" Louder, more terrifying. "You are nothing but hateful, greedy children. I should have left you long ago." Her face was ravaged.

She took a teetering step backward, holding her arm. Her anger bent her over, twisted her. "I can't take it anymore."

I watched, confused and numb. Sandy's face was impassive, as still as stone. She clutched our hands tighter, turned, and walked us toward the door. She looked back. "Good-bye, Mother. We'll be home by eleven."

Suddenly, Mom wailed. I thought I had never heard a sound as bad as that. I turned around. I watched in horror as she clutched her shoulder and her upper arm. "I think...I'm having...a heart attack." She sputtered; spittle bubbled out of her mouth. She fell with a weighty crash, facedown on the floor. One arm was pinned beneath her, the other flung out. Her legs were corkscrewed.

I was shocked. Lucy whimpered. Sandy let go of our hands. "Stay there," she instructed us.

She walked over to where Mom lay still and stood over her. To my astonishment, she lectured her. "Mother," she said sternly, though her voice was shaking, "you're faking, and we know it. We are not going to be intimidated by this kind of behavior anymore."

Mom didn't move, but Sandy went on speechifying, as though she had prepared in advance and was just waiting for an opportunity. "We love you, believe me. We are grateful for all that you do for us. We try as best we can to do our share. But we are leaving. If you die, we will miss you. But today, we are going singing."

With that, she turned again and grabbed our hands. Her fingers were cold. She pushed us out the front door. I heard the door close firmly behind me.

I was stunned. I wanted to run back, call the ambulance, help the medics load her onto a stretcher, hold her hand, and encourage her. "Live, Mom, live!"

Sandy shoved me into the car.

The car started.

But I was out of the car.

I ran to the front door. I pushed it open. I rushed in.

Mom was sitting up, brushing herself off. I was hysterical. All I knew was she was safe! I threw myself into her arms, buried my head in her neck, hugged her, patted her back, and cried, "Oh, Mom!" I choked, "I don't want you to die!"

I didn't then. But I did later.

She was quiet.

"Mom, *I'll* stay." I begged, "Please forgive Sandy, please, Mom. She shouldn't have said those things. She's awful not to stay." I buried my head deeper into Mom's lavender robe. "She'll go to Hell for this."

Mom very gently began to rub my hair. She put her arms around me, hugged me tightly, and kissed my head. She rocked me back and forth until my tears slowed.

"Oh, Kathy," she said, sighing softly. "Dear Kathy."

She pressed my cheek into the folds of her robe. "Sandy will be just fine," she said. "Just fine. She'll get along just fine in this world." She lifted my chin. "It's you I'm worried about."

Sandy left home. She didn't return.

———◆———

Eric and I headed for ZCMI. I knew exactly the token I wanted.

He waited while I went to the ladies' lingerie department. Lying on a table, under a sign reading "Let it Happen," were several samples of frilly underwear—sexy bras, old-fashioned garter belts, lacy underpants, all color coordinated.

I picked up a pair of panties and a matching silky flat-breasted camisole. Lavender.

"Charming," said the matronly clerk. "For your daughter?"

"For my mother." I smiled. "And for me."

CHAPTER 27

OUT OF THE VALLEY

———◆———

SANDY HAD ESCAPED INTO MARRIAGE. My flight was marked by my dark secret.

Thirty years later, Eric and I sat on the curb across the street from the Imperial Street house. The late-August sun drifted behind a large cottonwood tree, giving us shade. Finches flitted in and out of a bird-feeder. Eric picked up a small branch from beneath the tree.

"Oh my god," Eric said. "Remember that horrible, dreadful night?"

I had never spoken of it.

"Mmmm," I murmured. "It has haunted me forever." I felt like gravity was pulling my heart out of my chest.

"She was blue," he said dreamily, tapping the branch against the ground. "Blue."

"That night," I finally said. "You were so little, only ten. And I was so cruel."

———◆———

Hating the pandemonium and cacophony at Imperial Street, I moved to an apartment with a girlfriend when I was nineteen. I welcomed my independence. But I called home frequently; if Mom answered, I hung up.

Sometimes, I simply wanted to be there.

I was restless for reasons I couldn't define. I went home frequently when Mom was at work. I walked around the house, looking in all of the rooms, touching things. I was standing on an edge, wanting to jump off, scared to do so. I knew I had to leave, go far away. But where? When? And how could I leave my siblings?

The night Sandy left on her honeymoon, she held me in her arms, cried, and apologized. "I'm sorry, Kathy, I have to go. I have to go." I understood.

One evening I knew all the children were gone for the night. Lucy was sleeping over at Ninyah's house. Clark was staying with Aunt Rose and Uncle Thurston, with whom he would eventually live when he was a teenager. Eric was at a Little League sleepover. Mom had a night job. So the house would be empty.

I came to the darkened house, walked up the two steps to the back door, entered, and flipped on the light in the kitchen. No one was there. I called out to silence. It answered me in the way silence did, with an arm around my shoulder, an invitation: "Come on in, dear. She's not home."

Defiantly, I fixed myself a peanut-butter-and-jelly sandwich. If Mom unexpectedly came home and began to rail at my eating her food, I was determined to confront her. I'd been getting stronger: success in high school and now college, a teacher who had taken me under his wing, a job I was excelling at, and a sometimes boyfriend had sown a seed of self-confidence that was pushing out of my earth, vibrant and sun seeking. I'd been resisting Mom's accusations and demands. Even so, she could reduce me to tears, apologies, and lies.

And guilt. When I came to visit her, in the hope of a loving connection, she greeted me with a pathetic "So you finally came to visit your poor old mother." If I didn't call often enough, she complained, "What's the matter, your finger broken?" When I bought an old Chevy to drive to and from work, she whined, "Well, I see *you* can afford to live high on the hog."

I look back now and see her desperation. Sandy was gone. I was on my way.

That night in the kitchen, as a creature of habit, I cleaned the counter of all crumbs. I smoothed the peanut butter in the jar to make it look like none was missing; I stirred up the jam so it appeared untouched. I loosened the bread in the package to affect a full loaf. But I was nervous and anxious.

I was reaching for the chips when suddenly the back door burst open. In that moment, all my fear rose up in me and whipped around. My elbow caught the plate and sent it shattering to the floor. I burst into tears.

Something in me split open, and I lifted my arms. I would not take it anymore. I was nineteen years old. She could come to beat me, and I would hit her back.

"Peanut butter!" I wailed. "It's just fucking peanut butter!"

Eric stood there, his face mottled and fiercely red. "Kathy!" he yelled.

"Fuck you, Mom. Don't get on me!" I yelled.

"Kathy!" he yelled.

"I can eat the goddamned peanut butter if I—"

"The car's running. I'm sure—"

"You can't make me—"

"—get it open. You have to come—"

"I hate you. I hate everything about you. Everything."

It came out in a jumble of dissonance and complaint. My hands flew to my face. I was keening. "Aa-haah, aa-haah."

Eric was hysterical. His hands beat my chest, hitting and flailing. "Kathy!"

He began to pump his arms up and down, his breath coming in bursting exhales. His eyes were wide in terror.

I cried out. "What?"

I finally saw it was Eric. I grabbed his shoulders, bounced with him in his furious excitement, shouting to be heard. "What? What?"

Was Mom coming? Was he warning me? I had to stop screaming, but the rush of the sounds, high and piercing, overtook me. *We must keep it up*, I thought senselessly. *Mom won't enter a screaming kitchen.*

Our screams fed on our screams and rose in pitch—his decade of endurance, my decades of fear. Our tears would flood through the wreckage and wash her away.

Eric hit me on my arms, his slaps stinging. "Stop!" he yelled. He pounded at me, fists on my chest. "Kathy! Kathy! Kathy!"

He sobbed as he tried to form words. He fell to his knees, grabbed mine. I touched his head, which was hot and damp.

"Stop," I said. "Tell me what's wrong."

He let go of my ankles, stood, and grabbed my arm. He pulled me toward the door. "Come out. Please!" he cried. "I can't get the door open."

There was the door, and it stood open, as he had left it. Alarm seized me. My candy-eyed, ten-year-old brother, waist high to me, was frantic because he couldn't get a door open that was open.

I picked him up and forced him backward toward the door.

"Out! Get out!" I yelled. "It's open, don't you see? You can get out! You can go." I pushed him and he fell, stumbling backward, down the three steps to the small landing on the stairs.

I followed his fall and picked him up again to push him through the door, but he went limp, shaking. He was too heavy to lift. I was pulled down to his side as I tried. I held him on my lap, rocked and soothed him. He wrapped his arms around my waist; his head bobbed on my chest.

"I can't save her," he mumbled into my heart.

"No," I said, rocking. "No." I understood. His sorrow was mine—I'd wanted to save Mom, too. I brushed his hair and kissed the top of his head. I said, "We can't save her. If we try, we'll ruin our own lives. I'm only just learning that. But you—" I rested my cheek on his smallness.

He lifted himself and looked up at me, his blue eyes afraid. "So we should let her die?"

"Oh, honey," I said, "she's always dying. She's not going to really die for a long time, no matter what she threatens."

"But she's in there, dying. In the garage."

I pulled back. "What are you talking about?"

He looked to the open door. "In the garage. I can't get the door open. I heard the car running. I came back 'cause I forgot—"

I knew I should jump up, run to the garage.

"—the basketball, but the door was shut. I couldn't open it. I heard the engine. The radio—"

I knew I should run, force up the garage door.

I knew I should.

But I didn't.

I knew then what was happening. Mom was trying to kill herself. She was slumped down in the front seat of her old Ford Fairlane, sooty exhaust fumes thickening.

I sat there.

I imagined her drama.

I imagined she had written a note and hid it for someone to find. "I can't take it anymore," it would begin. "All I ever got in this life was sorrow." She would list her catalogue of losses, resentments, and complaints. "I gave everything I have to you children, and look how you repaid me. I would have been so happy if it weren't for you. I'll be better off without you."

I imagined she hid the note but not well enough that the adults wouldn't find it, pass it around. "Best you children not read this," Aunt Elaine would caution. "She writes she loves you very much."

"Oh, pshaw!" Uncle Thurston would scoff. "Why don't you tell them the truth?"

I imagined her dressed in her lavender nightgown. She walked to the garage and pulled the door down behind her, leaving a slit. She started the engine, tuned the radio to her favorite station, and twisted the volume loud to alert us.

She knew we would find her. We always found her.

"Kathy?" Eric looked up at me. I was still rocking him. "There's no crack under the door. And I can't get it open. She must have backed the car into it so no one can get to her."

"She knew we'd find her."

"No. She means it this time, I know. She didn't know I was coming home. And she didn't know you were, either."

I stared at the white curtain covering the small window in the back door. Two rods held it, the material gathered and threaded onto the rods. Dirt caked the ruffles. Who did the laundry, now that I was gone?

"Please. Can't we try?"

He leaped off my lap. He headed for the door.

But I sat there, dumb and silenced. A profound thought penetrated. A story formed. Here was my chance to escape. I could make it happen. I could kill my mother. I could finally be free.

———◆———

I would like to be able to tell you that we raced outside down the driveway, grabbed the woodpile ax, and broke open the door to the garage. That we grabbed the shovel and the baseball bat, and smashed in the car windows.

I would like to tell you that we cut our arms reaching in through the jagged glass to the locks. And that our arms bear faint white lines, the keloid scars of proof that we saved her.

I would like to tell you that we dragged Mom's heavy, limp body from the front seat to the cold pavement, dragged her out of the garage through the small passage between the car doors and the wall. How her head hit the concrete and bumped as we jerked her through the smashed door to the lawn. How her lips were white, how I slapped her face and breathed my saving breath into her lungs.

But I can't tell you that.

I just sat there on the step. I knew Mom was dying and that Eric could not save her alone. I wanted her to die. I felt the pressure at the base of my eyes, pushing into my nose, cutting off my breath.

I thought, *My mother has no breath; she is saturated with carbon monoxide, deprived of air.* I thought, *She is choking on fumes—colorless, odorless, and tasteless.* I thought, *She is drowning in absence. How does it feel, Mom?*

This was my flight, my soaring away. If I let her die, I would be free to leave. She would smother in her airless defeat. I would breathe.

This was my secret—I just sat, willing to let my mother die. I did not save her.

But little ten-year-old Eric must have, still a child. A beating heart, legs racing, arms swinging the ax, he must have grabbed and pulled the heavy, sagging weight of our monster mother to the ground. Her hair dank, body flopping, legs dragging, face caved in. A little boy lugging his mother while his murderous sister sat stiff backed and silent, grief pushing her out of the valley, over the mountains.

He must have sweated and strained to save our mother, while I sat in my strenuous silence and delivered myself out of the throes of suffering, as if I were being born again and she were dying in childbirth.

I had not saved her, but Eric had.

———◆———

Eric and I sat across the street from the Imperial Street house, staring at the back door through which he ran that night.

"I remember it as though it were yesterday," Eric said. He kept tapping the sidewalk with his stick. "How could we forget?"

I was silent.

"Man, that was a close call." He sighed, lifting and then collapsing his shoulders, scuffing a round stone with the toe. "Just think if you hadn't been there. I couldn't have done it without you."

Suddenly I felt chilled. My skin prickled.

He looked up at me, smiled sadly, and was silent himself for a moment. Then he spoke. "Though I'm not sure why we saved her."

"We?"

———◆———

As it turns out, we both saved her. Eric told me the story of our storming the garage, our furious struggle to drag her from the car to the lawn. We had cut our arms reaching in through the broken window to the locks.

As he talked, I remembered more details: the lace dragging from Mom's torn nightgown, her lavender slipper on the drive, her arm bleeding from scraping the concrete.

I leaned over her and pushed her chest to force her air out. I blew my life into her lungs and tongued the acrid taste of her breath as it mingled with mine, then filled her up again with my own heart's pumped air. Eric slapped her cheeks to wake her up. "She's safe now," I said as she began to breathe.

She sat up with a jerk and threw up on the grass. She looked at us and burst out, "Goddamn it!"

We helped her to her bed. I undressed her and washed the vomit from her face, dampened her brow with a cloth, put on a clean nightgown, and called the bishop, who came to pray over her and give her a Church blessing. She paid him no heed. We brought her water that she sipped through a straw, told her how much we loved her and that she had a lot to live for. She turned her face to the wall.

When the bishop left, Eric and I went to her bedside. She turned to us, her face cold and set.

"You're useless, Kathy," she said. "You can't even let me die."

Stunned, I said, "I wish I had."

———◆———

"You were kind of crazy that night, Katharine," Eric remembered. "Afterward, you acted like it hadn't ever happened."

I showed Eric a faint keloid scar on my arm. "I could never remember where I got it."

"Mine, too." He showed me his.

———◆———

I rarely spoke to my mother after that. She came to my wedding, but Ninyah planned it. I married as soon as I could and left Salt Lake City for Oregon. I carried a great weight of guilt for my unnatural desire to be rid of my mother, for my shocking willingness to let her die, and what I remembered as my failure to rescue her.

Decades later, sitting on the curb with Eric in the waning sunshine, I wept for a long time. Eric gave me comforting hugs, patted my head, and put his arm around me. "It's OK, Sis," he soothed. "We all wanted her to die." He was quiet for a while. "And look here. We have one another. That's one thing Mom did right. Almost until the end, she kept us together."

She had. Long before welfare or ADC, long before unemployment compensation and food stamps, without any child support from our fathers, Mom had kept us together.

———————

Eric and I shared many conversations during that trip—about Mom, Daddy, Eric's father, our grandparents. But most often we talked about our relationships with our siblings. We all operated on an unstated principle: Though we suffered in concert, each of us had to find our own way out of this family. We would do the best we could to help for as long as possible, but to survive, we had to eventually abandon our siblings—our individual survival came first. Later, we hoped, we would come together again.

Each of us made it, more or less, give or take. Now, as we approached middle age, we entered the shadows of our separate memories, step by step, sharing what we could of our secrets, marveling in our enduring love. And we acknowledged now the glue that held us together during our childhood, ironically making it possible for us to escape it. Our mother.

———————

Eric and I walked slowly up the driveway toward the side of the Imperial Street house. Still no one was home. I went to the back-door steps leading onto the small hall landing. I peered in the window and could see the dimly lit kitchen. I couldn't stop looking. It occurred to me that there had been milk in that kitchen. And bread, eggs, apples, cereal. In the locked closet, there had been backups. And cans and cans of food to be meted out until next payday.

On the table had been her ledgers, noting each scrap of income, each penny of debt, regular one-dollar or three-dollar payments, all balancing. In my basement bedroom, shared happily with my sisters, on three comfortable twin beds pushed close together we had talked into the night, scratched one another's backs, sung to ourselves, and listened to Mom upstairs, playing her beloved piano, lulling us to sleep.

Throughout the journey home so many years later, locked in my fully justified resentment, I had given little credit to my happy memories—the trips to Saltair and Bear Lake, all of us packed happily in the car; the reliable Christmas trees, the family decorating them together, singing carols; Mom's proud encouragement of our at-home performances, her clapping and huzzahing.

Now through the window, I could touch her poverty; I could see her bent over her books, overworked; and I could hear her weep in the night, lonely and disappointed. Yet she had not deserted us. She had stumbled along, raised her five children alone, her own parents against her. We hated her in good faith, but we must have loved her as well.

As dusk fell, Eric and I looked for mementos to place into our sacks. We walked slowly toward the side of the still-dark Imperial Street house, down the driveway. He picked up a sliver of wood lying at the base of the garage, peeled off from a few years of inattention. He sat down by the garage door, his head in his hands. "Give me a minute," he said.

Beside the steps was a long trough of stones and gravel. There I found a large rock, broken in two, the outside of which was dull and cracked. The inside of the rock was glossy, almost polished, and smooth from the split. Like an agate, it was colored. I took the two halves for my sack.

I paused for a long time, thinking. About Daddy. About Ninyah and Baba. Then I looked again and grabbed more rocks, several large ones, and a handful of smaller ones, a few pebbles—different sizes, shapes, and textures. I loaded the stones into my bag.

Eric looked at me quizzically.

"I think we might need these," I said vaguely.

CHAPTER 28

BEAR LAKE

———————

WE DROVE NORTH TO BRIGHAM City, our bags of tokens in the back-seat, and then northeast through gentle Sardine Canyon to Logan. We climbed up through the spectacularly beautiful Logan Canyon, over the high passes to the summit, from which we saw Bear Lake far below, half in Utah, half in Idaho, stretching seven miles wide and eighteen miles long.

From the air, passengers are astonished to see the most brilliantly colored lake imaginable. Bear Lake reflects limestone particles and calcium carbonate, so the surface of the lake shines through in more blues than the language has words for: turquoise, azure, cobalt, navy, sapphire, ultramarine, and midnight.

In the winter, the sky is a quilt of grays and blacks, and the lake sometimes freezes over into a vast steppe of white. Small ponds melt within it and shine through in crystal and ice blues.

All my best childhood memories are of the summers I spent there in Ninyah and Baba's two summer cabins on the lake: the Big House, a large old lodge converted into a house, and behind it, the Little House, an old icehouse converted into a smaller cabin.

The houses had no indoor plumbing for many years, so we trudged to the outhouse; no running water, so we pumped it from our well; no electric heat, so we fetched coal for the fireplace and stove. We washed our clothes in a wringer machine and hung them on the line with wooden clothespins. Each moment held my attention, and life was good. Here I indulged my best child self: hiking in the hills and caves, swimming in the lake when it was warm, and reading, writing, and dreaming. I roller-skated at Ideal Beach, where I got a job as a key girl, locking skaters' skates onto their shoes.

Ninyah often took me with her to Bear Lake for parts of the summer. If Mom drove us, she piled us out of the car and said cheerfully, "Go on, now. I don't want to have anything to do with you this whole week." Off she'd go, into the Big House to sit on the porch and drink. Later, she'd sunbathe on the beach, which fronted the house. We children were free to roam and play as we wished. Mom hardly ever spoke to us. It was a child's Heaven.

I loved the great spaces of the Big House: its sensible compact floor plan, square, with a huge central living room furnished with several overstuffed couches and chairs, all of which were upholstered with Ninyah's fashioned slipcovers. A massive stone fireplace reached to the ceiling. An upright piano stood against the wall. A bench with a padded lid held scores of sheet music, a hymnal, and piles of Broadway-musical songbooks. I remember very little of my mother's presence in the Big House, but I do remember her sitting at this upright piano: her cigarette on one side, the smoke curling up from the ashtray; her drink on a coaster on the other side; and her hands tumbling over the keys, her voice rumbling out "My Funny Valentine" or "Can't Help Lovin' That Man of Mine."

Through swinging doors on both sides of the living room stretched a kitchen almost the full width of the house, filled with a cornucopia of food. On the kitchen table for breakfast were laid great platters filled with bacon and sausage, pork chops, liver and onions, scrambled eggs, toast brown on both sides and buttered to the edges, cereal, oranges and apples, pancakes with syrup made from boiling water, sugar, and Mapleine.

Lunches were different. We were allowed to make anything we wanted whenever we were hungry. Ninyah put out an assemblage of sandwich makings—peanut butter and jams, baloney and lettuce, cheese, pickles, and bananas. Homemade soup simmered on the stove. And for dessert, Oreos, fresh fruit, sunflower seeds, or Popsicles.

Dinner was formal. Ninyah rang a dinner bell—a large metal triangle that pealed, loud and clattering—to call us from the beach, or the creek, or the scrub in which we played hide-and-seek. We washed our hands and faces, tidied our hair and clothes, and sat with our hands in our lap until Baba said the prayer.

On the dining-room table, great heaps of food circled around on the lazy Susan in the center. Ninyah bustled back and forth, bringing more of her succulent fried chicken, handmade mashed potatoes with no skin to be seen, beehive-yellow corn on the cob that had little handles sticking out the ends, soft butter, rich gravy, and bowls piled high with fresh-cooked vegetables. For dessert, homemade pie, filled with the raspberries we'd picked that morning, and homemade ice cream full of butter fat, straight from the Pickleville Country Store.

At the table we sat and ate with pleasure, laughter filling the air, politeness all around. Ninyah insisted that Mom behave, drink less, and make no snide remarks.

I was giddy with joy at the lazy Susan spinning with plenty and at the social intercourse. The children talked and giggled. Ninyah didn't stop our fun, so long as we didn't get too loud and raucous. She and Baba joined in, conversed, asked questions, gave answers, and solved problems.

"How can I sew a seam when the material is cut on the bias?" Sandy asked, and Ninyah told her.

"Why can't I wear long pants at church?" I asked. And Ninyah passed me the buttered peas. "Here, dear, have some."

Baba discussed serious issues with us. "Why do leaves change color?" Eric asked, and Baba explained photosynthesis and launched into regeneration.

"Why do boys get to rake the leaves and girls don't?" I asked, and Baba told me he would help me wash and dry the dishes.

The kitchen was open at all times and stocked with all the food I could eat. I even had a little stool that Ninyah bought for me so I could stand on it and get to the crackers, the chips, and the cold cereal. I stood on it and reached into the freezer for Popsicles, ice-cream sandwiches, and frozen grapes. I stood on my stool sometimes to eat, too much in a hurry to make it to the table.

The beachfront wraparound porch was U-shaped and screened; each side held a large bedroom, separated from the front porch by a heavy canvas blind. Blinds covered the screened sides as well, to keep out the wind and rain. Each bedroom had two separate bunk beds, so four children could sleep in each bedroom.

Adults preferred the inside bedrooms, but the children favored the porch, of course. We rolled the blinds up and down with a thick rope pull. When it was stormy out, the wind rushed in through the screen, lifting the rolled-down canvas blinds until they flapped against the posts that secured them. On calmer nights, we rolled up the blinds and watched the lake, the waves lapping on the shore, and the stars multiplying in a clear sky.

These rooms were secret hideaways, thrilling and cozy.

In the mornings, Baba dressed, stirred then banked the ashes in the fireplace, and added coal. In the kitchen he started a fire in the stove and put on the hot chocolate. When the house was warmed up, he woke us. We climbed from bed in our flannel pajamas, put on our robes and slippers, and came in from the cold porch to the living room. We snuggled into the couches in front of the fireplace, and Baba brought us hot chocolate on trays.

These were my idyllic summers, as liquid, as colorful, and as deep as the lake.

———— ◆ ————

Now Eric and I descended the mountain to Bear Lake, passed through Garden City, then Pickleville, and then past Ideal Beach. We drove down the long driveway past the Little House, toward the Big House we'd rented from our cousins. I looked up to see the roof's red chimney, where I'd sat for hours dreaming in the sun.

We parked the car in a patch of grass, where I had set out dinner for my dolls, feeding them grass as spinach and dirt clods as meatloaf. When we entered the house, I saw the bookcase that was always filled with interesting books—adventure tales, classics, and plays—from which I had invented many a tale of heroism and grandeur.

We unloaded our suitcases and our bags of tokens. I placed my bulging duffel-size sack on the floor of a front-porch bedroom. It was heavy, too full of too many objects, some picked up, some purchased. Tomorrow, on the lake, we would discard them and all they symbolized.

We lit a fire in the fireplace. Above the mantle hung a large framed print of an old aerial photograph of Bear Lake, on which we could pinpoint our grandparents' cabin. We sat in companionable silence, writing.

Tomorrow, each of us would say a word or two as we threw in a token. So certain of what I would say, I had written my script of good-byes to my mother, my father, and my Church before we had even started on the trip. But much had changed. So I wrote in my journal, preparing some different eulogies for the next day. As I wrote, I scowled or laughed, sighed or shed tears. Eric, too, smiled or frowned. All talk was unnecessary that evening.

Early the next day, we drove to Ideal Beach and rented our motorboat. The sky was blue; an autumn sun warmed the lake.

As children, we boated in our uncle's speedboat, jumping waves on water skis or simply skimming endlessly up and down the lake's miles. In the summer, storms could come up quickly, and sometimes we were caught in a darkening thicket of clouds. We headed quickly for shore, racing to beat the rising waves; Bear Lake took its dead quickly, without warning, and every summer boaters or swimmers were caught in its merciless storms.

Today the autumn sun was shimmering in the air, the sky was cloudless, and a blanket of blue stretched over the mountains. The lake was at its most resplendent, with navy, turquoise, and light-blue swaths striping from end to end—a perfect lake to accept our tokens.

We lugged our cumbersome bags into our rented boat. My bag had morphed into what looked like a gargantuan pickle, puffed up and lumpy. In a smaller sack, however, I carried the rocks and stones I had picked up at the Imperial Street house.

Eric had been no less the gatherer. He had a suitcase full of tokens. Inventive as always, he had crafted many of his own symbols from baling wire, twist ties, pipe cleaners, and electrical tape.

We had also packed lunches. Big lunches.

We set course for the middle of the lake. Boaters generally don't travel as far out in the depths as we went—the water can be rough and difficult to navigate. But it was calm and serene, and when we finally turned off the motor and listened to the silence around us, it seemed as though the lake had been waiting for us.

We planned to throw our tokens into the deep waters one by one. We would speak spontaneously for some; for others, we had written out our good-byes as a song, a poem, a prayer, a summation. We expected this ceremony to take hours.

We began to unload the objects from our enormous bags. I pulled out the slipknot, the aspen switch, the Mormon hymnal in which I had marked all of my grandfather's hymns, and the Book of Mormon in which I had marked passages that had tormented me and others that had inspired me. I uncurled the leather belt and unfolded the lady's lavender panties and camisole. Dirt from the iris rhizome fell to the floor of the boat. I lay the manila folder holding the sheet music carefully on the seat of the boat, with the Playbill from Kingsbury Hall on top.

What made up the bulk of my bag, however, was the food! The weight of it in the bag had crushed the loaf of Wonder Bread, and we laughed as I placed it on the floor beneath the seat among other tokens—the now soft-sided orange-juice can, the pack of Marlboros, the pint of vodka, and the pork and beans.

Eric unloaded his bag, which was even bulkier than mine. He had among his tokens a hangman's noose, a brick, a bag of tools, a sliver of wood, a microphone, some fake vomit, a stuffed bear, and a set of plastic dishes.

The boat was becoming alarmingly cluttered, but we kept unpacking. I had discovered a child's star chart at Deseret Book Store; I also had torn a page from *Newsweek* about important Southerners. Eric had purchased a toy sled and a box of canning wax.

We looked at the piles around us. Eric started to laugh, unleashing the tension. "Look at all this crap. Can you imagine what we look like?"

"Hmm..." I smiled. "If someone were to see us, they might think we were two crazy hippies taking turns chucking things into the water and giving speeches?"

"What if the Save Our Planet folks saw us tossing that can of pork and beans into the water?"

I giggled. I picked up the beef potpie. "Oh my god, do you think we are killing the flora with potpie?"

"And a leather belt—what the hell will someone think when they pull up a leather belt on a casting line?"

"A stuffed bear, Eric? Will a stuffed bear sink? Or just float faceup, eyes wide open?"

No one could hear us, so we cackled and guffawed, laughing louder as we expanded on the ridiculousness of tossing our tokens into the pure waters of Bear Lake.

What if a seeker of truth found a Book of Mormon floating in Bear Lake? Immediate conversion? Would someone report Eric's noose to the police? What if a child surfaced from a dive wearing Mom's lavender lingerie?

Soon we were hysterical, conjuring up the ludicrous consequences of our pollution, slipping on the boat's now-cluttered bottom, catching ourselves off-balance. The still water began to undulate under our vigorous incantations.

"OK," we agreed, as we tried to calm down. "Only vegetable matter." This sent us into another tailspin of good humor. I scrambled through the grocery sack for the canned peas. But I had forgotten a can opener. And besides, would peas be good for the fish? We were off again. How about the vodka? Can fish get drunk?

Our attempts to be serious finally prevailed, less exhausting than our hysteria, and we settled into a plan: instead of the actual tokens, we would use rocks and stones. Later, we took the actual tokens back to the house, wrapped them up in sheets, took them to the Bear Lake Landfill, and tossed them, shrouded, onto the heap.

In preparation for the throw, I had already selected six special stones, expecting to use them as additional tokens for a special purpose. I set them aside. We divided the rest between us.

A stone for the Book of Mormon, pebbles for the sheet music, a handful of gravel for the bits and pieces of food dribbling down the dining-room wall, a cobbled rock for the belt. Each stone became a castaway memory, embodied in the sandstone, shale, limestone, silt, and mud— in the sedimentary, igneous, and metamorphic rocks—all the origins of my land, my mountains.

So we began.

But we began lightheartedly, laughing as only we children laugh— half-hysterical, half-sad.

First we gave away Mom's phrases of derision. Eric had collected chicken bones that he'd saved from our dinner and tied together to look like fingers on a hand.

"Well, Mother dear," he intoned, "if you worked your fingers to the bone, may your bony fingers snag on seaweed." He tossed in a stone.

"Yes." I joined in, throwing a stone. "And may the seaweed be you at the end of your rope."

"And here's for 'I've had it with you.'"

"And here's for 'You'll be sorry when I'm dead.'"

"We should have brought a pair of false teeth." Eric clacked his fingers together. "Oh my god, imagine a swimmer finding false teeth."

"And a wig. Her wig would have floated." We rocked precariously, imagining Mom drowned and floating, only her wig showing.

"Imagine if a water-skier—"

We gave away the name calling.

First, Eric tossed five of his stones, one by one, as far as he could throw. "Here we are, your five little sons o' bitches—Sandy, now Kathy, little Lucy, invisible Clark." He threw the last stone the farthest. "And me," he said, "the love child you never loved."

I followed. "Here are all the curse words you used—you are tied to them, and may they sink forever." I tossed a handful of pebbles.

"Ungrateful wretches."

Eric lobbed a rock. "Shitheads."

"Pains in the ass."

"Worthless."

"Little bastards."

"Nothing but brats."

I felt a huge sense of relief as we delivered these derogatory phrases to the lake. We were killing the words. They would never rise again from her lips, or ours.

They had not been true.

Next we threw away her complaints about us. The stones flew.

"You drive me crazy." Eric was beginning to sound like Mom.

"You make me sick." I was beginning to sound like Mom.

"You think you're so smart. You're stupid, that's what you are."

"You'll never amount to a fucking thing!" I almost tipped over on this throw.

Eric and I looked at each other—now the big one. We would do this together.

I threw a large rock and yelled, "I would have been—"

He was right on top of my words with another rock. "So happy—"

"If it—"

"—weren't for you!" We yelled it together. We hurled with all our might. Laughing, tipping in the boat, regaining balance, we were euphoric, unburdened, and released.

Then we rested, quieted and somber, sitting in silent camaraderie.

"Want a snack?" he said.

We began laughing all over again.

———————

We threw in our stories. One by one Eric grieved and then threw away his father's desertion, his mother's neglect, his teacher's humiliations, his loneliness, and his fear.

I, too, threw my stones and pebbles in place of the tokens: for the shirt I'd ironed and my lost father; for the belt he wrapped around his suitcase when he left; for the Book of Mormon, the hymnbook, and the promise of an eternal family; for the withheld food. A stone for the star chart on which Daddy had marked Kolob in every sky, where God had lived and disappeared. A stone for each betrayal, all the confusion, and the deep sorrow.

We tossed the stones as the sun crossed the sky, the lake transforming itself from blue to blue. We shared our lunch, and then we began again.

I watched Eric's shoulders sag as he recited his sorrows and knew that both of my brothers, and each of my sisters, had crumpled under a similar weight. Eric and I sat facing in the boat. His face curled up like a child's. His eyes squinted from hurt and from sunlight reflected on the water. His hands cupped his face to the sky. His lips pursed together until, finally, a clutch of sobs opened them and a soft cry flew out into the sunshine. He began to weep, unrestrained, letting the poison drain from him.

Without touching, we held each other and let the tears come.

After a while, we began again solemnly, listening to dismissals and dedications. When we came to what was left in our stores of rocks, we threw them out one by one, without speaking, each of us banishing in our own silent way the damage each stone symbolized.

Into the deep.

———•———

The night before, unable to sleep for the anticipation, I revisited this journey into and out of my history. It was as though I had become the conduit for something working through me but also for me. I sat up, turned my light on, and held the six special rocks I had chosen, each for size, weight, color, and texture. For each one I had written a dedication. I had practiced the dedications as though I was to give a performance—my best performance yet.

Now, in the boat, I took out the rocks, turned them over in my hands—some of them ugly, cracked, jagged edged, and dull in color, and some of them lovely, smooth, and colored deep red, rust brown, and dark gold.

The first rock was rough, gray, gouged, and half-darkened by its own broken shadow. It represented the damage I had suffered in the Mormon Church.

I stood and steadied myself in the boat and began my dedication.

"You, my Church of Jesus Christ of Latter Day Saints," I began. "To the darkest waters of Bear Lake I consign the racism, sexism, and intolerance I have learned from you, the attempts you made to crush my adventurous and inquisitive spirit, and the hammer of judgment that fell so cruelly on my mother and me, and on all of us who did not conform."

Mine was the only voice in the air. No answer contradicted me. I threw the rock. It arced up into the sun, which was lowering in the sky. Because of the light, I didn't see it fall.

———•———

I reached for the second stone.

The morning before we came to Bear Lake, we had visited Temple Square at last. I was taken aback by the sense of serenity and peace I felt while walking on the Temple grounds. In the information building, bubbly ladies and kind men, friendly and affirming, approached and welcomed me. Wandering through the grounds, I remembered my Church as I had refused to remember it for the decades before my return to Salt Lake City—the harmonious hymns, the glory of the Tabernacle Choir's luscious tones, the rules I came to live by, and the warmth of the Church family into which I was drawn, which harbored me, and which, within its walls, protected me from assault.

I was not unaware of the contradictions, the complexities, and the dangers the Church held for me. Yet I was not unhappy on this visit to Temple Square. I felt safe. I gave myself to the sense of spirit and grace I had felt as a child.

I picked up the second stone. It was lustrous, oval, not quite smooth but with curves soft and cool to the touch. This stone, deep red, almost purple, also represented my Mormon Church. There, in the waters of Bear Lake, I would consign the values it taught me, which I have held fast to all my life. There, in the cerulean blue, they would be present for me forever.

"Thank you," I addressed the Mormon Church, "for loving and sheltering me as a child, for teaching me to love my neighbor as myself, to value my family, to feel charity toward all, and to give service to all humankind."

I immersed my hand in the water by the side of the boat. I opened my fingers and let go of the stone. Without a sound it was welcomed.

———◆———

I reached for my third rock. This rock was black, pocked like lava. It had weathered poorly. It was cracked in several places, chips flaking away from its surface. This was the saddest stone, with its surface of loss. My father. I held him out in front of me. I spoke to him:

"To the darkest waters of Bear Lake, I consign the sexual violation you visited upon me, the abandonment you served upon me, and the man you finally became, locked in your own shell, impenetrable, flicking out like a poisonous snake at wounds that never healed." My voice cracked. I swallowed, straightened my back, and went on. "You no longer hold the power of my love for you. I throw you away."

I threw him away.

The rock coursed so high, with such force and speed, that it fell like a bullet to the lake and must have sunk into unfathomable depths.

The fourth stone was flat and thin, polished to a shine, silvery and incandescent. It skimmed across the water, flashing light. Daddy. I spoke again:

"Thank you, Daddy, for the star chart and the stars and the moon, for your hugs and kisses when I was a little child, for teaching me about the Wasatch Mountains and how to run away, for the typewriter and the will to write stories, for the white shirts you trusted me to iron, for your songs of promise and your faith in me, for the nights in your arms and the safety I felt you gave me. More than anything, thank you for teaching me hope, strength, optimism, and the will to live."

I had brought to Bear Lake a small bottle of Old Spice cologne. I poured some in my hands and placed my hands to my face to smell the best of my father. I did not blame myself for the longing I felt, but I knew it was over. I emptied the cologne in the lake and skipped the stone across the scented water. I washed my hands clean in the blue water.

The fifth and sixth Imperial Street stones were two halves of one that had broken. Both were rough and pitted on the outside, but the break had been clean, and the heart of the stones remained smooth and calm, in harmonious color, pale and golden. My mother.

These were the most complicated stones, bumpy and awkward in my two palms, but cool and comforting when I closed my hands over them.

Half of the torn rock I tossed in a long trajectory, reciting a sad eulogy of blame. "I discard you, Mother, for deriding me so meanly, for screaming at me so unpredictably, for hitting me, for being drunk and complaining, for ignoring my lying and thieving, for missing my Christmas concert, for manipulating and misusing me, for not feeding me, and for not loving me like I deserved to loved."

The half rock tumbled into the water with a great splash.

I would throw the other half stone into the endless blue lake, to be there whenever I returned. I wept as I held it, standing still in the boat, my shoulders shaking. Eric was up from his seat and holding me, patting my back. Then he stood behind me in the gently rocking boat, his arms around my waist. I held the stone low, and as I pitched it into the sun, it fell perfectly through the water in a brief, quiet splash.

Thank you, Mom, for allowing me your parents—my beloved Baba and my incomparable Ninyah. I am sorry they loved you so poorly while they loved me so well.

"Thank you for keeping us all together as long as you did and as best you could. Thank you for working all those jobs for so little pay and reward. Thank for the evenings by the piano, for the trips to Bear Lake, for the stories, for the singing and the music, for those wonderful moments when you weren't depressed, or drunk, or crazy, and for your rare moments of gentleness and kindness.

"Thank you, Mom, for teaching me, by your example, to endure my sorrows and disappointments and to never give up trying.

"Thank you for encouraging me to be strong and rebellious, curious and demanding, and adamant about achieving justice for all.

"And thank you for making me understand how cruel and ruthless life can be for children, how a child can reach out for a savior. You were not my savior, Mom, but though you turned your back on me, you turned me to face out at the world, and you led me to find the work I do."

CHAPTER 29

PROMISES, PROMISES

"MOM IS DEAD." I SPOKE into the phone receiver from the concave booth outside the Washington State Memorial Hospital ICU.

"So," Clark said, hardly pausing, "the old bag finally kept her promise."

After I married and left Salt Lake City in 1965, I had almost no contact with my mother. Sixteen years later, she died, in 1981. It would be another decade before Eric and I would return to Salt Lake City and Bear Lake on our redemptive quest.

During my estrangement from my mother, my siblings kept me informed. Mom had married and divorced three more times. When Eric and Clark were in college, she moved to Seattle to be near my sisters, both married with children, both still Mormons in good standing and both on cordial, if cautious, terms with her.

For Christmas of 1980, Lucy invited me to Seattle for a family gathering as a possible start toward reconciliation. I was thirty-six years old, practicing law in Portland. I was hopeful and cautiously expectant.

During the visit, however, I realized that not much had changed. I had been considering taking my mother to see the downtown holiday lights, but when she whined about how long it had been since I'd called or seen her ("What's the matter? Haven't you got a finger and a phone?"), I balked. When she told me that a good daughter would take her mother to see the Christmas lights, I refused to do so.

"You might not get another chance," she said. "I might be dead and gone by next Christmas." This was a warning she had issued many times in my childhood. I rolled my eyes. Dismayed, and oddly disappointed, I didn't see her again. The following March, she was hospitalized in the last stages of emphysema, from which she died.

Eric, my sisters, and I stood vigil at the hospital during her decline. Clark stayed in Salt Lake City. Though he had graduated from college and was employed as an actuary, he had survived our childhood primarily by drinking, and by becoming the welcome clown, the delightful life of the party, the stand-up comedian who hides his sorrow and pain through humor. He riffed on all of our tragedies and turned them into funny anecdotes. When Mom complained of being too warm, he would quip, "Hot as a June bride in a feather bed, huh?" When I talked about how Mom taught us to cook, he chortled, "Yes, indeed, the H. Rap Brown school of cooking—'Burn, baby, burn!'" When Mom whined her demands with the threat "I may not be around much longer," he sighed dramatically. "Promises, promises."

He could turn anything into humor, often a joke I didn't really want to laugh at—clever but sarcastic or sad, with just an element of truth. When I called to tell him of Mom's death, and he joked about it, I laughed, unable to stop myself. But embarrassed, I looked around to see whether anyone was listening.

I gave Clark the final details of our mother's quick slump. He responded with his excuses for not coming for the funeral. He lied: "I can't get off work."

I could have confronted him: "That's just your excuse, Clark. What is the explanation?"

But I knew what he would say: "Well, aren't we the entomologist now?"

And I would play the game: "It's *etymologist*, Clark."

"See?" He'd launch a riposte. "Oh, I was just *bugging* you, Sis." So our shameful sibling habit of lying would be lost in banter and malapropism.

I already knew the reasons for Clark's refusal to respond empathetically to Mom's dying. It was the same for all of us to one degree or another: her death was a relief. Here was another door to shut, more distance to put between us and her.

Clark wrapped his sense of failure to be noticed and loved around himself, using humor as the only comfort he had. It was his way of finally taking power over her.

———◆———

When I presided over juvenile offenders at probation-violation hearings, the young people offered me every possible excuse for violating the conditions of probation. A girl missed her counseling appointment and claimed, "I forgot where it was." A boy tested positive for marijuana and justified himself: "My stepdad was tokin', and I must've inhaled the smoke." A boy skipped school: "I couldn't get to school, 'cause Mom wouldn't give me a ride and my stepfather was drunk."

I leaned over the bench and looked at him until he looked at me. "That may be true," I said, "but it's just your excuse. I won't accept any excuses." I continued to hold the gaze. "But you may give me an explanation."

"What d'ya mean?" he snorted.

"Explain something deeper than your excuse," I suggested.

"Like what?"

"Like tell me what it is that really keeps you out of school—do you think you aren't smart?"

"Well, I ain't."

"And tell me about your stepfather. Let's talk."

"What do you care?" he scoffed, but he was interested.

"Because I'd like to know you better."

Some children smiled. Some didn't. Some talked. Some refused. Some were remorseful; others tried to con me. Yet these offenders were still young enough to believe that someone could really care about them. Children were so eager to have someone's love that they cleaved to the probation officer, or to the lawyer, or even to the judge. Most of these youngsters *wanted* you to know their hearts and help them find their way back to innocence.

When I was able to gain their confidences, their explanations were poignant and clarifying: "I'm pretty miserable. Actually I think of killing myself." Or "Mom tells me I'm stupid all the time." Or "My stepdad's an asshole; he hits my mom." Many of these children eventually found a way out of delinquency through their own truths.

———

My siblings and I did not reveal our truths. We had our excuses down to a fine art. We no longer looked behind them for the deeper explanations. Often we lied.

"I have a commitment," I'd say.

"I haven't the money."

"Longtime friends have just come in from Cleveland."

We told lies when the truth would do, a pathology we'd honed into a survival tool to protect ourselves from Mom's angry punishments and debilitating disdain. It spilled over into the rest of our lives. Even into adulthood, I lied. If I was sick, I would say I had car trouble. If I had car trouble, I would call in sick. "I'm busy," I would say when I wasn't. I said yes when I meant no. Somehow the truth wasn't adequate. I denied it or exaggerated it.

The only way I've made sense of this terrible habit is to understand that I had to make things *different* than they were: usually bigger, more difficult, tragic, or exciting. I had to deflect attention from what was real and hide behind my barriers. I feared the truth was never going to be the right way to stay safe, so I moved it around. I try now to always tell the truth. Even so, my first impulse is to lie.

"You don't need to lie," I told Clark on the phone.

"I'm not lying," he lied.

———

Sandy, Lucy, and I took turns attending to Mom in the hospital. I rubbed her bunioned feet, fed her Jell-O, and combed her now-insubstantial strands of hair. Sandy and I sang hymns to her and songs from musicals, even when she lapsed into a coma.

Sandy had made her peace with our mother six months earlier and was at peace during Mom's death. Lucy had actually befriended her: found her an apartment, played cards with her, cooked meals for her, and encouraged her to date again, which she did. Mom fell in love again, married, divorced, and then remarried the same man. In the few years preceding her death, Sandy and Lucy told me, she had been happy.

"Define 'happy.'" I was sarcastic.

"You sound like Mom," Sandy said wryly.

I am ashamed that, at first, her death's-door powerlessness thrilled me. Thin wisps of her whitened hair flew about her head like cirrus clouds, not covered by the wigs she usually wore to cover the loss of follicles, of beauty, of a chance to snag a man. Absent her false teeth, her mouth curved into itself like walnut flesh, and when she opened it to call to me, to try to smile, to ask for a kiss, I had to stifle a laugh.

When I was a girl, I had watched her upside-down face as she leaned over me, a face that I found slightly repellent and macabre, her beady eyes slanted wrong in her chin, her nostrils pointing to a slim-arched frown. As her face crumbled toward death, I saw that face again, washed into a skewed shape, beaten by all those cigarettes, the screwdrivers she'd drunk, and by us, the children she had damaged.

When I had shown any tendency toward affection or compassion, she had steeled herself, devoid of comfort. I'd hit a blistering wall of rejection. As she lay helpless and scared, I felt the possibilities open up before me. I could torment her without repercussion; I could insult and berate her; I could tease her with her coming death and visions of the Mormon Limbo in which she was destined to float, unloved, for eternity.

Clark wisely didn't come; he might not have refrained from such revenge. Yet I refrained. Barely.

Her death unfolded before me and showed me a woman who was vulnerable as she had never been before. Strangely, I felt something in addition to hatred and relief. I felt afraid that she would leave, though I didn't want her to stay. I feared she would take with her something I did not know and needed to know. Though I'd been estranged from her for so long, I had the eerie sense that a gap would open and remain unfilled.

Shortly before she died, Mom called for me. I held her hand and answered her terrible questions. "I'm dying, aren't I?" she asked with a mixture of sorrow and fright.

"Yes, Mom, you are." Oddly, I didn't lie.

"Do you think I'll get to the Terrestrial Kingdom?" She laughed at herself. "Oh, dear, don't answer that."

I spooned some applesauce into her mouth. She ate and then sat quietly for a few moments.

"Was I a good mother?" she asked.

"No, Mom, you weren't," I said sadly.

She was less surprised at my answer than I was at giving it.

"But I taught you to be strong, didn't I?"

"That you did." I smiled.

"And I promised I'd never leave you, didn't I?"

"Yes, you did."

"And I didn't leave you, did I?" She placed her hand on mine.

"No, Mom, for the most part, you didn't."

As I sat by her side during those final hours and watched her slip away, as her body quieted and her facial muscles relaxed, as the time between breaths lengthened, I saw glimpses of her childhood innocence, her adolescent beauty, her wifely rebellions, her professional disappointments, and her unrelenting efforts to save herself from a future that nevertheless dragged her down. I saw her as a woman flailing in a hostile sea, trying to lift her children up for saving, yet climbing on them and pulling them down in her panic and terror of drowning.

Then she died. The flat line buzzed on the monitor; the sunlight came through the curtains in silvery motes that floated over her bed; the colorful balloons shifted in the air, as though a spirit had risen and fluttered. Low murmurs drifted in from the nurses' station, but the room itself was utterly silent. Mom's face relaxed, smoothed in her release of pain. I laid my head on her chest and felt her breathlessness. I spread my arms up to her pillow and felt the warmth leave her body.

"Good-bye, Mom," I whispered. I thought, but didn't say, *Good riddance.*

———

For years after her death, when my mother's five children met together or separately, we regaled ourselves with tales of our alcoholic mother and her vicious tirades, manipulative tantrums, abuse, and unreasonable demands. We talked about how she pushed us to Church, lectured us on Christ's principles, yet was deceitful and decadent herself. How she pitied herself and blamed everyone else. How she hit us and withheld food from us, using it to punish and reward us. We laughed heartily at her. We gave ourselves credit for surviving and congratulated ourselves for turning out OK in spite of her. Our laughter spent itself and died down to a lingering silence, each of us turning to our own thoughts. A heavy cloak of memory spread over us.

When we recounted her endless threats that she would die, one or another of us would invariably say, "It's the only promise she ever kept."

But this had not been so. She had kept the most important promise.

"If you hate us so much," we challenged her, "why don't you leave us?"

"Never," she said.

During the months and years that followed her death, I let my hot coil of hate and resentment curl around itself and harden like a trilobite, a fossil burned into the earth as a permanent reminder of life as it had been.

It would be another thirteen years before Eric and I returned to Salt Lake City to exorcise her.

CHAPTER 30

LEGACY

———◆———

AFTER ERIC AND I COMPLETED our ritual at Bear Lake, I returned to Oregon renewed and jubilant. I never again doubted my work or had questions about how I got there or why I stayed.

I know now how I endured the sorrow and the suffering I both saw and felt in my work, the exhaustion, and the terrible disappointments—not because I was punishing myself or being punished, but because, along with the other men and women who work for children and families, I was pulling against the currents, hoping to channel lives fraught with muddled genetic underpinnings and turbulent environmental influences, onto a course to the open sea.

I am seventy-one years old now and have been retired from the bench for several years. I live in Salt Lake City again. Recently I read an article in the *Salt Lake Tribune* about a month-old baby girl killed by her seventeen-year-old father, who shook her violently to stop her from crying. I couldn't stop thinking about it. Each time I read such stories, I recall the many cases over which I presided, in which a father or mother, a stepfather or boyfriend, killed, abused, or neglected an innocent child. Sometimes the victim was an infant, sometimes a toddler, sometimes older, but always smaller than the killer. And in almost all circumstances, the perpetrator had been abused as a child. The legacy had been passed down.

Then I remembered.

I can't recall how small I was, or what age, or in which house I was living. I only recall a grocery store and a cart, my mother and I going up and down the aisles, my sitting in the cart, a red-and-gold package on a shelf, my standing up and reaching for it, Mom's yelling at me to sit down, my not wanting to, the burn of a powerful slap, her knuckles, and the bright lights in the ceiling, when suddenly I was on the floor on my back.

Then this: my mother picks me up, her hands gripping my arms, pinning them to my side. Her mouth is curled, her tongue looks fuzzy, her hair is wild, and this is what I remember most: my head is coming forward and then back, then snapping forward and then clapping back. There are faraway voices loud and alarmed, and I am flying forward faster and backward harder. Inside my head, I can feel something roll up hard against my forehead. Then I feel my neck wrinkle as my head flaps back and things crash inside my ears.

My head hurts and the voices get louder. All I can think is that I am an airplane. There is thunder and lightning, clouds bumping, and we might crash, but I am a pilot and I am flying. I go forward and backward, flying, and things are hitting the windows hard. There is a struggle. Suddenly, my plane is in a tree.

But I am actually in somebody's arms. Two men grab my mother, and there is the clatter of my mother being pushed forcibly against the cans on the shelf. She is held there with her arms spread. I am crying because I am saved in the tree and somebody is saying something; an angel is holding me. I can almost remember what she says.

Thankfully, I have only this one memory of Mom shaking me. I call my sisters and ask whether they remember being shaken; they don't.

———◆———

I hung up and put the *Tribune* article aside. I went grocery shopping. Grocery shopping brings me peace. I was in the chips and crackers aisle when I saw a mother with her child, lime chips, salsa, and two boxes of Sprite in the cart. She came toward me.

The small boy, unstrapped, leaned out to grab something off the shelf. The mother yelled at him. "No! I've told you a million times, keep your damn hands in the cart."

I watched, concerned. They argued back and forth.

"Mama, please."

"Shut up. Just shut up."

"Mama, please, the cracker."

"If I have to tell you one more time, I'll smack you good."

"Mama, I want the cracker."

"Shut up!"

"Please."

"Fuck all, you little shit."

Smack. She slapped him across the face, and for me, everything stopped—the lights, the Muzak, the shoppers, all were arrested in time. I saw only the child as he toppled sideways, tipping, sliding, descending. I ran toward them, yelling, "Don't shake him! Don't shake him!"

She had caught him; he wasn't crying. She turned to me. "What the hell?"

Suddenly I knew what to do. What was it that came over me? The slow learning I had come to as I grew out of my home and my Church and my city? What I knew as a teacher, a lawyer, and a judge? And who had taught me?

I looked at the woman and confessed. "Sorry, I know this must seem so interfering, but I just wanted you to know that I *know* how you feel. Sometimes I felt like I couldn't stand being a parent anymore and like I wanted to just haul off and smack my kids."

"Who are you?" she asked, but she settled back on her feet. Her son began to whimper and hold his face. *Who am I?*

"I'm nobody, really. I'm just another mother who yelled at my kids. And everybody always felt sorry for my kids and never felt sorry for me."

"Isn't that the truth," she said, and then she looked at the boy in her arms. "Shut up, Layne, or I'll give you something to cry about."

"I thought maybe you'd like some help. I could take Layne while you shop."

"Well," she said, "but he probably won't go with you. He just clings to me all the time. Drives me nuts."

"Hey, Layne," I said to him, and then to her, "Can I give him a cookie? I have some in my cart."

"Yeah, I guess." She put him down, took his hand. The three of us walked to my cart, and I opened the one-hundred-calorie snack pack. Layne came to me then, dug into the box for a cookie, and sucked on it.

"You know," I said, "I worked a lot with kids, and I've learned that it's really hard for them when they get hit or shaken."

"I don't give a shit," she said. "He's hard on me. I've got four of them, and they're all brats."

"I know. It was hard for me, too. I think I did it because my mom did it to me. I hated it. But I stopped. And they were better behaved when I didn't yell."

"Yeah, my mom and dad yelled, too. Hit all us kids. Shitheads. But it shut me up, I'll say that. And it shuts Layne up. What's good for the goose and all that."

"Why don't you do your shopping in peace and meet us at the check-out stand. I'll go get Layne an orange juice."

"You sure you aren't some kind of pervert?"

I smiled and said, "I'm glad you care. Here, take my fanny pack. It has all my ID and stuff. I'll get it back from you in the front. Twenty minutes?"

"Yeah, OK."

I took Layne to the refrigerated shelves, opened up a Juicy Juice, and let him help me push in the straw. We sat down right there at the cooler bin. He ate another cookie and sucked his juice. I turned to him and said what I think the angel must have said to me when she held me away from my mother.

She must have said, "Kathy, your mama loves you very much. But she did something very wrong. She hit you, and she shook you. You may not remember this, but I will tell you anyway: no child deserves to be hit or shaken. Ever. For any reason.

"Now, can you say this? 'Don't do that, Mama. That's wrong.'" I couldn't say it when I was so young, of course, and neither could Layne. I hugged him and kissed the top of his head, and said, "No hit! OK? No hit. Not Mama. Not you. *No hit.*" He looked at me, startled by the sternness in my voice, and then went back to his juice.

When we got to the checkout stand, his mother was already done checking her groceries. "Where've you been?" she said peevishly. "I haven't got all day, you know."

She handed me my fanny pack. "We had a juice," I said lamely.

"Well, come on then." She yanked Layne by the arm and turned to go. "And quit your whining, Layne. That didn't hurt." She pulled him along, out of the store.

I got in my car. I'd forgotten to shop. I'd forgotten to pay for the cookies and the Juicy Juice.

I'd have gone back and paid, but she'd stolen my wallet.

I can hear my mother snort. "Why'd you even bother?" she would say. "Nothing changes."

I don't believe that's true. Legacies do change. It takes time, but I believe we can interrupt the cycle of abuse, perhaps even break it, and serve both the parents and the children. Lawyers, state child-service workers, court counselors, volunteer Court Appointed Special Advocates, Big Brothers and Sisters, foster and adoptive parents, church members, Citizen Review Board members, doctors, psychologists, and educators.

And parents. And strangers in the grocery store. You. And me.

Although I would trade them for happier ones, my childhood experiences have given me a deeper and more visceral understanding of the families with whom I work. Of all families, actually. We are complicated, we families, yours and mine. There is no such thing as pure evil and no such thing as perfect good. We can learn what to honor. What we discard will die in the dark, but what we nourish will grow in the light. Strong. Resilient.

Safe from harm.

I did not save my father or my mother, and my Church did not save me. But I learned the meaning of salvation, and I live it in my work.

ABOUT THE AUTHOR

KATHARINE ENGLISH SERVED ON THE Multnomah County Oregon Circuit Court bench, presiding for fourteen years over cases of child abuse and neglect, juvenile delinquency, and mental commitment. She then served as chief judge of the Confederated Tribes of Grand Ronde, Oregon, for another seven years. For more than twenty years, she was an invited faculty member for the National Council of Juvenile and Family Court Judges.

After retiring, she was a substitute teacher and tutor for seven years at Rowland Hall, a private school in Salt Lake City, until 2015.

She graduated from Portland State College, earned her law degree from Lewis and Clark Northwestern School of Law, and earned a master of fine arts in creative writing from Goddard College.

She has two brilliant and beautiful sons. She is now retired and living in Salt Lake City, Utah.